OPEN HER

Activate 7 Masculine Powers to Arouse Your Woman's Love and Desire

"Karen is 'right on' in her approach to teaching men about women. I have frequently said that when the male brain thinks it understands the female brain it will be wrong 98 percent of the time. Read *Open Her* and get it right!"

Robert Glover
No More Mr. Nice Guy

"*Open Her* is a soulful book that teaches men what women really want romantically and sexually. This is an insightful read for any man who wants to truly understand women, and create a deep, passionate, loving relationship."

Marci Shimoff
Love for No Reason & *Happy for No Reason*

"Most men spend lives of quiet frustration in the realm of relationship—trying to figure out what women want. Karen Brody's fascinating book, *Open Her*, changes the dynamic. She suggests that what women say they want and what they actually respond to, may be two different things. What ignites passion in women is far more likely to be a complete man, capable of bringing the full compliment of masculine energy and archetypes to bear in the appropriate moment."

Tom Crockett
Pillow Book: A Sacred Guide to Sexual Play

"*Open Her* is a goldmine for men who want to succeed at love. It contains everything a woman wishes her man knew about sex, love and intimacy."

Ana Loiselle
Marriage Coach Specialist

OPEN HER

Activate 7 Masculine Powers to Arouse
Your Woman's Love and Desire

Karen Brody

DreamStream Press
San Francisco

Published in 2014 by Dream Stream Press, San Francisco

ISBN-13: 978-0692273470
ISBN-10: 0692273476

Cover design by Vanessa No Heart
Book design by Tom Crockett

Open Her: Activate 7 Masculine Powers to Arouse Your Woman's Love and Desire is not meant as a substitute for counseling. The author is not dispensing medical or psychological advice. Whenever there is a concern about physical or emotional illness, a qualified professional should be consulted. The author shall have neither liability nor responsibility to any person or entity with respect to any loss, damage, injury, or ailment caused or alleged to be caused directly or indirectly by the information or lack of information in this book.

Table of Contents

Foreword

Sexuality is a treasure trove, but it's also a minefield. It's the one life arena that's fraught with both incredible primal energy, and also the possibility for endless pain and shame. And that's just within an individual – once partners are involved everything becomes even more heightened. To navigate this potent, tricky terrain, we need impeccable guidance. That's why I was so excited when asked to write the forward for Karen Brody's book. Karen and I met, and have found great common ground as educators of sexual and emotional intimacy.

I trust Karen's approach to sexuality and relationships, and deeply respect the message she has to share with men. When it comes to practical insights that unleash the transformative potential of sexuality within intimate relationships, this book is the gold standard.

What it's not: A way to get women into bed, or a way to get them to better serve your desires. What it is: A guide for evoking ecstatic sexual union with your partner.

Karen understands that such union is first and foremost about oneself, and that when a man learns how to open to his own unfettered masculine energy, only then is he capable of truly loving his partner, and of calling forth the same true love from her.

Getting there, even to the point of knowing the value of such a path, is not an easy road for most of us men. The rough combination of testosterone and cultural conditioning finds us, when relating to women, in the mode of hot pursuit. We want to conquer, possess, 'get' ours. All of which tends to shut most women down rather than open them up.

To make matters worse, few of us have the combination of looks and swagger necessary to pull off the kind of misguided seduction we crave. As a result, we're either left empty-handed or unsatisfied with the women we ensnare.

I experienced all of this personally in my teens and twenties. From an early age I felt both blessed and cursed by the amount of sexual energy that coursed through me. I had a wild sex life, but all on my own. That's because the women I wanted only wanted to be my best friend, and the women who wanted me I didn't want at all.

The resulting isolation, and sexual frustration, created a dark storm at the center of my existence. Luckily, I found my way to a great therapist. One day, I was complaining to her about how women only wanted James Dean, and how I could never be him.

My therapist asked me what qualities I attributed to James Dean. I told her that Dean (or really the archetype he represented) exuded such raw sexual energy that all he had to do was lean against a wall and women would throw themselves at him. At this point my therapist caught me totally off-guard.

"Would you like to meet your own inner James Dean?" she asked. I felt shocked, confused, challenged. What was she even talking about?

Using a practice called Voice Dialogue, my therapist had me move to another seat and began talking to me as if I was actually James Dean. When I joined in the dialogue, much to my surprise, I started to feel sexually confident. I could tell that I was radiating sexual energy in a new way, one that wasn't so bound up in fear and doubt.

Then came the kicker. My therapist went silent. She just looked at me. It took me a few seconds to realize that she was allowing her own sexual energy to enter the space between us in a palpable way. I felt wanted by her, as a man, as a sexual man, while knowing full well this was also a completely safe experiment.

We stayed in this incredibly charged silent gaze for at least five minutes. I can honestly say it changed my life.

But not in the way you might imagine.

I didn't go from feeling undesirable to supremely confident in my sexual attractiveness. Instead, I knew that the channels for sexual energy in me had just burst wide open. Before, my sexual energy was like a tsunami inside a garden hose – insistent, overpowering, focused narrowly on escape and release.

Now, the generative power of sexuality spread to every part of me like the waves of an infinite ocean. Its waves seemed made of light, illuminating every aspect of my being ripe for discovery and fulfillment.

Through sexuality, you might say, I gave birth to a new self, one that unleashed the man I'd always longed to be. This was also a man that women wanted naturally – the right women – and a man who could meet them in erotic connection without halting or hiding.

Which brings us back to this book. Besides being an exquisitely reliable guide in the realm of satisfying sexual connection, Karen is also a writer of great grace and insight. She shares from a fascinating feminine perspective all of those things women long for and so seldom find in their men. She makes incredibly complex themes come to life in a clear, accessible way.

Karen has developed a schema for opening yourself that cultivates what she calls the "Seven Masculine Archetypes." I didn't know it at the time, but in the aftermath of what happened with my therapist, that's what I did. Only I stumbled a lot in the process, and would have been enormously grateful to have this book as a companion on the journey.

That's exactly what you have in your hands, a true companion on the journey of awakening yourself, and also your love life. Either one would be enough. Together, they're irresistible.

Raphael Cushnir
July 2013
Portland, Oregon

Acknowledgments

I'd like to offer my deep, heartfelt appreciation to the following people, without whom this book and teachings would not be possible.

First, thank you to my mother, Gail, who passed away just before this book made it to publication. I wouldn't have the strength to walk this path had it not been for you and what I learned from you about men and love.

To my sister, Lisa, who's unending support and belief in me gives me a place to call home in the world.

Thank you, my dear Jay. This book couldn't have happened without you. You saw me so clearly and gave me the courage to step into my life's work. May you rest in peace. To Stephen, thank you for the amazing adventure, the heartbreak and the love. Fernando, your devotion, love and support helped bring this book to life.

To Tom Crockett, my creative editor, thank you for your masculine direction, your brilliant insights, and for providing the masculine practices that accompany the opportunities in each chapter. They're simply gold. Your belief in this project, and your consistent encouragement and feedback, made it possible for me overcome many hurdles and cross the finish line.

Thank you Raphael Cushnir for seeing the beauty in Open Her through your heart, and for writing a forward that inspires the awakened, masculine potential within every man.

Thank you, Betsy Blondin, for your excellent proofreading, and Vanessa No Heart for your brilliant, stunning cover design.

And thank you to these special friends who contributed in a variety of key ways to this book's completion: Kimmy, Lisa M, Adva, Allen, Gerard, Aysha, Peter O, Manny, Pattie C, Steve T, and Michelle K.

And a special thanks to all the men who hurt me enough, through love, to inspire this book and its wisdom.

Introduction

If you're reading this book, you're obviously not new to women. Because you're an intelligent, sensitive and caring man, you've probably had many women in your life and some success at love.

Nonetheless, if there is anything that can bring you to your knees and completely derail your forward motion, it's being in love with a woman! When she's happy and radiant, it fuels everything you do. The inspiration of her joy propels you forward and makes all your efforts worthwhile. On the other hand, when she's unhappy, disappointed, or not playing on your court, it can feel like your energy is being sucked dry. You lose focus. You lose that winning edge. And, at its worst, you lose your own sense of power and value, as if being with her is a dark hole from which you cannot escape.

The best of intentions and being a "good man" don't always have the effect of making your woman happy; you know this well. And so you keep looking for the magic bullet – the secret something that will land you in good stead, and from where you can coast along for a long time. Unfortunately, it doesn't work this way with women. Women are creatures of the moment, so coasting is virtually impossible. While it's not your duty to make a woman happy and cater to her every changing mood, understanding her at the deepest, most intimate level is an opportunity you should not miss – if you want an open, playful, and joyous woman in your life.

You need this book because this dance beckons you, and believe me, it's not intuitive at any stage of your life. In my coaching practice, I've known many men to wait decades to access information that changed their relationship in a day. So know that your choice to pick up and read this book is a really good one, and I assure you it will help you to be both a better man and a better lover for your woman.

Women clearly want different things in love than men. You've already figured out that piece. The question is: To what extent do you understand the intricacies of that difference? To what degree can you say you know your woman's heart, or the subtle nature of her desire? What is it that makes her crave you in one moment and refuse you in another? What triggers her respect and affection, and can you inspire that respect and affection now and in the future?

If you feel uncertain about the answers to these questions, take heart. Most men are perplexed by how a woman loves and what fuels her desire. Your masculine nature is to provide and protect, and that's likely where a great deal of your attention goes in relationship to a woman. Above all, you simply want your woman to be happy. This is a beautiful and noble intention. However, if not given in the right spirit, and from a place of power, it can backfire on your sense of confidence and undermine your success at love.

A feminine heart is easiest to understand if you think of it like a garden. Whether you garden or not, you know if you seed the earth properly and tend to it with love and skill, it blooms into a thing of beauty and wonder. In many ways, women are this way, too. Sure, you can just do a little watering now and then or throw a little food at your romantic relationship, and it will stay alive. But the relationship with a woman never thrives and blossoms until it's given the emotional and sexual nutrients and the care it really needs.

You didn't get to this point in your life without experiencing the dark side of a woman's heart. It's that moment when her smile has all but disappeared, her joy is gone, and her sexual desire has seemingly dried up. This moment is every man's worst nightmare; perhaps it's what compels you to read this book. And yet, it's exactly what happens when the feminine "garden" isn't tended to with loving attention (and I'm not talking about roses wrapped in plastic, or occasional lingerie). I'm talking about tending to love in a way that inspires a woman's deepest opening and a man's greatest sense of himself and his power.

Who and What This Book Is For

This book is not a guide for how to pacify women or win their approval. You will not learn how to become more docile, or how to masterfully conceal your masculinity and your sexual desires. On the contrary, the scope of this journey is far greater than your relationships with women. It's an opportunity for you to step up and be a better man in all the ways you want to be – and also to affect your relationships with women in a positive and satisfying way.

At the start of my work as "The Love and Intimacy Coach for Men," men came to me urgently wanting answers to their problems with women. "What do I have to say or do to get her to want me?" they'd ask, as if women were like riddles they could solve. Initially, I readily threw the answers at them, wanting them to succeed and believing they would. I thought surely the information would change things. But I quickly learned that handing a man "the answers" was akin to giving him a rifle without showing him first how to use it.

To succeed with women, a man needs to first come to know and understand his own power and how to leverage that power in a loving way with women. Few men have any idea of the kind of raw power they have. It's like they have a Ferrari in the garage, but they've driving a Volkswagen. So first, I want to show you where your power lives (in case you overlooked it) and how to use that power effectively in relation to women. If you're not getting the attention, affection, and sex you want, you can trust you're not using your power well.

The Seven Masculine Archetypes and How They'll Improve Your Life

There are seven Masculine Archetypes to which women everywhere have always been drawn. In one way or another, women find these aspects of masculinity irresistible as you might be drawn to the female archetypes of The Seductress, The Mother, or The Waif. You'll discover yourself most prominently in one or two of the Masculine Types – and smaller pieces of yourself likely throughout the others.

The archetypes are not intended to be the summation of a perfect man. Please don't waste your time feeling bad or regretting anything you didn't know in the past. Everything you've experienced until this point has brought you here, now. If you fall victim to regret, it will simply get in the way of a powerful opportunity to embrace yourself and experience greater success in relationships with women.

At the start of each chapter, you'll read a personal story of how I came to know that archetype, intimately, in love. These stories are based on real events and people. However, in order to protect the privacy of men who are featured, I've had to change their names, professions, and anything else I felt would identify them. You can trust that the essence of what I share with you in these stories is real. These are the intimate experiences that have shaped me as a woman and given me the inspiration to create this teaching.

Keep in mind that these stories are snapshots of relationships that were complex, and even messy, with men who were not perfect, as no man – or woman – is. They were men with all the flaws of regular, mortal men. But each was extraordinary in one particular way: he gave me a nugget of wisdom and a piece of myself I was able to carry forward in my heart. My desire is for you to know these aspects within yourself, both those you engage readily and those that are strangers to you, so you can play in a bigger field of masculinity. It's kind of like being able to play pitcher, catcher, first baseman, and shortstop all within the scope of a game. That "game," if you will, is your dance with women. Most guys just have a single position.

You will have the opportunity to intimately know aspects of masculinity you may have sensed only in passing or believed were reserved for other men. It's within this bigger scope that you'll be able to create and attract more of what you desire in your relationships with women, and be more of who you desire to be as a man.

Each archetype possesses a special power. You will learn how to activate that power within you. Each Masculine Archetype uncovers a piece of the riddle of being a man, and loving women, which gives him strength and ease. Each brings a gift to women and to the world that you may feel inspired to embrace.

I suggest you explore all the archetypes and notice where you see yourself and where you might have an absence of that archetype in your life. Then intuitively choose an archetype you'd like to know better. Perhaps it's one your woman would desire in you. Do the practices for that type that week and the next. Watch closely what you experience. Observe how your woman responds to you – and how all the women in your life do. Then, when that archetype feels natural and pleasurable to play in, take on another.

The attitude you bring to the material matters a lot. I don't suggest you engage it casually or put too much emphasis on results. This is a process, not a destination. Be with the process; invite your awareness. This means tuning in to a more subtle space, slowing down, noticing. I suggest you think of these practices and this information as a sacred gift – to yourself and the women in your life. Trust me: It's a gift that will continue to give and increase in value with your ongoing practice, awareness, and commitment.

Why should you listen to me?

I didn't always love men, nor did I have an interest in their empowerment. I started out like every other girl, loving and trusting the men in my life but had a caregiver rob me of my sexual innocence and choice. I would spend the next eighteen years in a variety of unhealthy states, trying to unravel the shame and the pain. My precociousness led to heartbreak time and again. I was also angry that nobody had protected me, and that men could be so unloving and hurtful.

Nonetheless, I had a lot of men in my life and many lessons to learn. I hurt many of those men with my anger, resentment, and inability to love. How could I love? I had no love for myself. I was a shell of a woman – really – beautiful on the outside but impermeable. At twenty-five, I began a journey (through books) to heal my wounds, and that journey culminated ten years later with my being spiritually directed to coach men. This included a major career change from journalism to getting my degree in counseling psychology.

Initially, the calling seemed insane. How could a woman who felt such pain and resentment toward men be of help to them? The hidden miracle in it was, of course, that when you help somebody, you can't help but empathize, and you can't help but help yourself. In this kind of work, the layers of judgment and separation fell away, and I was left with the truth.

I saw that men were hurting. They weren't the bad guys out to rob or deny women love; they were often victims of their own lack of confidence and self-appreciation. What I saw is how often men accepted a sort of second-class citizen status in their relationships with women – begging, bargaining, and dealing for love and sex – leaving their women hungering for a man who would love and honor himself. Of course, my clients thought they were doing the right things – being sensitive, listening, not demanding sex. But what they were unknowingly creating were sexless relationships, refining and reducing their masculinity until it was almost undetectable.

I've uncovered the secrets to empowering men that translate into deeply satisfying relationships with women. I'm certain that when you embrace the truth and power of your masculinity, the women you touch will be transformed and blossom.

May these insights serve and bless you a million times over,

Karen Brody

Chapter 1

The Artist

I met Chris at a party and was drawn to his eyes immediately; they were bright, interested, and on fire. The whole room seemed to disappear when we looked at one another. Chris was a photographer and, from what I could gather, a rather famous one. I didn't care much at the time about what he did. I was drawn to how I felt with him. I was seen, and it was intoxicating. I'd made my way through the entire party and engaged a dozen or so men, but Chris was the only one who made me feel a deep, authentic connection; and I found myself magnetized to wherever he was in the space.

I invited Chris to join me on the couch in the living room. I was nervous, but alone with him on the couch I knew I'd be able to feel him without the interference of other people's energy. As we sat searching each other's faces, he leaned into the big pillow and cradled his face in one hand. I felt a powerful quiet fall over me.

"Tell me about yourself," he said.

His way of being was so intimate, open, and focused; the walls came down. Sure, anyone can say, "Tell me about you," but surprisingly few men can say it in a way that rises above a pick-up line, and fewer still can say it in a way that communicates a genuine desire to know.

I noticed my entire body tensing, almost frozen by the intensity of his gaze and the connection. We laughed. "I'm feeling a bit nervous," I admitted.

"Nervous," he said, a smile crossing his face, "what about?"

"Your gaze," I said. "You're very focused."

"Well, it's kind of my job, though I will admit you make it easy."

My body was on fire with the delight of his attention. Staying focused on what I was saying was a challenge, but as I did, I saw that Chris became more and more intent on hearing me – not just my words, but me. His eyes intensified and shrunk down, as if he were sharply focusing on me, turning his ear slightly toward me when he wanted to hear more intently. I hardly knew this man and yet I knew I wanted him.

We made a date for a few days later. Chris said he wanted to take me to a water reserve set in a dramatic canyon. He packed a salad, sandwiches, and red wine; and we hiked into the canyon just as the sun set and arrived to see hundreds of birds dive into the canyon. It was visually spectacular and the perfect date, really, although I found myself yearning for that potent connection we had experienced that night on the couch.

When Chris called next, he asked me to take a trip with him on his motorcycle, about an hour out of town. If I were open to it, he'd photograph me. "Don't worry about how you look or what you wear," he told me. Naturally, I worried about what to wear but settled on a pair of jeans and a tight, white T-shirt. My excitement soared as I remembered that feeling his presence had created throughout my body.

He took me to the high desert. The ground was a stark white with cacti about three feet high – a beautiful backdrop for his photographs. As I watched him put his equipment together, I noticed he wasn't nervous setting up in front of me. And he didn't seem to need to perform either. The set-up was simply an eloquent, focused execution. I liked that a lot.

Chris then stepped behind the camera and told me to look at him. The tone of his voice made my heart start. "Look here. Take a deep breath." It was powerful how quickly he took command, and I was shocked at how easily I turned myself over to his command. I was standing there wide open to him. There was a flat rock behind me. He said I could sit. I was fully dressed but felt naked.

As he began snapping away, something in him changed. His sexual energy was suddenly palpable, or was it mine? He seemed gripped by a passion to capture something in the moment that I might exude. As he moved in and out of proximity to me, I felt myself become soft, open, and vulnerable. "Yes, yes, beautiful. That's it, wonderful. Yes, let me have it."

I think I would have done anything he asked, but Chris stayed at a very seductive distance – a place intimate and yet not intrusive. Sexual energy poured out of me like a river without restraint. Try as I did to draw him in, to get him to kiss me or to take me, he remained the master observer, and this turned me on even more.

At one point, I lay back on the warm, flat rock and allowed my heart and my feelings to open into the light. I felt completely safe, completely at ease, and one with my body and heart. I was pouring out into everything, in a state of total ecstasy. I felt like the most beautiful woman in the world. It was so freeing to be totally expressive of my love and simply to be seen in that beautiful way. As Chris began to wrap up, I sat on the rock feeling jubilant, like a little girl again. All I wanted to do was have Chris make love to me. And yet, I was afraid to break the spell of this magnificent feeling.

After he got the equipment wrapped up, he came and sat with me. He looked into my eyes. I loved his eyes because they didn't need anything from me. The power of that was incredibly seductive. He then kissed me, intensely and slowly. We kissed like that, late sun falling on our faces, until it felt as if our mouths became one. He then lay down on top of me. Without even moving, I felt our energies dancing, merging. Our intimacy was so deep, like an abyss of possibility; but it had nothing to do with our words, commonalities, admiration, or agreement. We were like the earth meeting the sky on that warm, flat rock – breathing as one until the sun went down.

When we got back to Chris's place, he asked if I'd like a hot bubble bath. I'd gotten chilled on the hike back. I nodded, nervous but excited. I heard him start the bath and put on the kettle for tea. I was thinking most men would have taken advantage of my openness that day – on the rock. But it was obvious Chris was content and comfortable with the pace. He invited me to get into the bath. There was a robe carefully laid out for me to put on (in privacy). He guided me to the bathroom and said he'd check back in a moment with tea, giving me time to get in on my own. He didn't use these obviously intimate moments as seduction opportunities, as is so common with some men, and this intensified both my trust and my desire.

Chris sat on the floor, and we talked while I was in the bath. He spoke about his work, the land he lived on, and a little about his photography. I found myself drifting into romantic thoughts of a future with him and coming back to witness him finding himself within himself as he spoke. When I could no longer sit in the heat of the tub, Chris helped me out and dried me off. This, too, was a moment that was intensely erotic for me because he was so present and in control. By the time we got to his bed, I was without defense, without fear – just open and ready for him to have me.

It's hard to describe how good it feels for a woman to open to a man – to have no reservations or concerns. It is a kind of ecstasy unto itself to want so passionately that there is nothing else. I had that feeling that night. How Chris made love to me is secondary, really. What made it memorable and unforgettable was how he opened me. He was curious, interested, and focused, and he had a meaningful desire to engage me. He stands out in my memory because I felt gorgeous and feminine in his presence and under his touch.

Who is *The Artist*?
Why are women drawn to him?

The Artist is the easiest archetype for most men to identify with, because men tend to be highly visual. If you're a man with a pulse, you experience a powerful visual urge to look at beautiful women. That looking stimulates you and feeds your sexual appetite and vitality. What matters most is what you do with that impulse as it's how women perceive you and respond to you. Where does that sexual impulse lead you? Does it frustrate you? Do you find yourself becoming possessed of the need to have a woman because she turns you on? Are you given to anger or resentment when you don't get what you want? Are you distracted by beauty? Or, do women fuel your mission in life and energize you to make a difference?

If you find yourself captivated by a woman's beauty – by how the light dances in her eyes, the pitch of her laughter, or how she glides across a room – you already know what it is to appreciate a woman and femininity. You already know what it means to open to the archetype of The Artist in relationship to the women in your life, and in relationship to the world at large. The Artist isn't The Artist because he's an actual artist, but because he has a relationship to femininity and women that makes women come alive in his presence.

Within every woman is a powerful desire to be seen. Like women themselves, this desire may seem odd or mysterious to you. You likely don't have this same desire, at least not with the same intensity. The feminine in all of us identifies with the light and with being seen. The masculine in all of us identifies with the witness and the observer. When you animate your masculine energy by acting as the witness and the observer, ¬¬ you create a powerful polarity of sexual attraction with a woman.

Every woman, regardless of how you may judge her beauty, has a deep desire to be seen and appreciated by eyes that can truly see her. A woman may not have much confidence in her beauty and may have a hard, guarded exterior, but the desire to be seen and celebrated is there, waiting, like a seed to burst open to the warmth of the sun. Under the right conditions, with care and attention, the seed becomes a flower. As The Artist, when you see a woman – truly see her – her "petals" open to reveal her radiant, feminine essence. You've probably glimpsed this essence before: A happy, confident woman exudes it like a fragrance. Of course, many women never receive this gift from a man, even in relationships that endure over decades, because the men in their lives are oblivious to this aching, feminine desire. A woman can be like a dandelion among thousands of others for her man, or she can be a single red rose in a field of weeds.

For most men, seeing a beautiful woman tends to be a pelvic event. It simply activates a physical desire to possess that object of beauty and empty one's self into it. For The Artist, those sexual feelings arise but are accompanied by a desire to join a woman spiritually and from his heart. This isn't simply wishful thinking and a projection from a woman hoping some prince might act this way. In fact, it is what men who are successful lovers and partners have told me about their experiences. When these men learn to appreciate women and femininity separate from their own desires and satisfying their own sexual needs, they feel the power they have to affect how a woman feels about herself and how she moves and flows in the world. That's a pretty intoxicating thing to come to know and understand about being a man.

The Artist represents the opportunity to experience your masculine power through seeing and appreciating femininity. It allows you to be the kind of a man who can affect a woman deeply by reflecting her truest self to her, rather than simply chasing the effect she has on you. If you think about the time, passion, and commitment it takes to paint a portrait – the painstaking layers of color ¬that are applied to the canvas and the hours upon hours of looking, sensing and interpreting – you can imagine why a man who looks deeply and reflects what he sees has such a powerful effect on a woman. You don't have to be a painter or a visual artist to fulfill a woman in this way, to be her mirror. You need only the desire to have a positive and meaningful effect on her. It might be news to you, but you have a lot of power wrapped up in how you engage your masculine gifts, both with women and the world.

Awakening The Artist

As I've said, being able to live The Artist archetype – in relation to women and to the world – does not mean you have to become an artist as a job, or even as a hobby. It does mean there are ways of being you can practice that will positively and significantly impact your ability to attract, engage with, and maintain a deep passionate relationship with a woman. As The Artist, you have the opportunity to see the world, the women in it, and the particular woman in front of you at three important levels: her feminine essence, her unique physical beauty, and her deep inner beauty.

The first opportunity is to see a woman's feminine essence. This is not specific to any particular woman and requires you to see and appreciate what is universally feminine about her. It is important not to overlook this, as it is her feminine essence that actually attracts you sexually. It is the mysterious part of her that is most different from you and usually the source of most of the confusion men have about the women they love.

The second opportunity is to see her unique physical beauty. This is usually what you think is attracting you. It may be the shape of her legs, the curve of her breasts, the way her hair plays across her face, or the sparkle in her eyes. The trick here is to look past your typical sexual triggers and see something uniquely beautiful about her.

The third opportunity is to see a woman's deep inner beauty. And yes, inner beauty is real. The inability to see it and love it is simply a limitation. You might be thinking, "Yeah, she's a good person and loves puppies, but what really turns me on is the shape of her ass. Isn't all this "seeing her deep inner beauty" just kind of bullshit, just a sort of meaningless exercise?" Well, that kind of depends on what you want.

Every woman wants to be seen and to be deeply known. If you want a woman in your life who is emotionally fulfilled and playful and expresses sexual desire for you, yes, becoming acquainted with a woman's deep inner beauty is a worthwhile endeavor. A woman wants to feel that you welcome and appreciate her femininity (so you won't be constantly holding her to masculine standards of behavior or trying to make her be more like a man), her unique physical beauty (because she wants to know she is physically beautiful in your eyes), and her deep inner beauty (that is, what life experiences made her into the woman she is). If you leave out one of these ways of seeing and appreciating her, a woman will feel you don't truly know her and thus you cannot truly love her. If you've had a woman question whether you see her; if she has said to you, "You don't know me," then you've experienced a lack of The Artist's archetype in how you interact with her. You know from experience that a woman in doubt is never a fount of joy or an eager erotic partner. She's got too much of herself invested in trying to be seen by you.

My clients often tell me: "I just want a happy woman in my life," and yet, what they really seem to want is a woman who acts like a man by day and plays like a woman by night. They view giving to a woman as a chore or duty, rather than a powerful masculine opportunity. It's not just your woman who benefits by way of your seeing and reflecting her feminine essence; you benefit by coming to know the power of your masculine gifts.

The First Opportunity:
Seeing Her Feminine Essence

Essence is not an easy thing to define, but you know some women are somehow more feminine than others. You feel it in how a feminine woman affects you. Her femininity permeates and intoxicates you, and it awakens your passion and desire to give to her. If you love her, you're inspired to do good in the world, to be a better man.

A woman's feminine essence is very much like a river, flowing and unpredictable; this you know. It might be the very thing that terrifies you about women and loving them – this wild uncertainty. What you may not know is that a river needs riverbanks; it needs to be contained. Without riverbanks, the river isn't a river at all; it's simply a flood. The banks of the river offer support and a carriage. A man's masculine energy can be very much like the riverbanks for a woman, a source of solid, uncompromising support. Together the river and the riverbanks are a balanced force, equally powerful and equally necessary.

A woman wants to be supported with equanimity and strength like the river is held by the riverbanks. She wants to feel you respect her as a feminine being and that you take pleasure in the way she complements you as a man.

Women are accustomed to being desired for how their bodies look and feel. It's no surprise to a woman that the radiance of her smile or the shape of her mouth turns you on. ¬What surprises and captivates a woman is your fearless invitation to her to be the woman she is. I know this all sounds really poetic and wonderfully ideal, but you're probably wondering how it plays out in real life, with real women. Trust that a woman knows when she's accepted and loved for being a woman. She may not be able to articulate why she knows, but she knows.

You know when a woman accepts you for being a man, and you know when she throws it in your face as if it's a crime. You know how valuable a woman's true acceptance can be in terms of how you feel about yourself and how you live in relationship to her. Your greatest opportunity in loving women is that fundamental acceptance, and it begins with this deeper, more compassionate way of seeing and reflecting.

I had two business meetings this week with two very different men who responded to my femininity in different ways. In one case I felt seen; in the other I felt diminished. The first man was an editor I was considering hiring for this book; the second was a web designer.

The first man, Jesse, was attractive and professional, beautifully groomed, about thirty-five years old. He made an impressive entrance, but that's as far as the positive experience went. I found Jesse to be abrasive. He challenged my thoughts and ideas right off the bat – the way men challenge one another.

What he didn't understand and most men don't is that women don't respond well to masculine ways of interacting, like being challenged. We experience it as hurtful. It's a case of expecting a woman to be like a man. For example, I said something to Jesse about my own fears of rewriting (as I'm really bad at rewrites), and he contradicted me without even acknowledging what I'd said. "No, rewriting isn't a problem. You just have to buckle down and make it happen." He seemed to think countering me was adding value when truly it was only diminishing trust.

I'd also expressed concerns and feelings about hiring an editor and opening myself to scrutiny and greater vulnerability (this was my feminine way of moving into intimacy with him), and he threw out unsolicited advice that was critical and unsupportive. "You said the writing was good, so what's there to worry about? Unless you really don't think it's very good."

I could feel Jesse found me attractive, but his face lacked any hint of appreciation. When a man holds this tightly to his sexual energy, it makes him appear less powerful. It was clear to me that Jesse was afraid of losing control.

Overall I felt Jesse lacked sensitivity and didn't have the capacity to appreciate me as a woman, so it wouldn't be possible for me to work with him. As much as I knew he'd be an excellent editor (based on reviews of his work), having a man who felt threatened by me oversee my book project didn't feel like the best way to support myself. This is often how men (not grounded in their own power) react in the presence of a woman's expressed feminine essence – they feel a need to come up against that power rather than embrace it.

My second meeting was with a web designer who was referred by a friend. I felt instantly at ease with Tim because he was confident and gracious. It was clear from the moment our eyes met that Tim liked people and could make room for them to be themselves. When we first sat down together, Tim asked me to tell him about my book and what I envisioned for the website. "What would make you really happy to see on this site?" he asked. The openness of Tim's question put me at ease. When I shared what I imagined, he responded to what I said and encouraged me to tell him more.

Tim was a little older than Jesse but light years more mature. He was relaxed and at ease with himself, and this made him feel powerful and trustworthy to me. What I enjoyed most is that he respected me by inviting me to be myself, to express my inner most desires with him. "Tell me why you wrote this book," he said. I breathed deeply, feeling how right the moment was to have a man support me in such a caring way.

Where Jesse was trying to avoid feeling me, Tim was masterful at feeling me. He was centered and self-possessed, but also open – a rare gift in men. When I compared him to Jesse, it felt like the difference between chatting with a boy scout and authentically connecting with a scoutmaster. Tim was a leader and led well because he didn't need to step on my toes to establish his lead. I found this very attractive and empowering.

Defining Feminine Essence

By now you know how the sense of a woman's feminine essence is felt, but can you define it? The following quiz is designed to help you further cultivate awareness of female essence, so you can give a woman the feeling she wants to have with you and feel your own power more vividly with her.

Circle the top ten qualities below that you are most attracted to in women or that you'd most want in an intimate partner. No one is looking over your shoulder, so be honest with yourself and don't read ahead.

I want my intimate sexual partner to be:

Stable
Emotional
Expressive
Steady
Thoughtful
Voluptuous
Clear
Sensual
Beautiful

Competitive
Graceful
Loving
Directed
Radiant
Focused
Soft
Driven
Vulnerable
Penetrating
Aggressive
Spontaneous
Passionate
Strong
Protective
Receptive
Passive
Hard

Here are the feminine qualities. How many of them did you choose? Emotional, Expressive, Voluptuous, Sensual, Beautiful, Graceful, Loving, Radiant, Soft, Vulnerable, Spontaneous, Passionate, Receptive, Passive.

So do you really want a woman who is logical, predictable, relentlessly focused, directed, and centered? Not likely. If you do, is it a woman you want to be with, or a man? You might like a woman's masculine qualities seventy percent of the time, but when it comes to sexual energy and attraction, would you be turned on by such a woman? Is the lack of opposite energy sustainable for a sexually exciting relationship? Likely not.

If you chose an overwhelming number of masculine qualities, there is obviously an opportunity here to develop an appreciation for the feminine.

Practice:
Finding and Flipping the Feminine Essence Switch

Some women naturally express themselves in very relaxed, feminine ways. Other women express feminine energy in a kind of strategic way to manipulate and control men. But many women are not used to expressing their feminine energy at all.

Working in a masculine world or living in a depolarized relationship with a not-so-masculine man can make a woman feel unsafe or uncertain about expressing her feminine energy. However, it's a woman's capacity to express her energy in a feminine way that most attracts you to her. Even the most hardened woman wants a man who will find the switch in her that allows her to relax and be the feminine creature she longs to be.

1. Think about the qualities on the list above. Can you add other qualities that feel distinctly feminine to you? Remember every man and every woman has the capacity to express energy in more masculine and more feminine ways.

2. Look at the women in your life. Study them. When do they express those more feminine essential qualities? Is that essence like a well-guarded seed, or does it easily pour forth? Are there conditions you notice that need to be in place for those qualities to be elicited?

3. How does your masculine presence (steadiness, focus, and strength, among other things) affect the expression of her woman's feminine qualities? If you bring focus and direction, does she respond with radiance and receptivity? Become a connoisseur of these qualities in the women around you, but don't do it just to see if you can unlock those qualities in the women in your life.

4. The secret to this is in the power of polarity. Most of the qualities described above are polar opposites of more masculine qualities. By exercising or expressing a polarizing quality, you tend to animate its opposite in your partner. If you really gaze deeply at your woman and really see her, you will most likely elicit her radiance and glow. If you offer her loving direction, she will most likely respond with receptive surrender (though if she is not used to feeling your direction, she may initially not trust it and test your resolve to offer her direction). If you give her something solid

and strong to hurl her passion at, she will most likely relax into softness.

5. Make this your practice for the next several weeks. Don't be discouraged if it doesn't work right away. If she is used to providing her own masculine energy, she may not initially trust yours. She may associate masculine energy as domination and control, especially if she has never felt masculine energy coupled with love. Be patient. Find the feminine essence switch for the woman in your life.

The Second Opportunity:
Seeing Her Unique Physical Beauty

When you tell a woman that she's beautiful, it's nice. She likely feels you see her to some degree. But I assure you that the first thought that follows for her is, "What's beautiful about me?" Most of the time, she doesn't ask. It's a vulnerable question, but trust me: She's thinking it.

It's clear to any woman that beauty captivates. Beauty is what draws you to a woman. And yet, it's impersonal. It's like admiring a person you don't know. When you tell that person you admire them, it's sweet in its own way; but unless you know that person and can say so with some conviction, your admiration is about as deep as a wading pool.

Telling a woman she's beautiful is an opportunity to let her know you truly see her, but as an Artist, of course, there is an art to doing it. If you don't know the art, most of your compliments will fall flat. An artist looks at the many elements that make something beautiful, breaks them down, and puts them back together as a whole image. You want to learn how to see with this level of specificity.

You don't have to be a scientist about this or to paint anybody. My hope is to inspire you to embrace a new level of seeing. By now, you're aware of a woman's feminine essence, which is the way she uses or expresses her energy. Now the opportunity is to see a woman's unique beauty. What is it about her physically that lights you on fire?

There have been times when I've asked a partner of mine to tell me what (specifically) he found beautiful about me (after he told me I was beautiful) only to witness him freeze. Why? Likely he'd never thought about the specificity of what he found beautiful. For me, these moments were painful and excruciating because I believed if he couldn't name what was specifically beautiful about me, he couldn't have meant what he said. These moments are not only awkward for a man, but they also can make you feel like you're being cruelly tested. The truth is a woman is simply looking to know that your compliments are personal to her. She's not trying to make you feel bad. She just wants confirmation that you see her.

No woman wants to be like every other woman for you. A woman's greatest romantic fantasy is to be "the one." This means that something about her physical beauty (and her feminine essence) moves and captivates you like no other woman in the world. Can this happen for you? Of course it can, ¬if you develop this awareness. Does she have to be the only woman you find to be beautiful? No, of course not, but you better be able to make her feel like the only woman in the room and the most beautiful woman in your eyes. A woman who has to question whether you see her unique beauty and her feminine essence (and that you love this about her) will feel uncertain with you. If she feels uncertain, she won't express her desire or her loving fully with you. If you feel the woman you're with is holding back, that she lacks passion and expressiveness, you might look at how you're seeing and reflecting her.

I spent eight years with a man who told me multiple times a day how beautiful I was, but his words never penetrated me. I thought I must have had a problem with receiving. It wasn't until I spent time with a different partner who could express specifically what was beautiful to him about me that I was able to take in and trust words of affirmation. For a woman to trust what you say, it needs to be specific to her. Remember this and your effect will be meaningful.

Practice:
Finding the Jewel

This should be a fun practice, one that you find you are already good at. I want you to explore what you find beautiful about your partner. If you aren't with one partner (or even if you are), you can look for what you find beautiful in other women. I'm asking you to appreciate in detail what makes women beautiful to you. Find the jewels that make up a woman's unique physical beauty. This is a radically simple practice, so these are just a few tips to help you over the rough spots.

1. Get past the obvious. As a man you've grown up getting turned on and even masturbating to specific feminine images. For most men this is reduced to breasts, asses or legs. So do yourself a favor and make these off limits for a while. If you cannot appreciate a woman's breasts, her ass or her legs, what's left? That's your challenge.

2. At certain times in history, women wore so much clothing that a glimpse of neck or earlobe or wrist or ankle could be the subject of entire love poems. Is there some hidden feature you might be overlooking?

3. Eyes, hair, mouth, and skin are easy subjects for compliments, but remember that the best compliments are fresh and alive and avoid clichés. Also, keep in mind that most women put a lot of energy into the appearance of their feet. It never hurts to notice that.

4. Not all compliments need to be expressed in words. This is especially true of physical aspects that a woman might be sensitive to. If she is constantly worrying about having fat thighs, it doesn't help to say, "I love your thighs." It might help to demonstrate with your hands or your mouth or your body how much you love her thighs.

5. Be aware that what makes a woman physically beautiful is not always static or easily captured on film. The feminine is movement itself. Be aware that it might well be a gesture that you find most exciting about a woman.

6. As a real test of your prowess as a jewel finder, look for beauty in unlikely places. Most men have a kind of instant ranking system that classifies women into two and sometimes three categories: "hot," "acceptable," and "not my type." A real Artist can find the jewels in even a woman that falls into the "not my type" category.

7. Keep in mind this is a practice, not an excuse to stalk and stare at women. You should be able to appreciate without salivating. You should be able to compliment without attachment to an outcome. The minute a woman feels you are complimenting to get something from her, you've lost her.

8. Some women have been so wounded in regard to their physical

appearance that they resist accepting compliments. They brush them off. If your woman is automatically dismissive of compliments, first ask yourself if you are complimenting her in a genuine, authentic and original way. If the answer is yes, then force her to face the compliment. You can't force her to accept it, but you can use loving masculine force to press into her. Turn her to face you. Let her know this is not a casual moment. Let her feel how important it is to you that she knows this little detail. Then let it go.

The Third Opportunity:
Seeing Her Deep Inner Beauty

My friend, Danielle, who is a highly creative artist, is physically one of the most beautiful women I've ever seen. When I look at her face, I find myself trying to break down what specifically contributes to her breathtaking beauty. She's perfectly symmetrical, but there's much more to her beauty than meets the eye.

I often hear from Danielle how much she'd like to meet a man who could see beyond her physical attractiveness to her inner beauty. You might wonder why this is so important. Why doesn't she appreciate the gift she's been given, and why is being celebrated for her loveliness a problem?

It's interesting that when men feel intimidated by beautiful women like Danielle, they get irritated at the idea of being forced to look beyond what has them hooked. It's like, "Hey isn't it enough that I can't take my eyes off you?"

Having been blessed by the genetic lottery with what men in this culture find attractive, I admit it's not such a bad deal to be physically beautiful. However, there's also a deeper desire to be recognized for what is inside of you that gives shape and interest to that beauty. The beauty you see on the outside is only a fraction of a woman's total beauty.

Women like Danielle tell me that men often lose their sense of center and control with them. Instead of being men who offer comfort, love, and empathy, they behave like sycophants, pouring their hearts and souls into sexual attraction. How can a woman share her true self – her pain, her hopes, and her dreams – with a man who sees only a beautiful shell? A man can get so caught up in his own feelings around a woman he's attracted to that it doesn't occur to him that being beautiful comes with its own set of challenges and its own invisible heartaches.

Often women who are physically extraordinary end up taking radical measures to be seen beyond their faces and perfect bodies. They shave their heads, pierce their skin, and tattoo their bodies in order to convey: "I have an inside, too."

A woman does want to be seen as physically beautiful, but it's only one of the ways she wants to be seen. Danielle often tells me how few people actually know her. They think they know her, but what she feels is that they decide who she is based on how she looks.

When I was a girl, it became obvious to me that boys found me attractive. By age ten, I was garnering attention. Boys giggled in my presence, made silly comments, and even tried to touch me as I passed by. To go from being a child to a pubescent girl was suddenly very uncomfortable, and yet that discomfort grew into titillation. Being attractive definitely felt good.

By the time I was in high school, feelings of invisibility began to grow inside of me. I was depressed and despondent, but nobody seemed to notice. Under the surface of my cute sexiness, I suffered a lack of caring at home and a lack of intimacy with my family and friends. Even my girlfriends couldn't see how much pain I was in because I appeared so confident.

At fifteen, I met a boy who would change my life. He was a loner: a sexy, handsome boy who didn't seem to care that I was beautiful. He seemed to care that I was in pain and had experiences inside of me that were untold. He wanted to know who I was and what gave shape and meaning to the depth he could sense in me.

We spent day and night together, often for long stretches in silence, just holding each other. For the first time in my life, everything I felt and had experienced seemed meaningful rather than random, because it was no longer solely in me. I was no longer trapped inside of a lonely shell. Being with James made me feel real and unafraid of my own ugliness and the dark experiences I held inside. The other boys I'd known wanted only to take something from me to fill themselves and often left me feeling empty and alone.

Every woman wants you to know her pain, regardless of how she appears to you. She wants you to traverse her emotional landscape, to know the stories, triumphs, hopes, and dreams that live inside her. Where has she been? What roads, what turns, detours, and compromises has she made for love? How have other men loved her?

Love for a woman is everything. It's really the point. Sure there's work, sex, friendships, family, and passion, but love is the center and meaning of it all. A woman might be impressively successful to you in a masculine sense:¬ accomplishments, money, and even fame. But for a woman all of this pales if her success at love is marginal and does not fulfill her hopes and dreams.

If you don't take an interest in a woman's journey of the heart, you won't have a place in her heart. It's not about documenting the facts about each of her lovers (and how many she's had) on some time line; it's about having a sense of what has shaped her experience of loving.

When you next make love to a woman, look deeply into what makes her the woman she is. See her deep inner beauty (her emotional landscape) and her physical beauty together. It's as if you're looking at the bottom of the sea and the surface simultaneously. This will give her the felt sense that it's safe and good to open the gates of her pleasure and heart to you.

Practice:
Eye Gazing
First the bad news: Many men find this practice difficult. Now the good news: Done well, this couple's practice can be deeply bonding and really allow a woman to feel seen.

1. Begin by sitting facing your partner as close as is comfortable. You can sit knee to knee in two chairs or on the floor, or you can sit with your partner in your lap straddling you. Use pillows to support both of you long enough to remain in this position for a set period of time.

2. Start with five minutes and work up to fifteen or twenty. You shouldn't be looking at a clock to figure out when you are done. A piece of instrumental music playing softly in the background is an effective and non-intrusive timer.

3. Begin by gazing into your partner's left eye while she gazes into your left eye. Slowly bring your breathing into alignment. You can inhale and exhale together, or you can inhale on her exhale and then reverse it.

4. Without forcing anything, keep your attention on her left eye. Look deeply into her eye. Then look deeper than her eye. Imagine that you are penetrating her with your gaze. Let your breath deepen along with the depth of your penetration. Feel your way inside her with your gaze.

5. Feel into her heart. Feel her pain and her joy. Inhabit her body and heart and soul. If emotion wells up in you as you feel her depth and her beauty, that's okay. Tears are okay. Just don't break focus or get lost in your own feelings.

6. You don't need to accomplish anything here. You are merely giving her the gift of seeing as deeply into her as you can. You are giving her the gift of your absolute presence. You are penetrating her with love.

7. When the time is up, stay together a while longer. Hold her. Come apart gently and be gentle with each other afterward. Some couples feel like being sexual afterward, but that is not the point of this practice; and if your partner feels like this is just a prelude to sex for you, it will reduce the effectiveness of the practice.

The Shadow of The Artist

Every archetype has a shadow aspect. You might think of the shadow, or the dark side, of the archetype as what happens when a man gets fixated on just one archetype – devoid of the others. Or what happens when his expression of the archetype is separated from his heart and his love. If you've ever felt or craved the temporary satisfaction and adrenaline rush of manipulating a woman's desires to your advantage, you know what it is to taste the dark side of this archetype.

Every man walks on the dark side now and again. Every man imagines or even acts out what it might be like to manipulate, trick, or overpower a woman¬ with his body or mind. The key to not falling into the shadow archetype is balancing this energy and using it as healthy, manageable sexual fuel. The opportunity is to illuminate these places in yourself and understand what causes them to fester, so you can find your way into light and love with women.

Some twenty years ago in Chicago, a photographer approached a girlfriend of mine on the street and offered her an opportunity to model. She was flattered to be seen by a much older, seemingly sophisticated man, a man who told her that she had top-modeling potential. He complimented her and made her feel seen and beautiful and special all at once. I tried to warn her that the setup sounded suspicious and offered to go with her, but Jenny didn't like what I had to say. She left our apartment in a huff and accused me of feeling envy at her good fortune.

That night with the stranger was a traumatic one for Jenny. The man alternated between being sweet and charismatic and taking a hard line approach and pressuring her. He told her again in great detail how beautiful she was and how much potential she had, but followed that with asserting that no woman could make it in the modeling field if she didn't do swimsuit work and wasn't willing to show at least her breasts in photographs.

Jenny said she didn't want to get naked in the session, but he continued the pressure and accused her, cruelly, of acting like a child. He was in his fifties and she was twenty-four, so she was sufficiently confused and intimidated by his presence. Would a man of his age actually lie to her in order to seduce her? He was her father's age, and so there was an expectation of safety and protection that simply wasn't there.

Jenny ultimately acquiesced to the swimsuit photos out of a fear that he was right about her modeling career. The swimsuits he provided her were incredibly racy, and when she refused to disrobe fully, he threatened to throw her out of the house in her swimsuit, in the dead of winter. "You're wasting my time," he told her.

After six hours of being tortured to compromise her modesty, the pictures he promised to mail to her for her portfolio never arrived. Jenny spent days mourning the loss of her innocence, feeling dirty and violated. When she tried to reach him by phone for her photos, she discovered the number on his card was a false one.

Here was a man who figured out how to manipulate a woman's deepest desire to be seen by seeming to be a man who could see. The fact is he didn't see women at all. All he saw was an opportunity to exploit a desire he barely understood. I imagine that he felt a kind of "right" to Jenny's body and soul because she was a seeker of fame. He and men like him miss the point that until they learn to love and appreciate women, they will always be liars and thieves of the feminine spirit.

The dark side of The Artist isn't always a con artist; sometimes he's a real artist. Take Pablo Picasso, one of the greatest visual artists in history. Here was a man with a true gift for seeing. Picasso was known to seduce women, immortalize them in his paintings (while proclaiming his love), and then lie to and cheat on them until he broke them emotionally. He claimed there were just two types of women: goddesses and doormats, but he lacked the insight to see himself as a killer of feminine spirit.

Our stories tell us there are women who can transform frogs into princes with the power of their loving. Picasso could transform a goddess into a doormat with the shadow of his heart. He knew how to minimize a woman by refusing her what she most needed: to be deeply seen and appreciated as a woman. By spreading his affection and attention thin with other women and using verbal abuse to demoralize the women who loved him, he made women doubt their beauty and value. It seems this gave him a sense of power to walk over the heart of femininity.

It wasn't above Picasso to parade his lovers before his wives with shameless pride. One night, his mistress, Francoise, who bore him two children, witnessed him making love to one of his pottery students. She cried but said nothing. The next evening, knowing that she knew, he told her: "I go where I want; I see who I want; yes, and I sleep with who I want."

The shadow of The Artist is, unfortunately, a man who hasn't discovered the feminine as a complement and a source of strength. He feels his power is dependent on domination rather than cooperation. Seduction for him is always self-serving and limited. It has no depth. It's a goal-driven game that isn't sustainable. The distinction between boys and men is that boys need to diminish women for their sense of power. Men empower women, and this feeds their own sense of power.

The healthy Artist archetype sees himself in the feminine. He knows that we are inextricably intertwined, like the breath to the body. The only game the healthy Artist is interested in playing with women is one of mutuality and mutual empowerment. His gift is that he sees deeply, and what he sees is that he has the power to make a woman feel like a goddess. And he chooses to exercise this power and reap the rewards.

Men often ask me: Why do women like jerks? Why would a woman endure a Pablo Picasso or a man who is less than kind? The answer is simple and yet complex. When a woman becomes entangled with the dark side of The Artist archetype, it's usually because she's tasted a drop of something she deeply yearns for, and that drop carries a promise of what could be.

Imagine being lost in a desert, desperate for water. You find a tiny pool under a cactus and you lap it up. Fearing the vast brutal desert, you stay at that one spot for days hoping for more water. Some women live on a drop of water their whole lives. It's not that any woman likes a jerk; it's that hopes springs eternal in the feminine.

You can be a man who offers a drop of water or a man who quenches a woman's thirst. It's really a matter of knowing that you have what the feminine soul hungers for and finding the confidence in yourself to give it to her.

The Artist is the first important archetype for man. When you love a woman in the three ways of The Artist archetype – seeing her feminine essence, seeing her unique beauty, and seeing her deep inner beauty – you seed a garden for sexual pleasure and love. The more you care for and nurture that garden, the more it rewards you with erotic and romantic abundance. The Artist learns to attend to and appreciate a woman.

This is a powerful force to animate and leads to the next of the archetypes and the next key to a woman's heart: The Poet, he who learns to extend his deep seeing into verbal appreciation and celebration.

Chapter 2

The Poet

I met Mark at a party on a gorgeous fall evening. I'll never forget how I took him for a sailor or a moneyed entrepreneur, elegantly leaning up against a wall, studying the room. He was neither of those. He was basically a brilliant, broke writer, but by the time I discovered this, I didn't care. I was hooked on how he was with me.

That night we talked for hours, holding hands and caressing one another in a warm, soft corner of the room. I barely remember what we said. It was the energy between us that mesmerized me like a slow-burning flame heating every cell in my body.

The following weekend we met for coffee. I felt excited to spend intimate time again with Mark. We laughed over some of the moments we had observed at the party and made small talk for a while. At some point, we got onto the topic of love and our past relationships, and Mark paused to gather his thoughts.

"I'm not going to try to hide this from you, Karen: I think you're amazing. I've been thinking about you ever since we met. You might even say it was love at first sight."

"Wow," I said.

"Yeah, I'd say wow is how I'm feeling."

Mark looked at me for a good long while and let that idea settle in. As I looked into his eyes, I knew I too had been feeling something very similar, and yet, I'd felt a need to resist it at the same time.

"I watched you for hours at that party," he continued. "I watched you laugh. I watched how you moved. I watched you flirt with other men. I watched you eat. I realized that I could watch you for the rest of my life, and I've never had that feeling before. The pleasure of watching you was immense for me. And when we talked in that corner, I felt that I was home. I know you're probably thinking that it's because you're beautiful and I have some sort of adolescent crush on you, but your beauty is such a small part of it. When I look at you, I see myself in a frame that I like. I like myself when I'm with you. Does that make sense?"

Did it make sense? Oh my God, I thought, it certainly did.

Mark paused to sip his coffee, and I held my breath. Part of me wanted to protect myself, to make sure this wasn't a momentary high from which he'd soon crash.

"Karen, I've known a lot of women. I won't lie about that. I've had many lovers. What I want in my life is a woman who lights me up, who is the song of my heart. I knew the first time I saw you that you could be this woman. When I look into your eyes, I see amazing possibilities. I don't think I've ever felt this before."

"Yes," I answered softly, "me too."

"Really?" He seemed to be looking so deeply into me, as if he could see my truth if he looked hard enough.

"Yes."

"And," he went on, "while this all sounds incredibly romantic, I think we need to get to know each other . . . you know, like all those messy little details that make us human."

"Right, because you may not feel this way in three months," I said playfully, with a laugh.

"Oh, yes, we need to get to know each other," he said, looking down into his coffee with a warm and sexy smile on his face. I was thoroughly hooked.

Three months later, Mark's love and desire for me were not only still very much alive, but that flame I felt so clearly was ablaze and never ceased to burn. His way of engaging me deepened, taking me to places that both terrified and surprised me. The giddiness of new love had faded as I'd feared, but what stood in its place was as solid as a redwood tree.

He saw me. He always had. That was clear. But I didn't expect how his ability to reflect the real me would open me to being the person I'd only briefly known before. Even more remarkable was a kind of radar he had for my inner states. Without my saying a word, he could pick up on my thoughts and feelings.

One day, after seven months together, I was despairing of my ability to complete projects in my life. When I compared myself to Mark and his impeccable follow-through in his life, I felt small. I was in the kitchen in this dark mood and he took me by the hand to a spot under a tree in our garden. "Karen, do you have any idea how gifted you are?"

I began to cry.

"I don't need to feed your ego. I'm talking to the real Karen here. You have something people need. And when you don't give that gift, other people suffer. I see you no matter what you do. You can't hide from me. I don't care if you gain weight, change careers, or color your hair. I'm in this with you – heart and soul. There is nothing artificial about how I see you or what I want from you. I want you to see yourself this way and stop playing this game of 'I'm not good enough.'"

We never talked about it again. And I was different. He didn't leave me any space for pretending anymore.

I was so in love with Mark that I wasn't the Karen I thought I knew. I'm not talking about romantic love – love that's out of body, a projection. I'm talking about pure love – love that would be there if he left, love that would remain if he chose another woman. My love was pouring into everything, and my desire to give to him was unprecedented. I'd never wanted to give to a man so freely without also holding back. The walls of fear simply dissolved.

Mark's claiming me as his – asserting his love daily with action and his beautiful words – taught me to trust and to let go. In bed, before Mark, I'd always held back. It wasn't something I tried to do; I just did it. One day I noticed that safety net wasn't there. I was flying in my body. I completely surrendered and trusted his love and mine, and sex moved from a nice, pleasurable experience to one of deep merging and unspeakable delight.

Being fully seen and accepted meant I could surrender and be myself. I didn't have to hold tight to some shallow image of myself that I figured he loved. I didn't have to try to be some unchanging picture. This was one of the greatest gifts I'd ever been given by a man. Mark chose me and expressed that clearly. He also celebrated me through his words and actions and, finally, he claimed me in a way that every woman is terrified of and secretly yearns for.

Who is *The Poet*?
Why are women drawn to him?

Cyrano de Bergerac was a 16th century poet and playwright famous for his poetic seduction of an intellectual heiress named Roxanne. You've likely seen a version of the play about his life by Edmond Rostand or one of the movie versions. Steve Martin played an updated version of Cyrano in the romantic comedy, Roxanne. If you don't know this story, you need to. It's one that makes every woman's heart sing.

The story essentially goes that this poet, who also happens to be one of the most skilled swordsmen in France, has a gigantic nose that makes him believe it is impossible for him to be loved. And yet he is deeply in love with his distant cousin, Roxanne. One day, he discovers Roxanne is in love with a man named Christian. With no idea of Cyrano's feelings for her, she confides in Cyrano and asks him to befriend and protect Christian in battle. He does so out of love. He soon discovers Christian is distraught over his own perceived weakness – that he cannot write, and that Roxanne has requested a letter from him to express his interest and caring for her.

Cyrano writes a series of letters, captivating Roxanne with the explicit and heartfelt words that express his own love for Roxanne. Then Christian dies suddenly in a battle. Not wanting to destroy Roxanne's pure love for Christian, Cyrano takes the secret to his grave. Even in his last moments, when Roxanne discovers it was Cyrano all along, he never admits his love.

When Roxanne initially read "Christian's" poetry written by Cyrano, she said: "I would love you even if you were ugly, because you have touched my heart."

The reason women love this story is because we adore a man who can see and express his love in a way that is deeply personal and attuned with who we are and how we want to be seen.

Clearly, Cyrano saw that Roxanne was beautiful, but his capacity to give voice and context to what he saw was rare and compelling. We've explored how The Artist sees a woman's three dimensions of beauty. The Poet gives that seeing context and language. To see a woman is one aspect of loving. To tell her what you love is a different kind of expression.

Finding that in yourself is the challenge, as giving voice to what you see brings a kind of vulnerability. It's emotion expressed, and in that there is always risk. And yet, it's this ability to express what you see in a woman – explicitly and distinctively – that gives her a gut-level desire to be with you.

When Roxanne asked for the letter from Christian, she wanted confirmation. Many men "loved" Roxanne. She was intelligent, beautiful, and passionate. What she wanted were words that would confirm Christian's love as personal and authentic – words that aligned with her truest sense of herself.

Awakening the Poet

The Poet isn't necessarily a poet, just as The Artist isn't necessarily an artist. Again, this opportunity is about animating one aspect of masculine loving. The Poet is a man who can take what he sees and feels about a woman and communicate it with feeling and meaning. Being a generic, sappy, poet is not attractive to women and won't get you very far.

A woman needs specificity to trust you. If you tell a woman she excites you, that's sweet, but it doesn't say that you know her. Poetic language is meaningless unless it's personal and she can feel it as meant genuinely and solely for her.

You don't have to flaunt a sophisticated vocabulary or pen the flowery words of Cyrano de Bergerac to seduce a woman's heart. When my partner, Mark, said he saw me through all of my doubt and drama, his words weren't poetic, and yet they were poetry to me because I felt that what he said was real and from his heart.

There is something powerful about being able to take what is inside of you and offer it to a woman in language. I've been working with couples for more than ten years and often experience how men confront describing what they feel. I don't think it's so much that they don't have the feelings (as women often think), but that they haven't learned how to translate those feelings into words. Saying "I love you" is important and meaningful, but it doesn't create a bond of trust and certainty with a woman. Learning the skill of The Poet is a powerful opportunity to deeply experience a rich part of you that has yet to be expressed.

We're going to explore three opportunities to give voice to your feelings – three ways a woman secretly hopes to be touched by you. Your woman – the woman you truly desire – wants to be chosen by you, clearly and explicitly. She wants to be celebrated by you in a way that suggests you know exactly why you have chosen her. And, she wants to be invited by you to a place that surprises her. Of course, when these three aspects of loving are combined, a woman's desire and affection for you soar.

The First Opportunity: Choosing Her

Once there was a man who walked the long, lonely beaches of life in search of the perfect seashell. Every day he scanned thousands of seashells in hopes of finding the perfect one, but years and decades passed to no avail. Although many of the millions of shells were beautiful and even captivating, none of them seemed to speak to him.

One day after a turbulent storm upturned and rearranged the landscape of the seashore, the man heard a whisper in the early morning light as he made his usual trek. His eyes were drawn to an unusual flickering in the sea of shells. The voice seemed to call to him.

As he made his way toward the sound and the flickering light, he felt a pulsing and a quickening of his heart. Something told him, "This is the one." His long search was over.

He plucked the shiny body from the sand and it was radiant, just as he had always imagined. Smooth, alabaster, perfectly formed: a creation of total beauty. It was as if it were made for his hand and for his soul, and he was home. This is my one, he thought, as he slipped the shell into his pocket next to his heart and completed his final stroll along that long, familiar beach.

In a woman's romantic fantasy, she is your "one." She wants to feel that you chose her, whether you engage with her for a night or a lifetime. Choosing a woman doesn't end at choosing Jenny over Sasha, or even at marriage. These choices are just a beginning, just the opening dance. To be with one woman is a choice you keep making and keep communicating throughout your time together. You might think that choosing a woman once as your girlfriend or wife demon-strates that she is your "one." You had many choices and you chose her, right? So why should you have to prove it again and again?

The fact is that no one choice is permanent. In love, you have to keep choosing, as frustrating as that might be. There are no free days. If you love a woman, you have to keep choosing to love her – and the moment you stop, she will feel it. If you want meaningful and fulfill-ing sex, you have to keep actively choosing to make that happen. Your woman wants to know that you keep choosing her as your woman, because anything less is not alive and present. You're living in the past if you're not making a choice. Communicating your choice of her is not simple. You can't ride on the coattails of a poem you wrote to her forty years ago. Your choice needs to be communicated.

I call a vast number of men in the world "wide-net fishermen."

These are men who, for lack of confidence in themselves and a lack of understanding of women's hearts, cast a wide net in hopes of getting some sex and love – any sex and love. Some men do this even beyond marriage, always on the lookout for that next lucky catch.

That wide-net strategy is really about trying whatever it will take to catch a woman. Wide-net fishermen often catch a variety of wom-en because they throw their interest at any woman who will have them. Whether you're single or have been married for twenty years, the women you choose, or the woman you choose, must know you are choosing her – not that her being with you is some accident of fate or the "luck" you had with your wide net.

The problem is that when a woman feels she is one fish of many, she loses respect for herself and her attraction for you. No woman wants to be someone you dredged up by chance. She wants to be the one you found because you were looking for her. Every woman wants to believe she will belong to a specific man, and that he is looking for her and will find her. Like that one special seashell among millions of others washed ashore, you see her and you know. She's the "one." Now, you might not be looking for your "one," and the women you meet might not be ready for marriage, but nonetheless this romantic idea is alive and well in every woman you meet.

I've known hundreds of men in my practice who were wide-net fishermen. Getting them to give up this broad approach to getting women is never easy, as the net becomes a crutch. If you lack the confidence to believe you can imagine, manifest, and seduce the woman you truly want, you'll likely cast a wide net. You'll try a variety of methods in the hopes of netting any woman.

There is nothing worse, as a woman, than finding yourself really attracted to a man and then realizing his "choice" of you was no choice at all. The fact that he may feel lucky to have caught you is no source of comfort either.

In a confident masculine state, you want to choose and claim a woman as yours. It's a powerful masculine impulse. When you're not in your power, you actually believe a woman needs to choose you. So you do everything in your limited power to make that happen. You chase, you bargain, you compromise, and you cast a wide net – all in hopes of being chosen. The problem is that you miss the point. A woman wants to feel that you chose her from among all the women you could have, that you exercise that level of confidence and power. It fulfills her deepest desire to be seen and celebrated as a unique feminine being.

Practice:
The Language of Choice

While the fact that you are constantly choosing the woman you are with may be obvious to others, the language of choice is an intimate one. When you are expressing your choice of her, it is first and foremost between the two of you. When was the last time you communicated in a convincing way that you would choose her again, or are, in fact, choosing her again, moment by moment? Why do you think women invented the idea of the renewal of wedding vows? It's because after everything they've been through with you they want to know that you would do it all again, that you would still choose them.

1. You can't express your choice if you don't know why you chose her. Take some time to write down why you chose her over any and every other woman to be your partner (hint: because the bartender just announced last call is probably not a good reason). Do this once and then ask the question more deeply. You don't have to write sappy greeting card statements. Be honest. Once you have some real reasons, you are ready to express them.

2. Choose her with casual ease. In a relaxed moment with no agenda (not to get any outcome and not as an apology for some slight), touch her gently, and with simple honesty let her know that you would choose her all over again.

3. Choose her with details. The best time to express your choice of a woman is when she is least expecting it. The best way to express your choice is with specificity.

4. You're probably hoping for some examples here. You won't get them. You're a guy, and it's just too tempting to borrow someone else's expression of choice. If you really don't get how to do this, force yourself to watch four or five romantic comedies in a row and take notes. The romantic films that women love most (the ones that are most popular) are the ones in which the writers put just the right words into the mouths of the actors as they choose the woman who is the main character of the story.

5. You're probably hoping that if you do this really well and find just the right words, one time, you can check this off your manly to-do list and be done with it. Think again.

The Second Opportunity: Celebrating Her

When you initially meet a woman you are attracted to and enjoy, you find yourself in a state of celebration. You're on fire with the excitement and anticipation of being with her. You're inspired to please her, delight her, and take her somewhere.

But celebrating a woman is more than a state of revelry centered on sexual excitement. It's a state of ongoing, renewed appreciation. Naturally, if you don't think about your pleasure and delight, it's missed, and the celebration of her and what she brings to your life is lost.

Celebrating a woman is about putting attention on your good fortune. It's a demonstration of your delight. The feminine in a woman wants to be the center of your attention, and she wants to feel you celebrate being with her, today, and always. Celebrating is a way of saying, "I still see you. I still want you. I still love you."

Often, men stop celebrating women once they have them, because they think of celebrating as a strategy for conquest. But it's the way you celebrated her that opened her heart to you. To stop after the first seduction feels like a trick. How often have you heard a woman complain that the romance was over? That means she has stopped being the center of your attention. And when that happens, it feels to her that she's no longer appreciated and desired. She is no longer a source of delight for you.

For a man, this will seem grossly unfair, but it's a woman's nature to forget what you did the day before to celebrate her – because as a "feeling being," every day is a new day. What you did for her yesterday, was wonderful, but it's gone. She wants that feeling again, that reminder, when you touch her and connect in celebrating your love and desire for her.

While choosing a woman is an intimate act (even when it is done publicly – think wedding vows), celebrating a woman is a public act. It is about taking her places where she is seen, and how you are with her in those public settings. When you initially date a woman, you want to show her off. You want to be seen with her. You celebrate her beauty and her presence in your life. You take her out where she is the center of your attention. You tell people she's yours, and you cater to her needs. All of your demonstrations are a celebration of sorts. In a woman's body, mind, and heart, this feeling is incredible. Of course, as she falls in love with you, she believes this warm, eager attention will last forever. When it collapses after you get her, a part of her hope and excitement for your relationship collapses, too.

Is it any surprise that women love Mother's Day and Valentine's Day? It's kind of sad that women have to rely on a holiday in order to be celebrated, but it's obvious that it makes women feel important and loved.

When men celebrate women, something beautiful happens: Women become more generous and loving. A heart that is weary gets renewed. A body that is dull gets turned on. A mind that was closed is opened. Women are incredibly responsive to being filled by a man's demonstrations. The problem is that most men don't know this, so they let a woman's heart run down to empty. An empty heart is neither generous nor amorous.

When The Poet celebrates a woman, he makes it clear through demonstration that he is delighted. He takes the feelings inside of him and gives them form. That form is genuine for him, and it is how he expresses caring. For one man it might be a drive in the country and a picnic, for another a shopping spree, for another writing a song. Celebration is how you translate your appreciation and caring into physical form. A woman can know you love her, and that's a good thing. But if you don't demonstrate it creatively in forms she can touch and experience, you leave a lot of love on the table.

When a man cannot translate his feelings into physical and verbal forms of expression, he often feels passionless to a woman. A man's lack of passion feeds a woman's lack of desire. To be fully felt and experienced, love needs to be given voice and form.

Telling a woman: "You know I love you," demonstrates a creative limitation. She shouldn't have to "know it." She should feel it and experience it in your demonstrations. Her knowing is something that develops over time with your consistency. It's great if she knows it, but you don't want that to be a crutch for your immediate and most passionate expression.

The first thing to cultivate is your appreciation. Appreciation is a focus, but appreciation fades without attention. Every day, try to notice what you love about her. Is it how she inspires or supports you? Is it her smile? What about her can you celebrate? And then ask yourself how you want to give form to these thoughts or feelings. Is it with gifts? Is it with acts of loving kindness? Is it a card or a plane ticket, a poem, or a bouquet of flowers? What are you most moved to do? What ways are most satisfying for you to celebrate her?

Practice:
Paths of Praising

After the previous practice, you should have a sense of why you chose the woman you are with. This is the basis for what you have to celebrate about her. If you did not write anything down, that may be okay, but how prepared are you really?

Play this little thought game: You're walking with your woman down a city street and you pass a local news crew out doing a human interest story in honor of Valentine's Day. All of a sudden you find a microphone in your face with the question, "What is it that attracted you to this woman?" or "What is it that you find most attractive about this woman?" Would you know what to say? How would your woman feel and how would you feel if you stammered and looked confused and said, "I don't know; she's a good mom."

Celebrating her can have two aspects in practice. One is the way you speak of her or support her or share her publicly. The other can be gifts or gestures that make her feel celebrated.

1. Praise her publicly. While many women will claim this embarrasses them, it is also something that they're hungry for. Praising her in public needs to be done with sensitivity. First of all, it needs to be honest. Don't make extraordinary claims (unless you are clearly being playful, though it is important to avoid sounding facetious). Don't praise her outlandishly in front of her friends. Women can be competitive among themselves. Praise her for things you really do find amazing or irresistible about her.

2. Praise her professionally. Praise her capacity or capability. You should know better than anyone what her gifts are. Let her know that you see those gifts by praising her for them in public. Again, you need to be sensitive to what you say about her in front of colleagues, whether coworkers, superiors, or personnel she supervises, but praising her professionally can be a beautiful gift.

3. Praise her intimately. By intimately, I mean praise her for what you continue to find beautiful or erotically attractive about her. Of course, this area also requires some sensitivity. It needs to be honest, and it is best expressed in relation to how you are affected by her beauty.

4. Praise her with gifts and gestures. You can express praise with gifts and gestures, but this is usually more powerful if there is no obvious reason for the gift or gesture (birthday, anniversary, Valentine's Day, etc.). It is also best if the gesture or gift is not clearly self-serving of some other agenda. Something sexy from Victoria's Secret might be the perfect gift, or it might feel like you are just making a down payment on anticipated sexual favors. Also, be aware of the fact that just because you found a particular gift or gesture that worked well once, it is not a license to simply stop thinking and stop being creative in how you praise her.

The Third Opportunity:
Inviting Her

When a woman is considering you as a lover or partner, she senses what is possible with you. Where will you take her? Not simply where will you go for dinner, but where can you take her body, mind, and heart?

As an emotional, romantic being, she wants the wild, exhilarating possibility. She wants the epic love story unfolding frame by frame, each scene more sizzling than the one before.

Does she ask herself literally, "Where can he take me?" No. But because a woman (being a feminine being) longs to be lifted off her feet and transported into love, she just feels this. To be taken somewhere has so many meanings – all of which are centered on being led and carried into experiences that create intense feelings of love and desire.

I think of the first boys who took me somewhere in body and mind. I remember the boy who taught me how to ride a horse bareback, to feel a kind of freedom I'd never felt before in my body and spirit. All our adventures together gave me this taste of freedom. There was the boy who taught me about the joy of giving to others as I watched him care for an old, lonely man on his Saturday nights.

And there were the men . . . like the one who first photographed me so I could see the beauty he saw in me and stop criticizing myself. He helped me see myself authentically, not just once, but throughout our time together. Of course, I will never forget the man who helped me heal my sexual wounds by loving me as I was and desiring me with equal passion. All of these experiences are so different and yet they left an indelible mark on me. In some way, each of these men or boys took me somewhere I'd never been, and they did it out of love.

If you look at women's romantic fantasies, so many of the metaphors are about being swept into love. The reason is that being swept up creates a feeling of physical lightness, which is a literal high for a woman. This "high" is created for two reasons: She is relieved of her focus on doing and deciding, and because being taken care of produces the hormone oxytocin in her brain. Oxytocin is the hormone responsible for feelings of pleasure and love in a woman. In a woman's romantic fantasy, she is often taken away from the drudgery of daily life and led somewhere that enchants and delights her.

When you meet a woman who excites you, do you catch yourself thinking one step ahead in any moment? When will I kiss her? Where will I take her next? Shall I invite her home? A woman, on the other hand, is thinking ten steps ahead. She's wondering: Would you travel well together? Would her friends like you? Would you make a good partner or husband?

What might happen with you is an incredible source of excitement. Love is built on possibility. Where will you go together? How will she grow and change with you?

Her picturing and conjuring of feeling creates a wave of growing excitement, but that excitement and expansion can quickly crash into nothingness if not met by your imagination and leadership. It's a key moment in a romance. And it's one that needs to be carried intelligently into a relationship.

If nothing seems possible with you – if loving you or wanting you is a dead end – a woman's heart contracts. She won't create this swell of feelings inside of her; she'll simply shut the romantic door. This happens whether there is no possibility with you, or whether you've allowed the romantic possibility in your relationship to dry up.

Men are generally great at stimulating a woman in this way in the beginning when passions are high and you're working to win over a woman. You do all kinds of things that stir the possibility pot. You talk about a future. You share dreams. You show up with a plan, sweep her off her feet, and take her to places that excite her. You feed the possibility by continuously building good feelings together.

When you stop taking her mind, body, and heart to these places, the romance dies. To a woman, it can feel as if she's been duped, as if you held out a promise you didn't fulfill. Her expectation – when and if she chose you – was that the romance would continue to grow and bloom. In fact, it was her dream that you'd always have this same excitement for creating possibility with her, while perhaps for you, that high-energy "moment" was all about getting her and sealing the deal.

Whether you've been with a woman for a month or a decade, she still has this same desire to be taken somewhere. If you don't lead in this, she'll look to someone who will, or she'll close down her desire for you. It's so much a part of what stimulates her sexually. Think about how different a woman is with you when you're on vacation or creating some future together, or when you're sharing dreams. It's because you are feeding the romantic possibility with her.

Where does a woman want to be taken? Every woman is different. I want to be taken to places I've never seen. I love adventure. I also want to be inspired by a man's brilliance and vision. Being taken somewhere in my mind and imagination is really powerful. I want to feel that my man is creating something of meaning in the world. This, too, is a journey.

I also want to be taken somewhere in bed. In other words, I want to be touched in a way I don't expect, or for a man's passion to surprise me. It's not just about new experiences, or wild and different experiences; it's about leaning into and expanding what is possible for you and for the two of you. Love is a journey: Where are you headed? Are you just going through the motions, or is there a bigger possibility for your sexual relationship and for your loving?

When a woman is talking about what you might do together or she wants to talk about dreams, she's looking to dive into the ocean of possibility with you. She wants to swim the waters of delight and explore the depths of where you can go together. These are the key moments when she's looking for that leadership and excitement. She'd love you to say something like: "Let's take that class we've always wanted to take," or "Let's find or build the home we've always dreamed of."

Of course, going along and saying you will create together and then conveniently "forgetting" can be very damaging to your relationship. You'll lose her trust and her love if you play games with her heart.

There's a kind of death that happens between a man and a woman when a man stops leading romantically. A woman turns her heart over to you in the hopes of you taking her somewhere. Sometimes it may be a place she could get to on her own, but there is simply more relaxed and open pleasure in being taken there; and sometimes a man can truly take a woman someplace she might not be able to get to on her own. Your opportunity here is to take her by the "hand" in all areas of your loving (romantically, sexually, and emotionally) and invite her into that next unexplored place of loving and pleasure, keeping in mind that The Poet gives physical form to what he feels.

Practice:
Mapping the Territory of Invitation

Most men today tend to experience the women in their lives as being very competent at running their own lives. This competence can actually spill over into a tendency to be controlling. Because of this, most men tend to default to either letting their women guide them or to figuring out where to lead their women by asking them where they want to go. This is certainly respectful and often seems to be what women want. But it is a guaranteed romance killer. So how do you know where to take a woman? How do you figure out the territory of invitation? As with most of the practices in this book, I can't give you a map to follow. Your woman and your relationship with her is a unique territory. The best I can do is give you some hints:

1. First of all, and this is really going to seem counter-intuitive, you need to find your center as a man, without consideration for her at all. Let go of any concern about her fleeting emotional wants and desires. Find your passion for where the course of your life is heading, and offer her a sincere invitation to join you on that journey. If you can find no woman who wants to accept that invitation, then live your life's passion without a woman. But I can tell you from experience that kind of passion is romantically intoxicating to a woman. You most likely will not be alone for long.

2. As The Artist, you learned to see into your woman deeply. With that capacity you may actually be able to see her more clearly than she can see herself. It is from that depth of seeing that you will know where to invite her, where to take her. At a most basic level, do you know what causes your woman to be more relaxed, more open, more sensual, and to radiate with more love and light? By trial and error alone, you should begin to find the kinds of experiences that amplify the qualities you most love about her or enhance the natural gift she is to the world. Those are the places, events, and experiences to which you want to invite her.

3. You also need to be aware that while you cannot force her to some place she resists going, if you truly believe that some experience or invitation would be truly enrich her life, then your

invitation must have that force of conviction behind it. Without attachment, you may need to bring insistence to your invitation.

4. Your invitations also may be shaped by simply listening to what she says. It may not be her specific requests, but what she talks about. If you have learned to really see her and listen to her, pay attention to what she talks about, what relaxes her, and what opens her. These will give you good clues to places to which you might invite her.

The Shadow of the Poet

Just as The Artist had a shadow side, The Poet also has a darker variant. The shadow of The Poet is often seen in men who are simply in love with being in love. This tends to rob their expressions of choice, celebration, and claim of anything personal. They romanticize their women to feed their own needs, rather than to reflect anything true about their partners' feminine hearts. At the extreme edge of shadow, they use words to manipulate women and satisfy their own ego desire for conquest and seduction. They use what gifts they have to possess and control: a kind of currency to buy love. The reason so many women get fooled by the dark side of The Poet is because so many women are hungry to be chosen, celebrated, and claimed.

Kristine always got a sickening feeling in her stomach when her boyfriend Patrick bought her a gift. Often the gifts were expensive – things she'd seen in passing and commented on, or things she'd mentioned briefly that she thought she might like. She loved the gifts themselves, but as she described to me, "I don't know if I really even wanted those things. They were the kind of things I just liked dreaming about. And for some reason, I don't feel good about accepting the gifts. I know I should be happy, but...."

Kristine had been with Patrick a year. He lived in another city four hours away, so the relationship felt somewhat new. She was concerned that Patrick was pushing hard for marriage. When she put his positive qualities down on paper, he seemed to be the ideal partner; but when she thought about actually marrying Patrick, she felt less sure.

Marriage was all Patrick could seem to talk about in the months leading up to my first session with Kristine. Each week he'd send two dozen roses to her office with a note that said, "Marry me?" While her business partners gushed over Patrick's demonstrations of affection, they left Kristine feeling empty and at times angry. Did he think she had nothing better to do than think about his proposal?

She also felt self-critical. Was there something wrong with her? She had what seemed like the nicest guy in the world asking for her hand in marriage, and yet she felt hesitant. At thirty-eight, she felt it was time to marry, and yet her intuition warned her that going forward might be a devastating mistake.

Patrick earned good money as a financial advisor – his ability to take care of her was never in question. If he stayed on his own trajectory, they could expect to live a very good life, something Patrick stressed more times than Kristine cared to hear. Was he suggesting she couldn't support herself?

Patrick liked to travel, dine out, and have fine things, and if Kristine was honest with herself, so did she. Kristine also admitted that she wanted a man who could express his feelings easily, and Patrick did so abundantly. But his poetry and declarations of love fell flat for her. They seemed oddly impersonal, and something about his urgency to marry made Kristine nervous.

Patrick was masterful at demonstrating what seemed to be love – with words, gifts and support – but something about his interest in Kristine didn't feel real.

Finally she got it: "I don't think it's me he loves. I think it's the idea of me. I think he's in love with the idea of being in love. It's like he's some kind of romance junkie and I'm his current fix. It's me now, but it could be anybody, really." She shook her body with disgust. "That's it in a nutshell. He'd do this with anyone. Last week he forced us to take one of those horse and buggy rides when we were out of town, and he had to propose to me in front of the driver. It was humiliating. And worse, it had nothing to do with me, really. It was like he was playing out a fantasy role he had seen in a movie."

Kristine and I agreed she needed to have a talk with Patrick to find out how much of what she was feeling was her own fear of love and intimacy and how much was her concern that Patrick's love was inauthentic.

I helped her create a clear set of questions designed to get at the heart of what they each expected from marriage and what marriage meant to them. Patrick agreed to the talk with me acting as a mediator. When Kristine presented the questions, what she discovered was eye opening:

"What about me feels right for you as a marriage partner?" she asked him.

"What about you feels right?" he replied in an annoyed tone. "What is this, some kind of audition? Have I not proved my love to you?"

"You have. But I want to know why me?"

"If you don't know, I don't know what to tell you," he said defensively. Kristine noticed in that moment that this was typically how he dealt with conversations of specificity.

"Please, Patrick. This is about my need, not about you. I need to know why you chose me."

"I chose you because you're the woman in my life. I can't think of any reason not to choose you."

"That's why you want to marry me?"

"Kristine, I want to marry you because we love each other. Isn't that good enough?"

"What do you love about me?"

"I love everything. I love how we look together. I love how I feel with you. I love your hair and your body and your smile. I just love you." Patrick seemed to be growing frustrated. "Look, I give you flowers every week. I take you to the best restaurants. I make a lot of money, and I want to marry you. Don't you think you're over-thinking the whole thing? You're not exactly getting any younger."

"What did you say?" Kristine asked, incredulously. "I'm not getting younger? Are you serious?"

"Let's face it, Kristine, it's not as if twenty guys were banging down your door when I met you a year ago. I see your beauty, but how many men do? And frankly, I'm really uncomfortable with the fact that you needed a therapist to help you decide if you should marry me."

"What do you even know about me?" Kristine asked, bitterly.

"I know that you're less secure than I thought you were, and that you have an addiction to food, and that you wish you were the prettier sister, and that you love your business and hate your business partners, and that you generally don't like your life and wish someone would help make it better. Am I right?"

Patrick's face was priceless. I could see he believed he'd reflected her accurately, perhaps even lovingly, and that his comments were going to have a positive effect. I could see in Kristine's face that she had the answer she needed. The feeling she'd been getting all along was dead-on: he didn't see her and he didn't know her. He knew her habits and her fears but didn't know her heart. All of his demonstrations of love – the poems, flowers, gifts, and trips – were no more than props, substitutes for feelings.

I don't believe Patrick wanted his interactions with Kristine to be saccharine and shallow and essentially impersonal. I don't think he was a bad man. He was, in many ways, a natural Poet, but he had not learned how to manifest his inner Artist. He tried to jump right to choosing, celebrating, and claiming a woman without first learning how to see her.

These two archetypes, The Artist and The Poet work together synergistically. The Artist sees a woman's complexity, beauty, and depth, and The Poet makes his choice of a woman based on what he sees. The Poet then expresses that choice in celebration and by invitation.

When a man can animate The Artist and The Poet successfully, he's ready to explore the third archetype, a role that brings action and definition to an intimate relationship: The Director.

Chapter 3

The Director

In many ways, Vladimir was like a prince to me. He was handsome, elegant, powerful, and intelligent. It was a pure stroke of luck that we found each other when his taxi crashed into mine on a Chicago street on a blustery winter's day. It wasn't a major crash, but it rattled me. I got out of the car half-dazed, not expecting to see a handsome passenger smiling at me and assuredly calming his driver at the same time.

His looks were striking. He was tall with loose black hair, green eyes, and the beginnings of a beard. But it was his attitude that captivated me. When he stepped out of the taxi, it was as if he commanded the city. "Don't worry," he said to the anxious driver who had hit my taxi. "Nobody is hurt. Are you okay?" The driver shook his head and was obviously scared. He quickly scanned the cab I'd been riding in to assess the damage.

I walked toward the handsome man, and he began to move toward me at exactly the same moment. All I could do was smile when I looked into his face, and he did the same. "Crazy way to meet," he said, though he managed to say it in a way that suggested he was completely at ease with this kind of crazy.

It was one of those odd moments straight out of a movie where everything around us seemed to be on a kind of cosmic pause – as if we were exactly where we needed to be.

"The police aren't going to come," he said.

"Yeah, they usually don't," I added.

"How about we get some breakfast? I know a great place just

around the corner," he said. While I would not call myself an easy pickup by any stretch of the imagination, something about that moment just felt so odd that I found myself nodding.

"Yeah," I said. "That would be nice." Vlad, as he asked me to call him, took us to a little nook in his neighborhood, teeming with business at nine on a Tuesday morning. Most of the people were dressed in business attire or were shoulder-to-shoulder at the counter in puffy coats. The air was warm with the scent of pancakes and sausage.

Everyone knew Vlad. "Meet my lovely new friend, Karen," he said again and again. "We just crashed into one another in the street." I loved the way he smiled as he introduced me, as if to say, "Look what I found. Isn't she amazing?" I also liked how he'd wrap his arm around my back and pull me closer to him in a way that was at once protective and also suggested that we were long-lost friends.

Vladimir was Russian but born in the US. He was divorced with a sixteen-year-old daughter and owned three upscale city restaurants. His life was very busy, but it was obvious he enjoyed it and had a lot of friends. I noticed that even though everyone around us knew him, or seemed to, his attention was very clearly on me, and he showed a genuine interest in hearing what I had to say and in knowing me.

"Tell me what you love to do," he said, as we sat together after breakfast.

It wasn't hard to tell him, because there was something about him that made me want to experience all the things I loved with this man. "I love Latin dancing, travel, adventure, dining, being in nature, movies, and art museums. I love trains and drives and airplanes."

"OK," he replied, as if some important point had already been decided. "Let's get on a train."

"To where?" I asked, laughing.

"Nowhere, anywhere, everywhere." His relaxed confidence made it seem like a perfectly reasonable suggestion.

"You're crazy," I said, smiling.

"Yeah, probably, but why not come be crazy with me? Let's see where our impulses take us." The way he looked at me in that moment was unforgettable. He didn't flinch or laugh. He just looked into me deeply as if he were seeing an "us" in his mind's eye. I got the feeling there was nothing random about our meeting that day.

"First," he added, "I want to cook for you at my place tonight. After that, we'll stop by a friend of mine's place to hear some incredible jazz. It's his birthday party, and I'd like to have you with me. What do you think?"

"Yes," I answered with a lack of hesitation that surprised even me, "I'd love to."

I dressed in a long, sleek black skirt with a silver bustier and a tight velvet jacket. I was pleased with the "me" I saw in the mirror and felt a tremendous sense of excitement.

Vlad's place was a gorgeous townhouse on the north side of the city – masculine and elegant, warm, and homey. He was dressed beautifully in a button-down white shirt over jeans, open at the chest. He was even sexier and more handsome than I remembered.

The dinner was exceptional as promised – linguine with fresh clams, salad, warm crusty bread, and a Pinot Noir. I loved the feeling of exquisite relaxation in being with a man who knew where he was in life and where he was going. I didn't have to make him feel good, nor did I feel that I could disappoint him. It was easy simply to enjoy each other as neither of us had any unrealistic expectations. I sensed that whatever I might want or need was only a gesture away from being fulfilled. Vlad was a man who knew how to make things happen. That made my whole body soften, and I felt a constant desire to be held in his arms and his gaze.

I admit I didn't really want to go out. I wanted to spend the night looking at Vlad, hearing his voice and stories, and tasting more of his masculine presence. But as he promised, he took me to a jazz club to meet his friends.

As soon as we walked into the club, people began to light up and come forward to see Vladimir. It was obvious he was well liked and known. I'd been with other men who were popular, but it was different with Vlad. As I watched people interact with him, I could see they didn't like him just because he was rich or influential or hip; they liked him because he was a good man. They liked how they felt with him – seen and appreciated – and I was getting a generous dose of that feeling all night long.

Vlad wasn't merely successful; he was a man who gave back to his community. He'd helped fund a cultural education project for poor kids, which included trips to the opera, symphony, museums, art classes, and dance. Many of those kids went on to get scholarships to college because they had tasted a world of possibility.

Over the next several months, I was more and more drawn to be with Vlad. I figured I'd tire of his social appetite, but the truth is I never did, because his way of being socially was so easy and authentic. We didn't have to put on a "face" together and be something other than ourselves. Wherever we went, whatever we did, I was with a man who had integrity, clarity, a plan, and a calm, assured and almost effortless method of execution. I'd never been with a man who had so much ease at making things happen, and I had no idea how much I'd love it.

I loved being the center of his attention as he made things happen. And I thoroughly enjoyed how he took care of me. Whatever I wanted was handled with ease: no stress, just solutions. A wave of a hand, a smile, a soft voice. People were drawn to give Vlad what he wanted – not because he was rich or famous, but because he was confident and charismatic.

The pinnacle of our experience together was probably our trip to Jamaica. I was nervous about traveling together for the first time and admitted that to Vlad one night. "Of course you are. You'll be spending quite a bit of time with me. You're accustomed to space, and I give you that. Don't worry, Karen, I'll take care of you."

Strangely, I believed him and I trusted him. Vlad didn't take over and make all the plans. For some women, that might have been the perfect course of action, but he was always feeling into who I was, and he knew that I would want some sense of control over my experience. He suggested places to stay, and we chose together the one we wanted. In booking the flight, he asked if it would be okay if he went ahead and had it handled by an agent on dates we agreed upon. That also felt good. I kept expecting heavy-handedness, and it was never there. He had a way of navigating (or leading) that was considered and considerate and made everything easy, which made it easy for me to turn over the reins.

Some men try to do everything, and that's stressful because you know it's too much and you know it's not sustainable. On the other hand, some men can't make a decision at all and rely on a woman for everything, out of a fear of getting it wrong. Vlad was a dancer in this regard. He could lead, but he could also follow. I was in awe of how well he did this and how easy it made it to enjoy our time together.

The trip was deeply relaxing, almost eerily so. How do two people who had known each other for only four months find such a complete rhythm?

Vlad had done enough research to be knowledgeable about the locale, but there was no agenda. "Come on," he'd say when I didn't want to think, when I was groggy from lovemaking. And he'd take me somewhere excellent to eat or to drink, as if he'd been there before. Instead of planning everything, he would suggest things at what always seemed like the right moment. "Feels like a 'walk-on-the-beach' kind of night," he said one evening. How did he know? Having been with men who planned everything to the hour, I was grateful for the space and the freedom to flow.

When I needed time alone, he was equally sensitive. I didn't say a word. I just thought it one morning over tea. "How about I go into town and do a little shopping and you have some alone time?" he said. "I'll get us some nice wines and cheeses." But it wasn't a question. He kissed me and got up to shower. And so I had a spectacular morning walking and shopping for gifts for my friends and felt renewed when I saw him that evening. I realized, too, that I'd missed him.

In the time Vlad and I were together, he gave me the gift of masculine assuredness and loving leadership. These gifts are the deepest kind of embrace. It's like being lifted up and set free to fly. Being with a man who isn't afraid to lead and is energized by leading, gave me so much space to be creative and expressive in the way I loved him. I wasn't so caught up in thoughts like *Where is this going?* or *Where are we going?* His lead was as natural as walking. Everywhere we went, women saw this in Vlad and lit up. I had this strange impulse to share him, on occasions, so that other women could feel what I felt. I saw how women gravitated to his confidence and gallantry, and I knew in those moments that being a woman – his woman – was a gift.

Vlad decided to go to Europe for a year with his daughter to develop a business and invited me to be with him. I struggled with the decision for months and ultimately decided to let him go. I had too much going on in my own business and wanted to develop speaking engagements around the U.S.

I have tremendous respect for Vlad and his gentle-hearted, intelligent way of leading. And I have much gratitude for his wisdom, sensitivity, and the places he took me in my heart. He taught me how to let go and surrender controlling things – and to trust a man to lead the way in love.

Who is *The Director?*
Why are women drawn to him?

The gift The Director brings to women is the gift of leadership. To lead is to initiate, give direction, move forward, set on course. Good leadership is never about force.

Think of how a conductor leads a symphony. It's with respect, care, and deference. He can't force his lead on his orchestra. They have to know that his lead is both solid and permeable. This is the kind of lead you want to cultivate with a woman.

Imagine trying to lead an orchestra of musicians without confidence and the certainty that you could provide a solid framework. You'd have mayhem. The players would become angry and pull out. No one wants leadership that is weak or uncertain. We want leadership that is like a conductor's wave of a hand – swift, clear, and unequivocal.

In my experience as a coach for men and studying these archetypes expressed in men, The Director is the least embodied type. Most men have lost their confidence to lead women romantically and sexually, if they ever had that confidence. There are good reasons for this: Over the past forty years, our pictures and expectations of what should happen between a man and a woman on a date, in a relationship, and in a marriage have shifted dramatically. Men often seem at a loss as to how to act with women and therefore take up passive, uninspired roles.

With the rise of the wave of feminism that began in the 1960s, women demanded men become more sensitive to their needs. It came out of a general sense of inequality. We demanded we all be treated the same, as if we were the same. We confused equality with sameness. We figured if we were the same, we'd have to be treated equally. And in a sense, it worked. As women learned to act like men and close off to our feminine power, we got better pay and laws protecting us from sexual harassment. This was progress. But the fact is we are not the same. Trying to appear to be the same has greatly diminished our capacity for love and pleasure. We can only experience the full benefit of loving the opposite sex when we embrace and welcome each other as the different genders we embody.

I notice men have become afraid of women through all of this. They are afraid to say the wrong thing, afraid to make bold gestures, and afraid they'll be persecuted for overstepping sexual boundaries (which to men seem invisible). This hurts your confidence and is painful and unfulfilling to women. We don't want a tribe of men who fear us and tread on eggshells in our presence. We want men fully in their power, meeting us in ours.

When women demanded that men be less aggressive and more sensitive to female emotions, we didn't know we would lose your leadership and directionality. We didn't want men to share their feelings (like women); we wanted men to be more sensitive to ours. We didn't want men to stop leading; we wanted men to stop forcing their lead.

You don't know how much we welcome and desire the directionality and leadership you bring – when you have the confidence to bring it and when you bring it with care. We love the guy who can orchestrate, plan, and execute. It's incredibly sexy to be with a man who is unafraid to choose and make things happen. This is true whether you're a dad or a stockbroker. Your woman wants you to respond intelligently to her requests for directionality and to do so with confidence.

When she says, "What do you want to do?" it's not a time to say you don't care. She's asking you for direction. When she says, "What do you think?" and you reply by asking what she thinks, you're making work for her. If she wanted you to have her opinion, she'd express it first. When she says, "Where shall we go for dinner?" she's looking for leadership, ideas, and direction. "Wherever you want to go" is no help.

You might be in a relationship with a woman (or have been) who is directional. It will seem to you that she wants to make all the choices. This is what happens when you don't lead. This is what happens when women lose the expectation of a loving lead from their men. If you're telling yourself the story that you tried to lead once and she didn't like what you did, drop it. Sometimes you will fail. Sometimes you will have ideas she doesn't like. This is part of leading. You're not always going to please her or have things your way. Handing her the reins is simply a way of saying, "I give up and I'm afraid to fail." It isn't attractive.

When you assume your directionality and it is confident and fluid, a woman stops leading. I see this happen with incredible speed in relationships. Women are highly sensitive to the energy you bring. When you trust yourself and your choices and act on those choices, she will welcome handing over the reins and also sharing the lead.

If you're parked at a train station and you don't know where you want to go, the trains can't help you. I've known too many men who just stand in the station staring at the board, too paralyzed to make a choice, and hoping someone else will tell them what train to get on. If you want to lead with a woman in your life, you need to decide where you want to go.

When you don't lead yourself and your life or take the lead with the woman you love, you leave a vacuum of masculine leadership. That empty space feels unsettling to a woman, so she will step in. She'll become directional and pointed. She'll make the plans, tell you what to wear, choose your dentist, police your diet. And while you might think this is sort of a nice perk, I assure you she won't want to devour you at the end of the day.

Assigning a woman the role of taking care of you triggers a mothering instinct in her. This does not make her feel sexy or turned on; it makes her feel like your caregiver. You become a job, a responsibility – one of the children. It's wonderful to be blessed by this aspect of a woman's loving, but you don't want it to be the primary way she relates to you. Women do not have sex with their children! You want to enjoy a woman's nurturing, but she needs you to enjoy leading her in love.

Women also lead. Some of the most compassionate and brilliant leaders in the world are women. But you must keep in mind that our context is romance and sex – not business or government. If your wife is the president of the United States and you're a math teacher, you still need to make directional choices that lead her into a more dynamic and synergistic dance with you.

I know this might not seem logical to you as a man, but trust me as a woman. What I most long for in a man is that sense of skillful and loving leadership. I can build a fire in my fireplace. I know how to gather wood and paper and light it. But when my man makes that fire and takes care of me, I feel loved and cared for. Is this logical? Not really. I could do this simple action for myself. But a woman's deepest desire is to be cared for. So when my man does things like this, I feel myself soften. I feel warmly feminine. I feel my arms reaching to wrap themselves around him. I find I yearn for more of his masculinity. When he becomes distracted or forgets our dance and leaves it up to me to take care of all the details of my own care and his, I step up. But I become tired and irritable.

The key is not just that my man does things for me. I don't need a servant or a maid. The acts that make the difference are ones in which he takes charge. When he acts on a moment with creativity and leadership, I feel I'm being held, secure. This might be deciding to take us to dinner on a particularly hard day for me, or suggesting sleep rather than lovemaking when I have an early morning, or bringing me flowers as a romantic pick-me-up. Creative masculine leadership is a definite turn on!

The Director archetype presents the opportunity for being directional. The feminine is not this by nature. A woman can learn to be directional – because all men and women have both a masculine and feminine essence which can be cultivated – but the feminine flows in a woman. When you "just go with the flow" with a woman, you're acting in a feminine way. This may feel safe to you, but you can bet it doesn't play well for sexual attraction. You want to put your romantic and sexual interaction on course. Once you do this, you get momentum. The attraction, desire, and pleasure accelerate. A woman's energy expands when there is direction. You don't have to do it all; you just have to keep setting your interaction on course.

How do you know when you're on course? First, you're actually headed somewhere. You're not flowing with the feminine, like a woman. You're not following the lead she sets for your life and going along with a program. You're a creative force of forward motion.

You're looking at where you are and where you want to go, and you're putting one foot in front of the other and heading there. In essence, you're the captain of the ship, and she's on board for the ride.

If you're not on a course – whether you're dating or in a relationship – your love life is adrift. Your woman is complaining. She seems to want things you don't understand. She's not happy, and she's not turned on. You're tired and overwhelmed and starved for good sex. And if you don't have your directional wits about you, you'll fold. You tell her "You steer the ship. Take us where you want to go." And, reluctantly, she will. But then you'll feel a loss of your power, attraction, and sexual synergy. If you're like most men, you'll blame it on her. You tell yourself she's impossible to please.

I've shared quite a bit with you about the feminine desire to be taken somewhere. If you've ever hired a guide to walk you through a forest or jungle and guide you to obscure places in an unknown land, then you've experienced being led. I want you to recall how it felt to trust someone to get you somewhere and to do it well.

Remember the delight at those moments when your guide seemed to know just the right plant to point out or trail to suggest? Remember those moments when he opened your mind and impressed you with some obscure fact? Remember the awe you felt at his connection to everything and how he took you there with such confidence and assuredness? This is how a woman wants to feel in the lead of a man. She wants to go with the flow of the masterful direction you set, so she can feel the joy of being a feminine, spontaneous, playful woman.

Now, imagine your guide asking you to decide the best way to get out of the forest at dusk, saying, "It doesn't matter to me which way we go." You'd lose confidence. Not only that, the excitement and sense of freedom you had with his lead would diminish instantaneously. It does not inspire trust or confidence when the leader doesn't lead or when he haphazardly turns over that lead to someone else.

To be with a man who doesn't direct – who fails to move things forward – is a romantic disappointment for a woman. The journey lacks a certain pleasure and ease. I notice, for example, how bitter women with children become when the men in their lives force them into the role of family captain.

You don't have to be in a relationship to have this kind of negative or positive effect on a woman. I have a male friend, Rob, who is directionless. Even though we're not lovers, I experience tremendous frustration in his company. An evening out causes me immense stress. At a recent dinner, for example, he would not focus on the menu and decide what he wanted to order. He first had to know what I was having and then asked the waiter what he would have. And then he asked me to decide for him and surprise him. After I ordered for him, (against my better judgment), he changed the order! His meal then came undercooked. But rather than send it back and ask for exactly what he wanted, he ate around the center, pushing and poking at the meat! This drove me mad. When the waiter asked him how his meal was, he said, "Great!"

Rob's unwillingness to speak his mind and take charge of the situation made me very uneasy. I wanted to take over and handle it but resisted so as not to encourage his lack of leadership. After dinner we were in the street with no plan for where to go, and he said to me anxiously, "Where do you want to go?" Of course, I expected this from Rob. It's what he does. Nonetheless, I noticed it and wished it were different. This wasn't a case of where do we want to go, with him also considering my ideas. He put the lead entirely on me.

The more I am accustomed to being feminine with men, the more this is challenging for me. I don't want to take over. I want him to direct, with me functioning as a kind of co-pilot. It's an equal dance in my mind. I want a man to step forward first, and then I want to meet him in that step. It's like in a tango – the man steps forward and the woman's foot goes back. We move together, in agreement, with symmetry. But in any case, he leads.

Not only does Rob turn the lead over to me completely, he doesn't give me time to think. "What do you think?" he presses impatiently. Rob can't stand to be in a place of indecision, and yet, he can't force himself to decide. So I force him to decide. "You decide," I say. And interestingly, he does, but only after my assertion gives him permission.

In the street, as we walk to the next place, Rob switches the side of me he's on without notice. I find myself looking for him. Sometimes he's behind me or in front of me, and it leaves me feeling exposed, unprotected, and irritated. At the end of the night, I am happy to have seen him because I adore him and his many charms, but I am tired of having to make all the choices and be the "man."

Directing is a gift you give to the feminine; it's not a job. We're going to explore three powerful ways you can set love, sex, and romance on course as The Director and experience the power of choice and directional action.

The First Opportunity:
Having a Vision

When a woman sets goals and puts herself on track to attain them, she is often derailed by her feminine impulses.

It takes extraordinary effort for a woman to stay on task. It's not that women don't have focus, but rather, that a woman's focus is diffuse. Her brain is designed to feel everything. She can get sidetracked by what she feels and how it affects her in the moment. You know this if you've ever tried to get a woman out of her head after she's had an emotional upset.

Your capacity to see what you want and be unwavering in your commitment and desire to get it is what women appreciate and gravitate toward in men. It's not that you don't feel, but that men are capable of compartmentalizing emotion – it's how your brain works – and that makes you highly effective at moving forward toward a goal.

Women love focus and determination in men. It's what we admire in masculine, heroic films and why we love strong, masculine characters such as Russell Crowe in *Gladiator*, Tom Hanks in *Philadelphia*, Liam Neeson in *Schindler's List*, or Ben Kingsley in *Gandhi*.

We count on you to know where you're headed in your life, because this singular focus gives you strength and power. If you see where you're headed in your life, it's an easy next step to see where you're headed in your relationship with a woman. Without your own sense of personal direction, you'll find it very challenging to offer direction in relation to a woman.

If your "vision" is getting through this month or simply getting by, you'll be easily distracted, derailed, and frustrated by women. If your woman is your focus, you also have a problem. It can seem as though a woman wants to be your focus and that she wants you to be that sensitive, cuddly man she can cradle and nurture night and day, but that's an illusion. If you fall into this trap, you'll become the kind of dependent, needy man she absolutely does not want in her arms. Yes, she wants to cuddle you, and she can take pride in taking good care of you, but she also wants you to walk out the door and achieve your mission in the morning.

A masculine imperative or vision doesn't have to be epic in scope. It simply needs passion and focus. If you want to eliminate hunger, provide education to children, build a humane company, or simply be a great teacher, you need direction and focus. But you can't have focus without a vision.

A man without a vision is like a ship without a rudder. You put a lot of energy into getting somewhere, but there's no certainty where you'll end up. When you know where you're headed in life, forces align to help you get there. Women align to help you get there.

I see how men who lack vision tend to be afraid of women and of having women in their lives. Even men in a relationship (without vision) have a fear of being derailed (of getting trapped and caught up), so they fight their impulse to love and be loved. When you align with a powerful vision, you also align your loving relationships with that vision. It gives you congruency and power.

When you're clear about the ultimate purpose for your life and where you're headed, navigating obstacles becomes an achievable art and skill. You don't need to force yourself to stay on one track your whole life – quite the contrary. The key to being a successful Director is knowing how to set your life on a track. That's what gives you the power to create the life you want, and it is what makes you feel powerful to a woman.

What you're doing is really secondary to how you experience it inside of you. Is your vision alive with possibility? Does it energize you? Does it bring out the best in you? Does it strengthen and inspire you? A vision is a powerful focal point. It's like a compass that continuously guides you toward your highest reason for being alive. Seeing where you're headed is one aspect of being able to animate The Director archetype. It's your compass. The next two opportunities give shape and dimensionality to that vision, making it possible to take this power and align it with a woman in your life.

Practice:
Vision Quest

Native Americans, and in fact many traditional and tribal cultures, had some variation of what we call a vision quest process. This is where a man at various stages of his life would isolate himself from his community and his family in some wild place (a cave, a mountain top) or sacred ground and spend a prolonged period without food or water or sleep, praying for a vision. A man would essentially eliminate all distraction in his life and sit with the pain and frustration of not having a guiding vision (a thing he must accomplish before his death) until that vision came to him. Returning from a vision quest, he was essentially a new man, animated by a new purpose.

Modern men have lost the tradition of vision quest and yet they need it more than ever. It is the one practice I most highly recommend for all men. In fact, if you do not have some kind of life-guiding mission and a sense of clarity around your vision, then you should stop pursuing women all together, because most likely you are using the pursuit of women as a petty distraction.

You need a form of vision quest.

If you can participate in a formal vision quest process with an experienced teacher, take advantage of it. An experienced masculine coach will help you prepare effectively, keep you motivated and on task in that preparation, make sure your vision quest is intense and pushes your envelope without actually being life-threatening, and help you process your experience afterward.

If you have no access to that kind of training or leadership, you can still do your own vision quest if you understand what is at the core of a masculine vision quest. It is beyond the scope of this book to adequately describe and prepare you for a vision quest, but here are some basic tips I've gleaned from men I admire about what makes a vision quest successful.

1. Having no animating vision is essentially an empty and painful feeling for a man. In the face of that pain, men anesthetize themselves with distractions. By anesthetizing yourself, you get no closer to a vision but instead are distracted from the fundamental feeling of failure that comes from not having a vision – not knowing what your purpose is in life.

2. What you most urgently need to do is remove all the distractions in your life. No women, no TV, no sports, no video games, no music, no parties, no alcohol, no drugs, no workouts, no adventure sports, no internet porn, no computer, no smart phone, no books – nothing you traditionally use to distract yourself.

3. Just sit. Sit in a tent in your backyard. Sit in a room from which you have removed most of the furniture. Sit in a closet. Sit on the roof of your city apartment building.

4. Just sit. Sit through your boredom. Sit through your frustration. Sit through your self-recrimination. Sit through your certainty that sitting is a stupid waste of time. If you are religious, pray for a vision. If you are spiritual, meditate. If you have to go to the bathroom, go do that and come back to sitting.

5. Carve out a long weekend to do this. Turn off the phones and the alarms. Don't eat (unless you have a serious medical condition). Drink a small amount of water only. Sit on the floor or ground. Stay awake as long as you can. If you doze off, pay attention to your dreams.

6. How do you know when you are done? It can come when you realize there is something you must do or accomplish before you die. It does not need to be a full-blown plan. It just needs to be an animating vision you can begin to flesh out with a plan of action. The men I have known who have used a vision quest to find their sense of purpose have described a successful vision as one that feels motivating and inspiring and a little frightening. A useful vision will result in a major change in your life.

The Second Opportunity: Taking the Lead

Now that you know or have a clearer sense of what your vision is for your life, how do you align this with your love and desire for a woman?

You'll recall the story I told earlier in this chapter about my friend, Rob, who seems incapable of leading and causes great frustration for my feminine heart. To gain a woman's respect and devotion, you first have to choose for yourself.

This theme came up in the previous chapter, and you will find that being the kind of man women desire is deeply connected to your power to make and stand by your choices. You have to know what you care about and be willing to make choices to align with what you value. If you can't decide what matters to you, you're going to struggle with women or attract a very masculine woman to decide for you. No feminine woman wants to have to help you decide what is meaningful for you or to suffer your lack of clarity.

Women are drawn to aligning with men who have vision and directionality, because it's an opposite energy from theirs. The feminine is flow, but she can't flow freely without the riverbanks that your direction provides. Without those riverbanks, her energy is wasted in a flood. Leading with a woman is about choosing, but you must first choose for yourself. You have to be willing to step forward and declare what you want to demonstrate and lead.

Most men follow women. They sniff around for how to please a woman and then do what it seems she wants. It's less risky than being directional, and it's often reinforced by women who have assumed the lead in their own lives. If you've been cast into the "friends" category numerous times, even with your wife, you know that chasing her desires – and even fulfilling them – doesn't get you much sex.

Despite everything you might have learned about women, the woman with whom you want to be in relationship is seeking direction. How do you deliver direction in a way that serves you both? First you notice the direction you'd like to take. If you're dating, what do want to get out of your first interaction? A date? A kiss? What would be a success?

Then, act on it. Tell her you want to take her out. Tell her you want to kiss her. Tell her what you want! You have no idea how compelling this is to a woman. If you're in a relationship, what is the direction you want to take today? Instead of sniffing around for what she wants and what will make her happy, what are your deepest impulses? Is it to pick her up and throw her into bed? How can you act on that impulse and also be sensitive to her and where she is?

Leading, like loving, is a dance. You want to honor your physical impulses. You want to give voice and demonstration to these impulses. Yet, you need to recognize that, unlike a tiger or a bear, you have to be sensitive to the woman you want to take. She wants to be led but not without finesse.

Men who get a lot of sex act elegantly on what they want. Your opportunity in animating the archetype of The Director is to back up. Stop following. Feel what you want. Then, learn how to get what you want in an intelligent, sexy way without catering, bargaining, or begging.

Language is a powerful motivator. How often do you tell a woman what you want from her? Probably not enough. If you're following her, you're too busy trying to figure out her next step. Rewind here. You need to come back to the impulse, the desire, and the instinct. Then you need to tell her what you want. Why? Because you know what you want! It's simple. She is turned on by your clarity and confidence. It's a start. She may add to your lead, but you've initiated it.

"Let's get some lunch."

You feel hungry; you act directionally. That isn't a question, but a lead. She might say "I'm not hungry, sweetie." You then act on that. "How about I just pick something up for myself then?"

You're not shutting out her desires; you're identifying your own and acting on them. This is how one leads. At the end of a date, don't wait for her invitation. Tell her what you want. She wants to know. "I want to see you again. How about Saturday at my place for dinner?" Don't make the mistake of waiting for her to tell you she wants to see you. It likely won't happen. If you're hung up on clues and some certainty that she wants you, you're operating from fear of failure. Acknowledge your fear and act anyway. Tell her what you want. This is your masculine imperative.

You're irresistible when you know what you want and assert it with confidence. This is using "telling" language, which has a preverbal effect on a woman. You are not asking for permission or chasing her desires. Women are naturally accommodating to a man who is in his own power. If you use force or resistance to get your way, you won't get it. But coming from a place of unbridled desire – and wanting to share that desire – is potent.

Of course, a woman has her preferences and will voice them, and you need to consider them. But first you need to choose in a clear and unequivocal way some simple things like turkey or chicken, dinner in or out. Know what you'd like from her. If you don't know, you put the pressure on her to take the lead for you.

Consider the tango. It doesn't matter if you can dance it; I'm talking about the idea of it. You know that the man takes the first step. If he doesn't, guess what happens? Yes, the woman has to pull the man toward her. She has to make the leading move. The momentum is hard to kick-start from the woman's position because she's expecting to be led, and she's stepping backward. However, when you lead, as you should, her following is automatic. Once there is momentum, she can express her creativity within the dance. And you can trust that it will be expressed!

I had a partner for many years who was incredibly easy to be with. For the first two years, I loved how he'd let me decide everything. I loved it because I was young and somewhat afraid of his masculinity and leadership. I didn't want to be with a man who might threaten my power of choice.

As I matured and we grew together, I became increasingly annoyed at his insistence that I lead. Whether it was a choice of dinner, friends, the bed we bought, or the color of the walls, I had to make the ultimate decisions. This made me angry, but I couldn't identify why. How could I have known I wanted him to lead when I'd been taught that my power was at risk if I didn't?

Not only did I assume the lead, but I became quite demanding. I lost all confidence that Alex could get anything done for us – whether it was choosing a hotel or buying a loaf of bread.

I didn't like being Alex's boss and he didn't like it either, but we were stuck. The worst part is that I didn't like myself. I didn't like not trusting my man to decide, but it felt impossible to change. We were like a ship on course for disaster with no idea how to turn it around.

If Alex had just said now and again, "Get the pink paint instead of the green," or "Let's stay in tonight and cook," or "Take that trip. You need it," I would not have minded those moments when he said, "Whatever you think is fine." I would have welcomed his turning over the lead to me. But lacking key directional moments from him, I felt unrelentingly overwhelmed.

There is nothing worse for a woman than not trusting her man can and will lead. To think you won't make choices when they're needed leaves her feeling exposed and unprotected.

If a man points a gun at your face and asks for your wallet, a woman wants to know you'll choose well. Or in a more mundane example, if she asks you to get paper towels and the store is out of the usual brand, she wants to know you'll make the next best choice instead of calling to recite the ten brands on the shelf out of fear of choosing. Without this confidence in you, she feels forced into acting like your man and your bodyguard.

Practice:
Learning to Lead

If you're like most men, you've become gun-shy about leading the women in your life. I understand how you got that way and how hard it is to suddenly make a change, but it is important you do make a change. I suggest you start small.

1. After years of pretending you don't care about what restaurant you go to or what kind of food you eat, do you even remember what you really like? Figure it out. The next time the question comes up, have an answer. Sometimes it is true that a man might not really care what he has to eat. When men get involved in projects or lost in thought, food might not be a big priority. In that case, be proactive. Tell your partner what you would really like is for her to take care of feeding the both of you, because you are really involved in a particular project.

2. Have preferences. Have opinions. They are part of what make you seem confident and directed. But don't forget that your opinions and preferences are just that: opinions and preferences.

3. Once you actually know what you want, you can begin to take her opinions and preferences into account – not by reflexively deferring to her, but rather by feeling into what would please her, open her, relax her, make her happy. Then offer that as a lead as opposed to simply offering her the choice to lead herself. Consider this scenario. You both come home from a hard day at work and you can feel how tense she is. You love her and want to help her move out of her tenseness:

    •   Bad choice: Do nothing and hope the mood blows over.
    •   Bad choice: Offer to take her out and then refuse to make any decisions. "Well, where do you want to go?"

- Bad choice: Insist on going to the place you always like to go, on the theory that at least one of you will be in a good mood.
- Good choice: Pour her a glass of her favorite wine and invite her to take a bath. Offer to draw the bath for her. While she is taking a bath, cook for her or run out and bring home something you know she likes. Don't ask her what she wants. Take a chance.
- Good choice: Tell her you want to take her out for dinner. Tell her where you want to take her. Be completely present with her and pay attention to her body language. You will know in microseconds whether your offer is going to open her or create more tension. If it is making her tense, have two or three back-up restaurants ready to offer, but don't get frustrated and just turn the choice over to her. That will only make it worse.
- Good Choice: You'll know you've achieved a kind of mastery if you can actually anticipate her mood: i.e., know where she is going before she even knows, and help guide her out of her own tension. This would be having a plan for the evening before she even walks in the door. Remember not to cling too tightly to your "plan." The plan is not what's important. The goal is to move her out of her tension.

The Third Opportunity:
Welcoming Her Power

If you're going to build a company, you need a team. You need to hire the very best people you can find and then listen to their input. No one man can run a company alone, and yet turning over the reins is not as easy as it seems.

It takes a powerful man to let go and turn to others for support and input. As much as you might want this in your leadership, if you fear or avoid your own choices, you will fear other people's input and choices, including your woman's.

The third step in directing is learning how to share and incorporate a woman's lead. You choose a woman to spend time with, or spend your life with, because she brings a sensibility, wisdom, and perspective you don't have. Your leadership with her is only as good as your ability to embrace her power. No woman will follow your lead if you aren't open to and welcoming of her input. If you use force, criticism, threats, or control, she might cater to you, but she'll never follow you.

Following isn't passive. It's an active choice. When thousands or even millions of people follow a certain leader, it's because his lead permeates. It moves through others like air, as inspiration. And likewise, he doesn't breathe without drawing on the energy of those around him.

Leadership with a woman is an invitation. It's your hand reaching out with an initiative, an idea, a suggestion. If that invitation is less than considerate, less than gentle, or less than certain, you will get resistance. Leading is about making directional choices and following through on those choices to the benefit of you and your woman. Eloquence and sensitivity are required to lead well. You don't want to step on a woman's toes, yet you want your lead to have sufficient force to move her.

Every leader needs to ask for counsel at some point. No leader brings about his vision without help, without other people. But getting others to follow and support you doesn't happen because you wish it. You have to be trustworthy (meaning you can keep your word and follow through), confident, and passionate about your mission, and willing to take risks other people won't take. It's clearly a synergistic relationship between a leader and those who get behind him. They need to feel there are benefits and a mutually desired outcome, or the mission will fail.

You might believe you don't need a woman's counsel to be successful in life. I agree. You don't need a woman, and it's best not to think you do. Keep in mind, too, that a woman does not need a man to direct her life or to bring a directional focus.

However, if you want the beauty and love a woman can bring to your life, and you want to have a satisfying and meaningful relationship with her, welcoming her feminine wisdom and support is wise, just as it's wise to rely on the experts you enlist to help you create a business.

I'm reminded of a man I knew intimately who believed he was an island. He was my stepfather, Jack.

When I look back on how he lived his life, I understand that in many ways he was a very lonely man. He spent most hours of the day and night working to support us, and in the moments he had at home, he was silent and brooding, wanting nothing to do with any of us. He often made indiscriminate decisions about our lives – like where we could sleep or events we could attend – without asking my mother's opinion or seeking to understand the circumstances of our lives. He literally had no clue about who we were or how we lived, and he yet assumed a certain authority in deciding what was right for us.

We saw Jack only for dinner on Wednesday and Sunday nights, and he forbade us to speak at the table. Jack knew he was disliked and disrespected and that made him angry, but he had no idea why. He thought he knew why – because he was in charge and had the tough job – but the true reason was that he wouldn't let us love him, and he certainly wouldn't let himself love us.

It was apparent in his fatigue that Jack felt his job in life was hard and that we couldn't understand his plight. How could we? He never shared a single detail about his life. Jack spent his days and nights alone, afraid to let us in. If he'd simply shared his struggles to any degree, we would have opened our hearts to embrace him, serve his needs, and offer comfort. But his resentment of us, and his life, made us resent him and everything he provided.

If only Jack had been able to embrace what we brought to the dance, we would have joyfully loved him. If he could have seen how much we wanted to be a part of him and what he did in the world … we could have happily loved and nurtured his spirit, and he ours.

A woman wants to know deep in her heart that she can inspire you. She wants to know that her love and presence as well as her wisdom and beauty inspire you to create something of meaning in the world. She wants to pervade you like breath or sunshine. If her love inspires you and moves you to make a difference in the world, she is a success.

Often our highest imperative as women, to love, has no physical or tangible result. To see the results of our best gifts given in love manifested through men as action in the world is a powerful triumph. It is the ultimate "win" in love.

If you're not a confident man and haven't learned to embrace a woman's power, you may think your woman's input or guidance is driven by a desire to undermine you or question your power. You might feel she lacks confidence in you, so you shut her out and refuse to share your life and its details.

The problem is, if you can't or won't make room for her and her power – which is her loving – she will try to disempower you; she almost can't help it. If she doesn't feel you value her as a partner, she'll feel fear and lack in herself, which generates negativity toward you and your vision.

How can a woman support a man who doesn't recognize or value the loving she brings to his life? And if you do not feel that she contributes to your sense of inspiration and power in the world, why are you with her?

You don't have to take your woman's "advice." But if you are a leader worth his salt, you'd be a fool not to consider it. While women might joke about these things, no woman wants to be the power behind the throne, but she does want to have your ear and know that you value the particular perspective she brings as a woman.

One of the ways a woman offers herself in friendship is to reveal the details of her life. When she trusts, she shares her details. It's really challenging for a woman when you don't open to her with your details. It's hard, too, when like Jack, you don't share your pain, because it seems you don't trust or love her. Be aware, however, that a little bit of your feelings goes a long way. She wants to know when something big has happened. She does not want to be the one you whine to about your frustrations every day. This is a balancing act. You don't want to do a lot of emotional processing with her because it can make her doubt your sense of direction, and as a masculine person, you probably will not be empowered by processing in her feminine way. She invites you into this space because it makes her feel good to be trusted and needed.

Your opportunity is to seek a woman's guidance in a way that empowers you, because that's the whole point. Her power becomes yours if you can let it in. You can tell her: "I may not act on your opinions, but they're valuable to me." This gives you the space to consider what she says and also to act on your own truth.

You are not catering to a woman by asking for her input. And if you are, stop it. You're asking a woman's opinions because she brings sensitivity to your endeavors that you do not have. She sees your blind spots. If you're afraid of this, it's a good indication there are aspects of your life not in complete integrity.

Naturally you have fears of the feminine. Sometimes a woman's perspectives will be hard and unforgiving. She may tell you you're not living in alignment with your truth. She may show you your greed or your lack of care. The truth is never easy to hear, but it is necessary; it's why you're with her. It's why you need to incorporate her power. Her viewpoint helps to make you impeccable. Your woman doesn't need you to do everything she suggests and wouldn't want that, but she does want to know you value and consider what she has to say. This, in her eyes, makes you a powerful man.

Practice:
What Does Your Woman Have to Offer You?

A good leader in business, politics, the military, or other endeavors knows himself and his team. He knows his strengths, and he is acutely aware of his own weaknesses and blind spots. He also knows the blind spots of his team members. But more importantly, he knows their strengths offset his weaknesses.

1. You may have never thought about this in any kind of an organized way, but do you know how your intimate partner supports your mission? If you don't, you should. There is no right or wrong answer here. But if you know what strengths your partner has, you have a better chance of making good use of those strengths and making your woman feel valued and honored. Here are some possibilities:

2. Remember that women naturally sense the movement of energy better than men. In a social setting, you might be so focused on the task at hand that you miss a subtle emotional undercurrent that is arising. The more feminine your partner is, the better a barometer she will be for the movement of emotional energy.

3. Women communicate in different ways and pick up on different communication cues than men do. In a business meeting, a man might need only to hear another man's words, but a woman will

be interested in how the man said those words. Your feminine partner can give you good feedback about just how committed someone might be to what they are saying.

4. The feminine is also a good gauge of integrity. Your woman might not be able to articulate exactly what is wrong in an interaction, but if she says there is something she does not like or trust about someone, you would be foolish to ignore it. Remember that this does not tell you what to do about a situation; that is still your responsibility. It does tell you to stay alert.

5. If you recognize that you don't have the best people skills, ask your woman for advice in addressing challenging interpersonal conflicts.

6. If you know you tend to get lazy, procrastinate, or cross ethical lines too easily, let your woman and her emotional feedback offer you the kind of course correction warnings that will keep you on track.

The Shadow of The Director

In the film *Casino*, about the inner workings of mob-centered Las Vegas, James Woods plays a hustler and drug addict (Lester) caught between his relationship with former prostitute Sharon Stone (Ginger) and her husband, casino boss Sam Rothstein (Robert De Niro).

Lester has known Ginger since she was a girl and a young prostitute, is clearly a master at how to manipulate her need to be loved and accepted, and plays on her longtime addiction to survival and drugs.

When she meets the powerful Sam Rothstein, who proposes to her, Lester encourages her to go ahead and marry him, even though she's not in love with Sam. Lester tells her to "take him for everything he's got." Ginger takes the deal with Sam after he guarantees she'll be taken care of for the rest of her life if she has a child with him.

Ginger has that child with Sam and gains everything monetarily she could possibly want (including a million dollars in jewels as a guarantee), and yet she finds herself drawn time and again to Lester, the hustler. Each time she hooks up with Lester, there's some drama surrounding getting him money and consuming drugs. Lester's interests are directed toward getting the jewels Ginger has stored at the bank and cashing in on Sam's good fortune, but Ginger is so caught up in her addiction to caring for Lester that she interprets his motivations as love. At one point, the two of them threaten to leave the country with Sam and Ginger's child, pushing Sam to the edge.

It's excruciating to watch Ginger keep turning to Lester the loser, the guy who is nothing but a hole looking to be filled, when she has a man like Sam in her corner. Sam is powerful and responsible. He loves her and wants to take care of her. Ultimately, Sam ends up taking back Ginger's jewels (her guarantee) and forcing her to return his child or leave the marriage broke.

At this, she goes berserk and tries to enlist the support of Nicky (played by Joe Pesci), a mob boss. She offers him the only currency she has – her body – in order to gain her freedom from Sam. She asks Nicky to kill Sam, but he says there's no way he'd hurt Sam, a man he's known thirty-five years, just for her. He also realizes that she's created a real mess for him, because the last thing Nicky wants is for Sam Rothstein to know he's been sleeping with his wife. He doesn't need that kind of beef with Sam.

So there's this sexy, tension-filled set-up with a triangle of three powerful men, all involved with Ginger. Despite being such an obvious loser, Lester is good at one thing: directing Ginger to get his own needs met. He's a master at how to hook her with certain emotional anchors from their sordid past. It's clear they have an "us against the world" addiction to one another, and each feels bolstered by controversy and drama.

It's also obvious that Ginger is addicted to making Lester happy, as if somehow if he's happy, she has a chance at happiness, too. And while Lester's clearly directional and uses directional energy to command Ginger, his leadership is focused on satisfying his own petty needs. Nothing he does is solely for Ginger or serves what she most needs. He embodies very little of The Artist or The Poet – other than to mention Ginger's sexual power in reference to her long legs. Mostly, he manipulates as a Director but lacks the integrity of self-control and caring to be truly powerful in The Director archetype.

It's useful to notice that Ginger is hooked on the empty gestures.

This is how compelling directional energy can be for any woman. His commands make her feel safe; so much so that she's able to forget or turn a blind eye to how self-serving they are. With Lester, she knows she can turn over the lead and act helpless, like the girl she was when they met.

Being commanded by a man like Lester is like having a dysfunctional daddy – a daddy who loves you when you're bad and holds unconditional space for you no matter what you do. She gets the total acceptance she's always yearned for from "daddy" and gets to act out, too. Of course, Lester has nothing emotional invested, so he couldn't care less whom she sleeps with or marries, which makes it easy for him to "love" her.

Sam, on the other hand, is the consummate Director. Impeccable in his leadership, he's elegant and refined, and also dangerous. He can be counted on to keep his word, to follow through, and to do things right. And he can just as easily order a guy's legs to be broken or have his wife killed if she doesn't behave.

The attraction is clear with Sam. He's also a bit like a father in that he asks Ginger to marry him, knowing full well she doesn't love him. She is a beautiful ornament or prize. He expects virtually nothing of her, which is a recipe for disaster. He even buys a house for them, fully furnished, and presents it to her after the wedding. She's expected only to grace the space with her beauty and panache. Of course, with this setup, she ends up relating to him like a father figure – acting out against him by running to other men, who are less fatherly and rigid, behind his back, seeking the kind of passion and fire she feels with Lester.

And yet, the attraction to Sam is obvious. He can make something of her and her life. He can make her respectable and get her "off the streets," so to speak. She feels cared for in his presence where no wish goes unfulfilled. It's a fairy tale come true. As much as this life with Sam is a dream (everything she's ever hustled for), Ginger's fuel is adrenaline, and Sam's direction lacks an edge she can't live without.

Ginger's desire for direction in her life is clear. All of these men present her with leadership and direction, but none of them offer direction beyond getting their own needs met. Lester allows her to turn over her power, act helpless, and indulge in drugs and fantasy.

Sam expects little of her and tries to fulfill her with things, and Nicky is willing to bed her as long as she agrees to need him and be a mindless sexual partner.

Ginger is drawn to fragments of The Director because they feel better to her than no directional energy at all. She has no idea what it might feel like to be with a man who can see her and celebrate her for who she is – a man who would refuse to enable her dependence. So she finds herself in the arms of men whose own feminine aspects are virtually nonexistent.

At this point, you understand how to create a solid base of masculine archetypal energy in relation to the women in your life. You know it is important to the feminine to be seen, and so you have animated the inner Artist to better see her. You know the feminine needs to be chosen, celebrated, and invited into something greater, and you've learned how to animate your inner Poet to give those gifts to her. And now you understand how important it is for a woman to find trustworthy masculine direction in her life. This is not because she is helpless or lost without it, but because she cannot be both surrendered and open to the dynamic possibilities of life and in charge of every aspect of her life at the same time. The inner Director is the gift a man brings – not just to his woman, but also to the world. It is the capacity to offer real direction in support of a clear vision and mission while honoring his partner's feminine power and intuitive gifts.

You are now ready to explore the next masculine archetype: The Warrior.

Chapter 4

The Warrior

When I met Patrick, he was a CPA and avid cyclist. His motto was: "Live hard; play hard." We were definitely physically attracted, but Patrick's way of life held little appeal for me. I loved that we could get a little crazy together over a game of pool or on some daredevil mission, but I wanted a man who was more present in his heart as my lover. Instead of pursuing a romance, we became good friends.

About a year after we met, a car hit Patrick on his bicycle. It wasn't devastating but it was bad. He sustained a head injury that made it impossible for him to do his work, and he was terrified to get near a bike. Things that had been easy in the past, like crunching numbers, were suddenly excruciating work. He was beside himself with grief, feeling in some ways that his life was over. The faith he'd always had that he was "bulletproof" was crushed.

Patrick was not a man to sulk or to wallow in his feelings. He'd spent thirty-nine years achieving and living life full out. But the accident killed that forward momentum, and Patrick drank a lot of whiskey to fill the void. Those of us who loved Patrick knew it could only go one of two ways: he'd kill himself or he'd wake up. He'd already lost about thirty pounds and looked like he'd aged ten years. While he refused to answer almost all communications from friends and family, I was able to get through to see him and asked him what he was doing.

"Are you trying to kill yourself?" I asked.

"I'm already dead," he said flatly. His eyes were moist, on the verge of tears. I didn't know what to say to Patrick. But I knew he was in trouble. He was more depressed than I had ever seen anyone. I went to his side and held him, his head to my heart, for a good long while. It seemed the only way to communicate, the only thing I could do.

When I left, Patrick was asleep. I was extremely disturbed by what I'd seen. His place was filthy; he was unwashed, and he was practically unresponsive. It was very unlikely that he'd be able to turn his situation around on his own and sending in "help" could land him in the wrong place. I went home with his future heavy on my mind.

I got up at 5:00 a.m. that next day, unable to sleep. There was an email from Patrick – a big surprise. He hadn't sent out emails to anyone for a good two months.

It was titled, "Thank you," and the message was short and sweet: "I appreciate you being there."

I was acutely aware that day of how we need to trust love. I hadn't known what to say or what to do with Patrick, but by simply following my heart and holding him, I'd helped change his state. He was back in the world again.

A month later Patrick called me and sounded excited. "I know now why all this had to happen, Karen. I've always wanted to do what I care about, and now I have no reason not to. I'm going to do what I've always wanted to do. You know I love animals and can't stand to see them suffer, but so far in my life that has just meant turning away from it when I see it. Now I actually want to do something about it. None of us knows how much time we have here, and I don't want to waste any more time."

I was a bit shocked. He might as well have said he wanted to become an astronaut. I'd had no idea that the issue of animal cruelty was so important to Patrick. He was a vegetarian, but we'd never actually discussed why.

"That's beautiful," I said.

"I've wanted to do something about it my whole life, but I've spent most of it behind a desk hooked on some lame view of the Bay. I'm thinking of contacting that animal rights group, PETA, and seeing what openings they have."

I was curious and queried Patrick, "Why this thing, why now?"

"How can we access a higher consciousness when we torture the very animals we eat? We can never evolve if this continues. I can't evolve by pretending that I'm not part of the problem. What kind of person am I if I know what I know and turn my back on this kind of cruelty? It's bothered me my whole life, and I want to do something about it. I'm going to give notice at my office and move forward with this."

I was astonished at Patrick's turnaround. Last time I'd seen him he was lifeless, and everything around him was falling apart. He did give notice and within three weeks was on the PETA team. They said that if he agreed to hold tight and take odd jobs, they could get him on staff as an accountant. Early on, Patrick went out on field investigations, assisted with publicity and emails from the public. He was on fire with excitement and purpose. The stories he told me about the animal cruelty they faced each day were horrendous, but the energy he was running on was incredibly attractive. Suddenly, the friend I never thought I'd actually date was looking very appealing.

Patrick asked me to have dinner with him. We went to one of San Francisco's best vegetarian restaurants to celebrate his new job. Patrick was on fire, glowing with excitement and pride. "I'm just loving what I do," he said. "I'm making squat for money, but for once in my life I'm genuinely thrilled to be alive."

We toasted.

"You always seemed so happy before, Patrick, so eager to be alive."

"Well, it was different. I was anxious, feeling at any moment that if I wasn't doing something and charging forward I'd slip into a deep sadness, a place I was terrified to go. This is different. It's often really ugly out there, the things we discover, but I'm fighting for what I believe in, and the energy I'm running on feels like rocket fuel. I'm not pretending, so I'm much less tired all the time."

"I'm really happy for you, Patrick."

"You got me here," he said and lifted his glass.

"No, all I did was show up one night. You did this."

We were quiet for a bit, just appreciating our connection.

"Karen, I've always wanted you, I hope you know that, but I just didn't have the confidence to pursue you. You're not the kind of woman who goes for a guy who's unhappy deep inside of himself, I knew that. If I didn't respect myself, how could I expect you to?"

Suddenly, the sexual attraction to Patrick made sense. I'd never understood it. We really were aligned in a most fundamental way. We loved the adventure of life. I was seeing something in Patrick that was primary in me. That alignment had just been buried under a heap of fear on both of our parts.

"I love what's been happening for you, Patrick. I'm not looking for a man who's always happy, by the way, or someone who's always living at the edge, but I do want a man who's self-aware and does what he loves. What you're doing now feels real and grounded, and even if it's not what you do for the rest of your life, what I love is that it's aligned with your truth."

Patrick and I became lovers and we became partners. He was passionate about everything. He gave me a lot of himself and focused on me intently, but I wasn't his everything. I liked his new life focus and the space and the time it gave me to miss and desire him. Suddenly he, who had seemed so boyish to me in so many ways, had morphed into this powerful man doing what he loved. I'd always admired his spirit and his social confidence (especially around other men) but his new way of focusing his energy inspired my respect.

Over many months together, what I came to know about myself in relationship to Patrick was that when a man fights for what he cares about, it inspires me to be a more feminine woman. His courage opened up a new kind of gentleness in me. I was there for Patrick, but he didn't need me. This was key. It deepened my desire for him. With other men who were there a lot and who needed me – whether it was my approval or my constant attention – I'd often find myself pushing away, seeking space. Patrick clearly wanted me and looked forward to our time together, but deep down I knew he wasn't attached, and I respected him for that.

About six months into working with PETA and having gotten his position as an accountant, Patrick became restless. He wanted to work in the field. He was bored behind a desk. I liked that rather than simply complain, he decided to speak with his supervisor and see what he could arrange. Patrick discovered there was a position opening in Manila for a campaign coordinator, and his name had already been discussed as a potential candidate. He'd not considered leaving the country before but was immediately drawn to the opportunity.

When Patrick told me the news, my stomach became a heap of

knots. I wanted to feel happy for him, but what did it mean for us? He said he was only thinking about it, but it felt like a foregone conclusion. His excitement was palpable. My feminine heart suddenly felt foolish, as though I'd been led down this bright, gleaming path that was really just a dead end with a lot of weeds. I thought about strategies to keep him with me, but at the same time I knew if he stayed something inside him would die; and I would come to resent him for doing what I said I wanted.

He mentioned he hoped I might join him in Manila. But I knew that wasn't going to happen. When Patrick and I had discussed the possibility of living together, weeks before, I was excited but cautious. It felt to me we were playing in a garden newly seeded, that there was much to watch, wait for, and see what would bloom. So when Patrick mentioned moving to Manila, my heart felt heavy. It was far too soon. I thought that someday I might follow him, but that he needed to get there first on his own. We'd have to see what would evolve between us.

I never did make it to the Philippines. Patrick married a woman he met there, and I moved on to another relationship as well, but we remain good friends. What I learned by being in a relationship with Patrick is that truly loving a man is about setting him free or helping set him on fire to do what matters most to him. Before Patrick, I might have fought to be the thing that was more important than Manila. I might have pushed him to sacrifice his passion for me, and I might have killed his love. I'm happy I made the choice that ultimately served us both in the best possible way, and that we were each able to learn something of great value by being together.

Who is *The Warrior*?
Why are women drawn to him?

Of all of the archetypes we've discussed so far, the Warrior is the one most bred out of modern men.

Oh, we have our armchair warriors – those men who love a good "fight" on the football or soccer fields, or a bloody boxing match – men who even get behind a good war, if it's happening on someone else's turf and on someone else's conscience.

But a warrior is of another breed altogether. He is not a man of "war."

He's a man who avoids unnecessary fights at all costs, yet is relentless in his determination to succeed at whatever cause he believes in.

To understand the true nature of a warrior, it helps to distinguish him from the soldier. A soldier is an active, loyal, or militant follower of an organization. Soldiers traditionally eschew one-on-one combat in favor of integrated and coordinated combat as a unit. A soldier is hired to execute an initiative, which has a beginning and an end. His objective is the objective of his commander. It's good to have soldiers if you're fighting a war because their job isn't to question the objectives of the war; their job is to execute the plan as commanded. It's also good to have men who will simply follow orders and work as a unit.

It is also worth mentioning that there are times when soldiers become warriors; this happens in combat when he finds that what he's fighting for is no longer ideals and objectives. If he finds himself in combat, what he fights for is the man next to him: the people he loves. At this point, he shifts from being a soldier to a warrior and will fight the fight to the end.

While wars can breed the warrior spirit in men, a man does not need a war in order to live his life as a warrior. A warrior is a man who demonstrates great personal courage and even aggressiveness in the name of an organization or cause. He will pay whatever cost is necessary to ensure a victory, and he doesn't play by anyone else's "rules." He makes the rules, and those rules are aligned with his internal sense of what is good and right. A warrior's dedication cannot be bought.

Many of the warriors who have contributed the most to humanity never made it onto an actual battlefield. Men like Martin Luther King, Jr, Mohandas Gandhi, and Nelson Mandela are not soldiers. Their battlefield is a field of love and compassion and justice. But they are warriors because they align their actions with their highest truth and don't relent until they realize a satisfying end.

Personally, I've not known many true warriors. They have graced my life in passing, but they are rare to me and rare in the world. There are certainly plenty of men who have the job of soldiering but precious few who understand what it means to be a warrior. There can be warriors on the battlefield and warriors on the home front fighting to end what they believe to be an unjust and unnecessary war, and neither is less of a warrior than the other. Unfortunately, it feels to me and to most women that there is a dearth of men who would fight for what they believe in, especially when it's unpopular or unsupported. These men are incredibly rare.

In previous chapters we've talked about how the feminine identifies with light and desires to be seen, and how this makes the archetype of The Artist attractive to a woman. We've explored the feminine desire to be chosen and celebrated, and how that makes the archetype of The Poet irresistible. We've looked at the feminine desire to relax and surrender herself to the direction of a trustworthy man in order to understand why women are drawn to men who manifest the energy of The Director. Beyond being seen, celebrated, and guided by the masculine, the feminine aspect in women also wants to feel a man's power and strength as it applies to her and to the world.

In the film *Gone With The Wind*, Scarlett is attracted to Ashley Wilkes, but she is drawn to Rhett Butler. Ashley Wilkes is a good and honest man, but he is not a strong and powerful man. Scarlett is attracted to him because she recognizes that other women are attracted to him. She is also attracted to him because of her belief that she will be able to control him. But the real sexual attraction in the story is created when Scarlett encounters a man whose passion and power and energy is as strong, if not stronger, than her own.

To suggest that a woman, or the feminine in a woman, is attracted to The Warrior in a man is not to suggest that women are weak or needful. Women can be warriors in their own right. But for much of the time we were evolving on the planet, women were vulnerable to attack from wild animals or other humans, especially while pregnant. The women who survived to become our ancestors developed a preference for men who could ensure the continuation of their genetic line by providing for and protecting them and their children from harm. That bias exists to this day in what women find sexually attractive.

If you can find and animate your own inner warrior, if you can become a warrior of the heart, you will find that women are drawn to you.

Reclaiming The Warrior

As I'm hoping you are beginning to realize, this book is not about techniques for seducing women or how to appear to be one way in order to trick a woman. Rather, it is about actually living that archetypal energy in relation to women and to the world.

Living The Warrior archetype is aligning with the truth of what matters to you and then finding the courage and the initiative to act on that truth. You don't have to save an endangered species or rescue every shelter dog in order to embrace your warrior energy. You simply need to stop being afraid of what you care about. Stop being afraid to engage, speak up, and act on what is meaningful to you.

What I see in so many men is a suppression of their warrior energy. Men have become so afraid of their own aggression, and of emotion itself, that they don't want to act on anything that has too much feeling. I see how the denial of anger and aggression also robs you of your passion, but it is your passion that makes you attractive and powerful to women. If you feel anger, you can feel passion. If you don't feel, and you control feeling, you become masterful at feeling nothing.

The Warrior isn't a man who looks for a fight, yet he doesn't live in fear of a fight. He's drawn into a fight when he cares, when there is something worth defending. He's not afraid to care about something because it calls him to speak out. He's not afraid to lose something because he has to choose what's right.

Unfortunately, most men have become so disconnected from their hearts (in trying to be more feminine and less aggressive) that they don't seem to care or feel. They're like soldiers in a negative sense – getting through it but trying not to be affected by it. Think of how rare it is to meet a man who expresses a passion for something he cares about. I've worked with men for over ten years in a very intimate way. And I've seldom seen that kind of passion spilling out.

On the contrary, I've witnessed how hundreds of men cannot admit to being angry, cannot say they're disappointed, and categorically deny caring about anything that will pull them into a fight. I'm not buying it. I know from working with these men that there is definitely anger – at life, at women, and at the expectations they are forced to live by. But to admit to anger would mean having to do something about it. Most men have been taught to leave the caring (for animals, the planet, other humans) to women and to simply channel their passion and caring into making money.

I used to find men's and boys' love and attachment to heroes a bit strange. But it's clear to me now how key these figures are to keeping the seed of the warrior alive in men and cultures. The hero – whether Superman, Indiana Jones, Luke Skywalker, or Jason Bourne – believes in something. He's willing to stand up and risk losing friends and popularity, even his life, to do what's right and good. Of course this is compelling to the male psyche. To live a life that means something – willing to risk body and soul for what you love – is the fullest expression of being a man.

What men sometimes forget is that The Warrior is not just the destroyer; he is the protector. He doesn't just fight for a cause. He defends what he loves. Therefore, it's love that drives his fight, not anger. Anger is clearly a fuel, but it's only a starter fuel. No real long-term fight can be fought on the energy of anger. Anger dissipates over time while love sustains and expands in force.

You might not think of a man like Mohandas K. Gandhi as a warrior. And yet, clearly he is a warrior. He didn't ask for a fight. Fighting is not what he valued. What Gandhi wanted was peace. In order for that to happen, he had to choose righteousness. He had to commit to the outcome he wanted. The fight that followed was a consequence of that choice. He was quite outspoken later in life when his philosophy of social change came to be known as "passive resistance." He argued that there is nothing passive about resistance, and that choosing nonviolent means over violent ones should not be seen as passive. In life, we can't know what circumstances will unfold when we choose truth and love (and if we did, it wouldn't be particularly courageous). And yet if we love truth, there is no other choice than to choose it.

When you stand for what you believe in – whether it's your kid's right to speak up in class or your lover's right to her feelings – you align with truth. This is a place of power, and it will align you with both forces in your favor and forces that will work against you.

Living The Warrior archetype is not without risk. The warrior is not the "go-along guy" that everyone likes. As a warrior, you will be called to sharpen your edge, and when you use that edge, you will at times offend people. But if you are afraid to offend other men and you let that fear rule you, you won't step forward and claim your warrior energy. Imagine Superman trying to get agreement on his actions, calling a committee to issue him permission to act.

When as a warrior you align your actions with your truth and match that with emotion, there is unstoppable energy. It seems that The Warrior acts alone, but in reality his alignment with truth and feeling causes forces around him to rally and support his cause. Men often fear taking a stance for fear of being alone. While aloneness is certainly part of the warrior's path, a man aligned with what he cares about always attracts a crowd. I don't think Jesus intended to have a party of disciples; I think it's simply what happens to a man who declares himself a warrior of the heart.

Power is the capacity to act. It's the capacity to affect the outcomes you most desire. To be powerful and harness your power, you have to know that you have power. In other words, you have to trust that behind your truth and aligning with that truth is a power beyond measure. It is a power beyond you and beyond your physical capabilities.

As you might have gathered by now, you do not simply awaken your warrior energy in your intimate relationship; you awaken it in your life. If you are in a relationship, your woman can be a good barometer of how well you are living your warrior energy. Remember that a part of her attraction for you is going to be based on her sense of whether you know what you really care about (the source of your power), whether you are willing to fight to protect her (in body and heart), and whether you are willing to fight for what you care about in the world. These are your opportunities for practice.

The First Opportunity:
Know What You Care About

It might seem rudimentary to talk about knowing what you care about, but do you? Do you feel confident that you know what you care about? And is what you care about bigger than your own personal needs and desires in any moment? In a given moment you might really care about having sex with the women you are flirting with at a party, but does that define you? When you die, do you want your obituary to read: "He really cared about having sex with women"?

Women know this secret and good men know it as well. Your real power doesn't come from how much money you have but from what you do with your money. Your real power doesn't come from your lifestyle but for what you would die. Your real power comes from what you love and what you would do to nurture and protect what you love, including your woman, your children, your values, and your vision.

When I ask my male clients, "Are you powerful?" It's a rare man who can say "yes" without hesitation. If he's financially successful, he'll think, "Well, I could have more." If he's not financially successful, he'll think, "No. I don't have money." It's unusual for a man to think of his power as arising from within him, separate from his ability to achieve and earn money.

Let me say this clearly and directly: your power lives in your heart. Having the internal awareness to know what's right and good for you is where your power comes from. This access to your higher self should guide your life so you can experience and do what you came to the planet to do. Without this access to your higher self, you will not feel powerful. You will have no sense of clear direction. You won't know what you care about. You will essentially be treading water, waiting to die.

I meet a lot of men in my practice who don't have an internal orientation. They are often master doers, but they don't know the power or value of having an inner life. They know if they follow A, they get to B. But outside of linear pursuits, personal power is a stranger to them. To be powerful you have to have a relationship with your heart.

If you have capitulated in your life and given up on what you care about, once or many times, you know how it feels not to be powerful. You know how it feels to compromise – whether for love or some material prize. A woman doesn't want her man to give up on his dreams, to lose his hope or ignore the call of his heart. Yet, it's commonly what happens when a man chooses the love of a woman and family. He sacrifices his dreams for those he loves and doesn't turn back. His woman or his family benefit, but they also lose a part of the man.

What is power, if not the ability to choose one's path in life? And yet, many men don't feel they have this luxury or freedom. A man often doesn't have the luxury of asking: Shall I work or stay home with my kids? Shall I follow my heart or get an advanced degree? Of course women weren't handed these choices. Women fought for the right to make these. Men now find themselves "oppressed" by the very same limiting paradigm women experienced fifty years ago when they were only allowed to ask: Will I be a teacher, a nurse, or a housewife?

Because men are encouraged to focus exclusively on success and forgo their heartfelt dreams, it makes sense that men bury feelings and soul-driven urges. Feelings and urges would only distract you from your mission to succeed. Why feel feelings if you can't act on them? And if you're like most men, you also sense that if you follow your heart you'll risk losing love – as a man's capacity to earn is so often tied to his chances at marriage or relationship. But here is the secret. As a man, you will probably have two holes that need to be filled in your life: a loving relationship hole and a life-mission hole. If you truly have a stronger masculine essence (you naturally express more masculine energy than feminine energy), that life-mission hole is going to be bigger and require more of your energy and passion to fill. If you forgo filling that life-mission hole in order to fill the loving relationship hole, eventually you and your woman will feel the huge compromise that you've made. In the short term, she may be flattered you chose her over your life-mission, but eventually you will come to feel weak and powerless to her. How can you truly know love (for her) if you do not follow your heart in terms of your love for the world? How can you trust the love that you create with a woman if it comes at the cost of your heart?

I won't deny that women are attracted to men who are financially solvent – especially if a woman wants or has children. I won't deny that your support and sacrifice make a woman's life richer and more fulfilling. But if these sacrifices come at the cost of you living your life in a meaningful way, how beneficial can they be for the whole? This is the question you want to be asking yourself.

A woman wants to align with a man who can be honest with himself and who commits to what he believes in. This may sound like a contradiction. And yet, this is the only sustainable model for love.

If you honor what is most meaningful to you, the truth is you may not earn as much money. You may earn more money. Your power lies in attuning to and giving voice to what is meaningful for you and trusting the outcomes will serve your highest good.

Recognizing choice is an affirmation of your power. You are always choosing, whether you recognize it or not. There is nothing more emasculating than to deny you have a choice in every way, and you are choosing the life you live. Where the feminine in all of us identifies with love and relationship, the masculine identifies with freedom and agency. If you believe you have no choice, you are not free and your lack of a sense of freedom is going to be perceived by women as something less than attractive.

Perhaps you tell yourself you can't choose the woman you want. Perhaps you tell yourself your wife or kids don't care about your choices. Perhaps you believe you don't have a choice in the work you do, as it's tied to a paycheck and people dependent on you. Whatever your justifications for turning away from your choice, recognize that there is a choice in all of it. You are choosing. If you deny the choice you make in everything you do, you deny the power you have within you to make different and empowering choices as you wish. And remember that if you don't choose the woman you're with (every day), she's not going to feel the certainty of your love. If she doesn't feel that certainty, her love will also be tentative.

No woman wants to think you settled for her because you didn't think you had a choice. Therefore, asserting that choice is important from the start and every day. No woman wants to stand at the side of a man who thinks himself a victim of his circumstances.

Practice:
The thing you care about—
The elevator speech of your life.

Imagine this scenario. You're waiting for an elevator on the ground floor. You're alone with a beautiful woman. You make small talk for a moment, but she seems genuinely interested in who you are and what you do. As you step into the elevator, she looks into your eyes and says with some urgency, "Assume we will never see each other again; tell me what you love and what you do."

What would you do? What would you say? Would you fumble awkwardly for some answer as the floor numbers strobe past? Or would you have an answer? Could you take her breath away? Could you make her fall in love with you in that short elevator ride, even if you never did see each other again? That is what your elevator speech is all about. It is thirty to sixty seconds of what animates you, what makes you get up in the morning, what you live for, and what you would be willing to die for.

If you're like most men, you will cringe if I suggest you journal this, but...

Okay, so don't journal it, but do write it down somewhere. Draft the elevator speech of your life and include the following:

1. What is the challenge that animates you (gets you out of bed in the morning and motivates)?
2. What is it you are doing to meet that challenge?
3. What's your vision of success?

If you find this hard to do for your whole life, can you do this for a specific project you are currently engaged in? This could refer to a social or mechanical problem you are addressing or to the building of a new business or the introduction of a new invention. As you are writing it, you should feel your passion rising, even if it feels awkward to put it into words.

Once you have your elevator speech, practice it. Practice in private with a mirror or practice publicly at the next party you find yourself.

The Second Opportunity: Fight for Her Heart

While knowing what you care about should be your foundation and is something the feminine soul in your woman will feel, it is largely your business to address. But there are two ways of expressing your warrior energy that directly relate to your being in relationship with a woman. The first is tied to her primal instincts. A woman instinctively gravitates to a man who can care for and protect her. This is the case whether she has money, or the money to hire bodyguards. It's instinctual to want to be cared for and protected by a man.

A woman doesn't need a tall man or a big man, and yet, most women are attracted to men both taller and bigger than themselves – because it feels right to be embraced and protected by a powerful man. If a man is not physically bigger than his feminine partner, he will still need to be energetically bigger than her in terms of his relationship to his power. The likelihood that you will ever need to literally fight for your woman is slim (especially since most men are aggression-adverse), but a woman wants to know that you will. If a man pulls a knife on the two of you, she wants to know that you won't run and leave her to defend herself. She needs to know you'll act in way that is clear, decisive, and perhaps even dangerous.

The problem is that masculinity in men has been so diluted by our fears of it that we women are left to wonder if our man will confront the intruder or run from him, which isn't a comforting thought. Because most men don't experience physical danger or threats in their daily lives, they don't think much about those situations and end up being surprised and even paralyzed when they occur. It isn't that they don't want to defend a loved one, but they have been caught off guard with neither a plan nor a highly developed set of reflexive actions. Most men don't study the martial arts anymore (and no, watching Jet Li movies or playing *Call of Duty* video games doesn't count as martial arts training). Women don't need you to be muscle bound or insanely jealous or have a hair trigger for a fight, but we need to feel that you will do your best to keep us safe.

Remember that your woman is most attractive to you and to the world when she is heart-open and relaxed and even playful. Can you create the kind of environment on a date or at a social setting that allows her to express herself in that way while still feeling safe because she knows you are there?

My friend, Tom, describes the way he and his wife, Kelly, experience social events like this: "Kelly is happiest when she can laugh and flirt and just be herself. That is a gift I want to give her, and she is the gift I want to give the other people at the party. That means I have to be aware of her without hovering too close. She and I both know she is not flirting in order to seduce some man or to get some particular outcome. She is flirting because it is her nature. I don't get jealous (or if I feel jealousy, I don't feel the need to act on it). What I do is simply be aware of when she needs an exit or if she is in any distress. Then my job is to extricate her from that situation with the minimum of anger or aggression or action. Rather than feel angry at some man, I end up feeling empathy. I find Kelly attractive; why wouldn't he? But my first job is to create that zone of protection for her."

One way a woman has of sensing the caliber of a man is to know or have confidence in his willingness to defend her. Another way is in his reaction to women being violated or attacked in heart, spirit, or body.

I asked a partner once, "If a man raped me, what you would do?" I admit it was kind of a stupid, testing question, but sometimes women ask these kinds of questions when they are feeling a lack in the relationship they can't quite identify. The hardest part, though, was the silence that followed.

What he said, ultimately, after much trepidation was that he didn't think it would be right to follow one aggressive act with another. It made sense, and yet it left me feeling sick to my stomach. It wasn't that I wanted to encourage violence, but to think that his first response wasn't a resounding, "I'd kill the man," made me question his power and how safe I was with him.

As a feminine creature, I'm a feeling creature. My analytical capacity might come to the same conclusion that it doesn't make sense to answer violence with violence, but my feminine feeling heart wants to know that you feel my pain and would want to kill the man as much as I would. I want to know that you have anger and passion.

The problem isn't the aggressive impulse you feel to kill a guy who hurts your woman or who cuts you off in your car. The problem is denying you have the impulse rather than learning how to manage it. Clearly there is a certain pride men have cultivated in seeming non-aggressive, in pretending this impulse doesn't exist. I agree that aggression is not a positive energy if it is not properly managed and channeled. No woman wants to witness a man pulverize another man (especially if it's irrational or unjustified), and yet, she needs to know in her heart that if something really bad goes down, you will do that unthinkable thing.

The difference between adopting a stance of nonaggression and one of The Warrior is that the warrior is prepared for a fight. He doesn't want a fight. But physically, mentally, and emotionally he's clear that if the moment presents itself to fight, he will not waver. That's the man I want at my side when we're looking down the tip of a blade or the barrel of a gun. That's the man I want in bed with me at night when there is a crash downstairs. If you fear your own instincts and don't trust your most powerful impulses, how can you know in a split second whether to act or walk away?

Practice:
Martial Scanning

How present are you when you are escorting your woman? Let's imagine that at one end of the spectrum you might be walking down a street in a big city with your woman, completely lost in conversation and oblivious to the world. That might feel very relaxed and relaxing, but it means that essentially both of you are in feminine mode. At the other end of the spectrum, you might be escorting your woman as though you were her Secret Service detail, completely focused on an ongoing threat assessment. This would be the opposite of relaxed and would probably make your feminine partner feel rather tense.

Your challenge is to develop the capacity for what is called martial scanning. This means a kind of relaxed attention to external stimuli (what or who is coming toward you, how people are behaving, your relationship to the physical environment) with the capacity to simultaneously put your partner at ease. Martial scanning is holding your body in a relaxed state of readiness.

Many years ago, a sociologist videotaped people at random walking down crowded city streets. He showed those tapes to prison inmates who had been convicted of crimes of assault (mugging, robbery, rape) and asked them to select their targets. There was amazing consistency in the results. The preferred targets were people who seemed lost in thought or who looked down as they walked or who were visibly tense. Those least likely to be assaulted met the gaze of passersby, walked with a relaxed gait, and looked up, ahead, and around more frequently.

You can give your partner the gift of allowing her to relax by knowing that you are maintaining external awareness for the both of you.

- Walk or stand with upright posture
- Soften your belly and breathe from your center
- Let your arms hang relaxed at your sides or in gentle contact with your partner
- Look up and around frequently

- Scan the horizon and monitor what is moving toward you
- Be aware of which direction you could move yourself and your partner if something becomes a threat
- Soften your focus to take in the full field of peripheral vision (this is actually more useful than allowing your eyes to dart back and forth)

The Third Opportunity:
Fight for What You Believe In

Beyond your willingness and readiness to fight for her or her children, a woman also wants to feel The Warrior energy expressed in you as the willingness to fight for what you believe in. This is important to a woman because it demonstrates a capacity for profound love.

It may be easy to think about fighting for your woman or your children or the house you live in, because they feel as though they belong to you, although these feelings can simply be expressions of possessiveness and dominance. But fighting for what you care about when it's beyond something that is obviously self-serving demonstrates a deeper capacity for love.

I think of Denzel Washington in the film *Philadelphia* as Joe Miller, a personal injury lawyer. He defends corporate lawyer Andrew Beckett (Tom Hanks) who was dismissed from his firm for contracting AIDS. Miller is obviously an outright homophobe as the movie begins. Even though he turns down the case, he goes directly to visit his doctor after shaking hands with Beckett, just to be sure he hasn't contracted the disease. Later, he is drawn in and changes his mind when he runs into Beckett at a law library and sees firsthand how Beckett (who asks for books on AIDS) is treated by others, with extreme prejudice. Miller is more disgusted by the inhumanity of the situation than he is by his fear of AIDS and decides to take the case.

The movie, based on the true story of Andrew Beckett, is such a powerful example of how one man (a not-so-famous lawyer) reached out beyond what was personal and personally affecting to embrace what was right and universally good. He takes on the case with incredible fervor. Throughout the film, we develop great respect for Miller, who transforms his fear and prejudice into love and righteousness. I think any lawyer would say the case was a long shot at best and that Miller was unprepared for its magnitude. I imagine every woman in the audience fell in love with the Miller character and every man wished he had his courage.

Joe Miller knew what he cared about. He cared about justice. Regardless of what rose up inside of him initially, he couldn't turn away from what he loved. This is The Warrior energy. As both a lawyer and a man, if he had turned his back on what he cared about, some part of him would have died. This is the kind of certainty you want to have as a man. You want to know you are living your life according to what you love, and that if you run astray out of fear, you'll come back home to your heart just as Miller did.

Think about it this way: Most young women who are still in touch with their feminine hearts imagine that they will be with a man who loves both them (Prince Charming) and the world (the Good King). If Prince Charming, who must eventually become the king, ignores his kingly duties and his people suffer, this is not the happy fairy tale. And yet this is how many of us build our relationships. I keep hoping that you will stay Prince Charming and focus only on me, and you keep hoping I will remain Snow White or Cinderella, forever swooning in your presence. Real love and lasting passion are built on something beyond fairy-tale princes and princesses. They are built on service and love for something greater than self.

When I speak of The Warrior I long to feel in the men in my life, it is the part of a man that loves the world and is willing to give his entire being for the love of a vision. That man has a well of passion deep enough that I never have to fear it will run dry. I do not underestimate for a minute that the pain a man feels at failing or losing in his quest is every bit as painful as what a woman feels when she loses a child or goes unloved. But a man who plays it safe by not seeming to care too much so he can avoid the painful risk of losing is only half a man.

Practice:
What will you risk?

Do you know what your bottom line is? Do you know what you believe in? Do you know what you would fight for? Do you know what you would die for? The majority of us never have to answer these questions, and that may be one of the blessings of being born in this time and place. Most men if pressed would say they would fight or die to protect the lives of their partners, children, family, or even friends, but even that is a kind of vague sense rather than a clear knowing.

As I was writing this book, the presidential debates between Barack Obama and Mitt Romney were much in the news. In the first debate, Obama's weak and lifeless performance was a disappointment to many supporters; and in the weeks that followed, his poll numbers began to slip, especially with women voters, a group that had previously supported him overwhelmingly. I wonder if the slip in the polls among women had more to do with the perception that the fight had gone out of him. This is something a woman can sense and feel.

So how do you know what you will risk or what you value before it is actually at risk? One way is to make your own personal list.

- What do you believe in?
- What are you willing to stand up for publicly?
- Can you identify or recognize when your values are in conflict? ("I want to say something about this, but I don't want to lose my job" or "I know what he's doing is wrong, but he's a friend of mine.")
- To what level does oppression or aggression have to rise before you will intercede and take some action?
- Is there anything that you would not tolerate, regardless of what it would cost you in terms of career, security, and reputation?

These are not easy questions, and the point is not to provoke you into rash action or to make you feel bad about the past; but men who live as warriors tend to be very clear about where their boundaries are in terms of how they live their lives.

Warriors are not warriors because they seek fights but because they are prepared to fight. Most men, given the time to think about it, could tell you what they care about. However, often the moment to stand up for what you believe has come and gone before you have even realized it, leaving your woman to wonder what it is that you truly care about enough to fight for.

The Dark Side of The Warrior

It's often easier for a woman to get hooked into the dark side of The

Warrior because there are more men who abuse this masculine power than who use it for good. You'll see more men fighting to win or to overpower others than you will men fighting for love and what they believe in.

Marianne, my client, repeatedly found herself infatuated and ensnared by Warrior types animating their dark side. These were men who abused power grossly, misunderstanding the true purpose and mission of The Warrior. And yet, their appeal on some level was undeniable and bears examination.

Marianne gave me permission to use the details of one such dangerous attraction (with names changed) so you can better understand how this ill-fated attraction occurs.

Marianne met Phillip at his city office in San Francisco to discuss her arrest on charges of pandering. She was deeply embarrassed about how she had made enough money to attend law school by managing sexual escorts for wealthy male clients. She also felt foolish for believing that since there was no real victim, it wasn't really a crime and, of course, she felt stupid for getting caught. Phillip, a defense lawyer, had told her over the phone that it was no big deal and not to worry, but Marianne was deeply worried that her own chances at becoming a lawyer were now in jeopardy.

The office was plush and put her at ease – and so did Phillip's soft, easy smile. After she discussed her case and explained how the police had entered her place, Phillip told her he thought they could get the case reduced to a misdemeanor based on illegalities in how the search warrant and search were executed. "Don't worry. This charge is going to go away," he assured her.

Marianne took a deep breath. What she noticed was how safe she felt with Phillip and also how attracted and nervous. More than an hour had passed and he was still allowing Marianne to talk through her ordeal – including all of the transgressions she experienced in jail. While she kept expecting he would conclude the meeting, he simply kept making space.

Two hours into the meeting, Marianne decided it was time to go and moved to get her coat. "How about we get a glass of wine and we'll go through this a little more. I know a gorgeous place overlooking the Bay," Phillip said.

Marianne told me in session that she had a moment of concern about having a drink with her lawyer but decided to go ahead because she trusted he wouldn't jeopardize her case, and that he knew what he was doing. Maybe she'd found just the perfect lawyer to help her turn this charge around. Why not have a drink?

Talking with Phillip was easy. They leaned into deep cushions in the magnificent space of a downtown hotel and talked about the details of the case. Marianne felt more than a bit embarrassed about what she was being charged with and wondered if Phillip judged her for it. Yes, she'd been guilty as charged and admitted so, but Phillip didn't seem to care about whether she broke the law or what she did in setting up men with her friends to have sex for money. His perspective was, "Let's make this go away in the easiest way possible for you."

That night, Phillip told the story of how he became a defense attorney and explained why he felt an imperative to defend people like her. "My father was killed by a hit-and-run driver when I was twelve. Nobody ever found the guy. Worst of it, nobody cared to find the guy. The investigation was shallow and turned up nothing. My mother was so devastated she attempted suicide a dozen times. We were never the same. Now I help people who feel helpless, like I did – people who need someone on their side to make the difference."

Marianne admitted to falling in love in that moment. Here was a man her father's age and yet so unlike her father. Phillip was so powerful, so dangerous in a sense: a man of passion, a man who would fight for something he believed in. Her father, Mr. Professor of Chemistry, never expressed anger, even when the boys in the neighborhood had ripped off her pants on the lawn and completely humiliated her, or when she was raped on a date at nineteen. Deep down, she admitted hating him for that.

"A man like Phillip was so exciting for me," she said, "because he snapped his fingers and things happened. What I always felt with my father was this sense of being permanently grounded – like we were on a plane that would never take off. You know that frustrating feeling when you're ready to go and you're not lifting off? Whatever was going on, my father insisted that we have no emotional response. When I was raped, he didn't get angry or cry. He just shook his head.

What did that mean? Did it mean that he blamed me? He shook his head and went to bed."

Phillip and Marianne had several drinks before Phillip drove her home. In front of the sleek high-rise building, they kissed passionately for a long time, and then Phillip suggested she invite him in. She did and in the morning Marianne felt some regret and had a major hangover. She began to wonder if she'd made a huge mistake. But when she soon heard from Phillip by phone, he assured her he was on top of the case and not to worry. "Let's have dinner tonight," he said. "There's more we should talk about concerning your case."

Marianne didn't believe there could be anything more to discuss about the case, but she wanted to see him, so she said yes. That night she discovered that Phillip was married and was unhappy that he hadn't mentioned it sooner. "It never came up," he said.

"Okay, but most people mention that when they are thinking of sleeping with someone."

"Interesting perspective, coming from someone in your line of work," he said. "Isn't it your job to set up married men with beautiful women?" He smiled warmly, but Marianne noticed there was a kind of edge to his response.

Marianne continued to see Phillip over the months leading up to her court date, because she felt vulnerable outside of the energy of his protection. When she was with him, she felt safe, like everything was going to turn out okay with her case and her life. When she wasn't with him, she felt fear rising up and gripping her. If she were found guilty of the federal charge, she'd never be able to practice law – her dream. And there was another growing concern that Phillip was dishonest. He had, after all, cheated on his wife with her, and she also learned that he had a longtime girlfriend he'd been seeing for five years. And yet, who was she to judge?

About three weeks before her court date, Marianne got a call from a friend who had been busted on a cocaine charge. She quickly referred her to Phillip. Afterward she had a moment of regret, as her friend, Samantha, was very beautiful. Would Phillip hit on her, too?

"Why do you want to defend me in my case?" Marianne asked one night at dinner. "Don't you care about what I do or what I did?"

"I plan to defend you because I don't think you did anything wrong."

"I broke the law."

"Ah, come on. You set a few guys up to have a good time. You're a college student for God's sake."

"What about upholding the law? What about caring about the law?"

"You think that is what this is all about? That I care about the law? The only thing I care about is winning. What I do is help people get the result they want. For me, it's not about what you did, but that you hired me to make it go away. That's my job."

Marianne was taken aback, but she wasn't completely turned off. She realized she'd been naïve, and Phillip's admission was a needed wake-up call. He was a lawyer, not a saint. He slept with her because she was young and beautiful, nothing more. And yet, part of her had to believe it was more. Part of her needed to believe it meant something to him – both their affair and his work.

It was the weekend before her case went to court that Marianne discovered what she really didn't want to know. Marianne called her friend, Samantha, whom she had referred to Phillip. Her friend was crying. When she asked her what was going on, Samantha hesitated.

"I don't know if I should tell you," she said.

"Why?"

"It concerns your lover boy lawyer, is why. And he said if I did, he'd make things bad for my case."

Not more bad news about Phillip, she thought. Marianne took a deep breath. "Tell me," she said.

"I told Phillip I couldn't afford his services. Everything was taken in the search and all my cash was gone. I already owed $3,000 to my sister for the bond. He said his retainer was $5,000, and I just couldn't do it. He suggested I come by his apartment to discuss it because his office was being cleaned that night. Seemed weird, but I was desperate. I needed a lawyer. When I got there, he offered me a drink. I took it. That drink led to another and another, and still we'd never discussed the case. He talked about himself the whole time. Finally, I asked if we could talk about the case."

He said, "I know the case. You're charged with a Class 1 felony and you don't have money for my retainer."

"Right," I said.

"What can you do to overcome that?" he asked.

"Well, it was obvious what he was alluding to by the way he undid his tie and looked down my blouse.

"I was disgusted but scared. So I said I'd do whatever would feel good to him to have him handle my case."

"What do you mean 'whatever'?" Marianne asked, now feeling a mounting anger.

"I let him do it all, everything to me. I don't really want to discuss it," she said, choking up.

"Now he says he doesn't have time to take my case. That he's suddenly booked. I threatened to hurt him, to turn him in to the bar association, and he said that if I said one word to anyone (including you), he'd have a talk with my judge and make sure I went away."

Marianne's head was swirling. Could this really be the man she felt so safe with? The man who was going to save her life? Could Samantha be lying? What if it was she who had seduced him? She'd been known to seduce married men before.

"I don't know what to say," Marianne offered without feeling. "This is more than I can handle right now. Let me call you in an hour when I can get my head straight."

"You can't tell him I told you," Sam said, but Marianne didn't know yet if she agreed with that statement.

Over dinner that night, Marianne decided she needed to get at the core of what was going on. Sam had never lied to her before. She was a good friend. Phillip was known to be a liar and a cheat, but this behavior? He could have sex with anyone; why would he need to bribe a client? She watched how a part of her wanted to deny the whole thing, to go back to feeling like she was safe and Phillip truly cared about her.

Phillip arranged for them to meet at a restaurant in a nice hotel. He was tense and preoccupied and began scanning the wine menu following a brief hello.

After food and wine were ordered, Marianne asked Phillip about his meeting. "How did things go for you in your meeting?"

"As expected," he said. "And your day?"

"Good, had a workout and a nice lunch and did a little computer work. Phillip, did you ever hear from my friend, Sam, about her case? I haven't been able to reach her and was wondering if she found a lawyer."

"She called, but I wasn't able to help her. She couldn't pay my retainer."

"Oh, so you didn't meet her?"

"No, I just said she called. I didn't meet her. Why?"

Marianne stared at the menu, unsure how to proceed. The scary thing was that he was so calm. There wasn't a single sign of discomfort. She thought sure he would blush or flinch, but nothing. It was as if she were talking to him about the weather.

"It's nothing," Marianne said. "I was just hoping the two of you could meet. Maybe it's better you didn't. She's awfully pretty."

Phillip gave a smirk, but he didn't laugh.

"Hey, would you excuse me a minute? I need to go to the ladies' room."

Marianne did something she hadn't expected to do. She called Samantha. "Get over here to the Palms Restaurant. There's something I need to discuss with you." Sam said she'd be right there.

The table had its back to the door, so neither of them saw Sam come in. Marianne had instructed the host to bring Sam to the table when she arrived.

Suddenly, just as salads were placed on the table, Sam was standing before them. Marianne looked at Phillip's face and saw his eyes drop to his plate. He poked at an olive as his skin flushed and glistened ever so slightly.

"Sam, how nice to see you. This is my lawyer, Phillip Grey. Remember, I told you about him?"

Sam and Phillip stared at each other without a word, and Marianne felt his contempt. He despised being put on the spot and being caught. Marianne knew in that moment that he had in fact met Sam, and everything Sam said was true. She didn't want to encourage Phillip to hurt Sam any further, so she said it was nice running into Sam and didn't invite her to join them. Sam took the clue and left the table. Marianne held back tears and mustered every ounce of strength inside of her to finish dinner (with pleasantries) and make her way back to the room with Phillip. She had a plan. She pretended to check her email where she found a note from her sister that her mother was ill. She'd need to get home immediately and make plans to fly out of town.

The lie didn't work on the high-powered defense attorney, though, even though she layered it with emotional drama.

"You walk out on me tonight, little darlin', and I'm dropping your case," he said, wrapping his arms around her waist.

"Guess I'll be looking for a new lawyer tomorrow," she said.

"You're not that stupid," he said with cold confidence.

"I gotta go, Phillip. Game is over here."

"You're not jealous of that friend of yours, are you?"

"Keep the retainer. We're done."

"I don't think you understand, little girl. I call the shots here. I decide who leaves. If you leave tonight, you won't be going to Columbia. I can assure you of that. Remember, the dean is a friend of mine. I can make sure you never get an interview."

"Are you serious? You'd hurt me? You'd hurt me because you slept with my good friend and I'm upset?"

"You bet I would. Now, you can have a nightcap with me and end our evening in an enjoyable, adult way or pay the consequences."

Marianne was reeling. Just that afternoon he'd been caring and protective, and now he was threatening. She couldn't let him ruin her chances at Columbia, her number one choice. The application was already under review and any one thing could change her fate. She wanted more than anything to get into Columbia and study in New York with her friends.

"A drink sounds good," she said with a feigned smile. "A drink sounds really good right now."

Marianne got into Columbia and became a lawyer in New York State. But the shame and guilt surrounding her affair with Phillip didn't go away. There were other men like him, too, who were seemingly powerful, who took advantage and left her empty-hearted. Marianne's choice to contact me came out of the desire to make healthier choices and to find one man she could love and who would genuinely love her.

The Warrior energy is undoubtedly powerful. It can be so intoxicating to women that they can find themselves ensnared by men who animate the energy solely for personal gain and manipulation. However, when this energy is awakened in a man out of love, it can inspire a woman's deepest love and respect.

In the next chapter, we'll explore the archetype of The Sage. The Sage further cultivates his own power and trustworthiness by aligning with what he knows and says, giving a woman an even greater sense of safety.

Chapter 5

The Sage

Brian was not the kind of man I would have picked out of a crowd. We all have had the experience of picking someone we were sure we wanted, only to later realize it was a bad choice. But this can also work in the reverse. We often overlook someone because they don't align with our internal attraction checklist, even though they may end up being a wonderful partner for us. Sometimes, it may even be a good idea to have friends choose for you. Had I relied on my own relationship patterns, I would have never met a man who greatly influenced my life and my way of loving.

I'd known a lot of smart men before Brian, but I had not known a lot of wise men. Brian was clearly wise. What I noticed right off was that he didn't feel a need to boast about himself or impress me. He knew a lot; that was obvious. He'd spent most of his life studying and teaching in one form or another. What impressed me most, though, is how much he knew about how to love. This was demonstrated in how he spoke of the people in his life, in the tone he took with me, and in his dedication to empowering people. I knew that Brian would be a teacher for me.

The day after dinner at a friend's house, where we were introduced, Brian and I took a walk through beautiful woods down to the ocean. We talked a bit more about our work. Brian was a marketing consultant. I found him creative and highly intelligent, but his being in marketing felt odd. To me, he seemed more like a spiritual teacher or a therapist. He was so thoughtful and deliberate. I trusted Brian almost immediately. I trusted that he cared about people. I trusted that he cared about me, regardless of what would happen between us. That's a pretty powerful thing to know after two dates, and yet it was clear.

I think what most inspired my trust and admiration as we got to know one another was how Brian listened. I felt enveloped by it. I'd never before identified how powerful a man feels when he's able to listen to those around him. I thought of monks and rabbis and priests and their capacity to hear at such a deep level that people were shifted in their presence. I experienced this with Brian at social and business events we attended where the people to whom he listened would unfold before our eyes.

Brian was on the board of a private girls' high school where the girls were educated to be leaders. It was not a high profile position; in fact, very few people knew about it. It took a lot of probing to get Brian to open up about his work with these girls. Initially, I didn't understand it. It didn't bolster his business, it didn't give him publicity, and it didn't seem to have any kind of measurable payoff – and that's exactly why he didn't want to talk about it.

Brian didn't do things necessarily because they gave him forward motion or results. He did things because he felt an internal alignment. He liked results like any other man, but results weren't his motivation. He was inspired to serve. In watching Brian navigate his work with this organization, I was able to see that there was a tremendous benefit toward the greater good, in doing something selfless. It's not about being some kind of martyr. It's purely doing for others because you want to see them thrive. None of the girls who were recipients of Brian's brilliance and generosity would know that Brian created programs for their empowerment. He didn't need them to know. His reward was in knowing that they worked.

I trusted Brian more than I had trusted any man. It's simply because I could count on him to do what was right even when it was hard. I'd known a lot of men, both as friends and lovers, who would give up or sell out when an effort was required. I'd also known plenty of men who did the right thing for recognition. Brian did the right thing because it was all he could do.

I remember vividly how he dealt with a former business partner who stole $20,000 from him. His investment was his time and his expertise, but when it came time to dissolve the business and sell it, she chose not to pay Brian a cent. At the time, Brian had a lot of her files on his computer, files that she needed to turn over to the new owners. Brian also had personal files of hers that were very important and could affect her legally.

There were many ways Brian could have retaliated and sabotaged her progress, but he didn't. One day, this woman had the nerve to ask Brian for those files. I asked him if he planned to turn them over. Brian gave me a little smile and then changed the subject. As much as I pressed, he wouldn't talk about it. Months later, when I asked what he had done, he told me he had given her the files. Initially, I was angry. I felt that he didn't respect himself, that he had let her take advantage of him. But as time passed, I came to know that Brian always did the right thing and not because anybody was watching. His former partner may have acted without integrity, but Brian always stayed true to his values. I came to feel I could trust Brian with anything, even my life, because his integrity was unwavering.

One of the obstacles Brian and I came up against was that I didn't know how to trust love. I knew how to love and how to be intimate, but I didn't know how to trust there would be any future in that. This made it difficult for me to commit to something long term. It was great for now, for today, and this week, but beyond that, I didn't feel the kind of faith in love itself other people seemed to feel. I have found that this is not an uncommon problem among women who have put great value on their freedom, independence, and ability to manage their own lives.

There was a moment in our relationship where something in me had to test the love Brian and I had, to know if it could last. We were at a friend's birthday party where I chose to spend most of the evening blatantly flirting with another man. I caught myself doing it but felt a destructive need to continue. We'd been coasting for months, it seemed. No fighting, no passion. Brian was loving, of course, and I was feeling not loving enough. I can see in retrospect that I was wondering if I deserved him, and it had contributed to a need to push the edge, to test and see what our relationship could endure.

At the end of the night on the drive home, Brian asked if I'd had a good time. There was no sarcasm in his voice. "Amazing time," I said, hoping to provoke an argument.

We were quiet for a while and then he said, "You know, Karen, I want you to be happy. Whatever you need or want, I want that for you."

"I know," I said.

"I want you in my life. There is no doubt in my mind about that. But if for some reason that doesn't make you happy, I want what is best for you."

I suddenly felt scared. My game had backfired. I was quiet and tried to center myself. I realized in that moment that although Brian was kind and honest, he wasn't a fool. I realized I could lose him. His willingness to cut ties with me in order that I'd be happy struck a deep chord. I guess the "test" was to see what his love was made of.

I said, "You know, Brian, I've been asking myself for awhile now, 'What do you love about me?' Lately, I haven't liked my answers. Often it's had to do with what I had accomplished, how I looked, who you believed I could be, or how I was for you in bed. Suddenly, I understand something I have never understood before."

"What's that?" Brian asked.

"You know you truly love someone when you want what's best for them, regardless of how it will affect you or what the outcome will be. It's so simple, and yet this is the answer that's eluded me all of my life. I'd been questioning whether you loved me or I loved you, and now I have my answer. We want the best for each other, regardless of how it affects us personally, and I think that's the definition of love. This is something I feel I can trust and lean into."

Over the next days and weeks, I had some profound revelations. I realized there had been men in my life who wanted to hold onto me even though I was deeply unhappy with them. And if they couldn't have me, they didn't want me to have anyone else. I had never trusted a man's love before because the men who said they loved me didn't trust themselves. They didn't trust that love didn't need to be a vice or be held together by fear. Brian trusted himself. He trusted what he knew, and he trusted in the goodness of things. He trusted that even if we broke up, everything would work out for the best – so he didn't need to cling or to create dependence and fear.

The turning point in our relationship would happen in our third year together when Brian began to do a lot of traveling. Initially, it was good for both of us. We had time alone, and there was the excitement of coming together again. But after many months of Brian being gone two weekends a month, I began to wonder. I wondered if he was playing with other women. I wondered what he did with his sexual energy for twelve days out of the month. I began to feel suspicious. My trust in Brian was breaking down. Suddenly, everything he said or did seemed to ring of a lie or some hidden agenda. His eyes seemed less interested in me. His attention felt less intense, less desirous. I found myself probing to find out where he'd had dinner on his trips and what time his head had hit his pillow.

I didn't know how to ask Brian without a big emotional charge. So I waited a while until I felt centered and calm. Then I invited him out for a picnic where we'd be able to talk free of any distractions. At one point when there was some quiet, I said, "I've had a lot of questions come up for me lately, and I'm wondering if we might talk about them."

"Of course, Karen. We can talk about anything," he said.

"With your being gone a lot this past six months, I'm noticing that I feel a little uncertain. I find myself wondering a lot about what you're doing when you're away. I know you're a very sexual man, and I wonder how you deal with that when you're not with me. And let me say that I don't want to intrude on your privacy. I just feel if we can talk about this, it might help allay my fears."

"What is it that you'd like to know, Karen?"

"Well, you meet a lot of women who are powerful and beautiful at the conferences. You have a lot of dinners with a variety of women, and you're in a really stimulating environment. I guess what I want to know is how do you manage and express your sexual energy on those trips? Is it porn? Do you flirt? Go out dancing with other women? Get sensuous massages?"

"Okay, I get it. But I don't think you do, yet." Brian said. "Here's how it is, Karen. I do spend a good deal of time with other women, some of whom are beautiful. When I look at them, I think of you. You fill me. Do I get turned on by these women? No. There are moments when I think What a beautiful woman. But since the time I dedicated myself to you, I don't go there in my body, in my fantasies, with other women. It's not how I choose to direct my sexual energy."

"You know, it would be so easy for you to sleep with other women and I'd never know. And I don't want to stop you if that's what you want. I just want to know the truth. My fear is having secrets or you feeling trapped and me feeling like your captor."

"Here's the thing: I don't choose not to sleep with other women for you. I do it for me. I do it because I have chosen you and because I want to devote my energy to you. When I decide where to put my attention, it's not a sacrifice. It's a gift to myself. Most of the time when I'm away I don't even masturbate because I want to save that energy for you. Am I turned on? Yes, when I think of you I get turned on, and I choose to channel that energy into other pursuits."

I understood something in that moment. If his "devotion" were given to me instead of for him, there would always be this sense that he was sacrificing his desire for other women because of me. I'd known hundreds of clients to feel this way.

Brian's choice to be monogamous with me was about what he wanted. It wasn't imposed. Wherever he was in the world, he would apply his own choice. He wasn't on a string that could get weaker with distance and time. Suddenly, he was the most powerful man in the world.

"I can't tell you how much this means to me – to know that you do this for you," I said. "It really deepens my love and respect for you."

Of all the men I've known and loved, Brian taught me the most about trust. To be trustworthy is an inside game. It's not about how you appear to others. It's how you are within yourself. It's the daily actions you take that strengthen the integrity of who you are. Brian demonstrated trustworthiness by honoring his agreements with himself. He also demonstrated trustworthiness by showing up the same way, day after day – regardless of how I was, or if I rewarded him.

It's not that Brian was bestowed with a special power. He developed his power by choosing to align his actions with his word, his energy with his heart. The truth is that he worked at it, and I received the gift and the teaching of that work.

Who is *The Sage?*
Why are women attracted to him?

The gift The Sage archetype offers a woman is one of creating an unbreakable trust.

Most men don't recognize how paramount trust is to a woman. For a woman to turn herself over to you – heart, mind, and body – she has to trust that your foundation is strong. Rome wasn't built in a day, and neither will the trust between you and a woman. Trust is built action by action. Don't look to do one good thing and earn a woman's trust. Rather, think of trust as the frame and carriage of your relationship. Is it solid enough to carry you into the furthest reaches of love?

If a woman frequently doubts what you say you will do, if she's afraid you won't be there for her when she reaches out, if she tends to back-lead you, her trust in you is not certain. She's not going to jump into a net that has proven to be full of holes.

If your woman trusts you to take care of the home you share when she's out of town and you fall through on your promises, a little bit of her trust is lost. If you say you'll plan a special trip for her birthday and conveniently forget, trust is lost. A woman counts on you to be impeccable in what you say and do . . . because what you say and do are the building blocks of trust.

For a woman, trusting a man's words and actions is as important as trusting the earth beneath her to be solid when she sets her feet upon it. Thing is, she doesn't have to think about whether the earth is solid. You want her experience with you to be this way, too.

When the foundation under her is questionable, she is constantly looking for safety, bracing for disaster. Instead, you want her to know that your presence and actions create a solid bridge for love.

An unbreakable trust doesn't mean you won't screw up. Sometimes there will be breaches of trust – it happens when two people dance intimately. What makes it unbreakable is the spirit in which trust is created. Trust is cumulative so once a woman feels it with you, it doesn't go away because you forget to bring home the milk.

Not having a foundation – or just doing trustable things every now and then – is like building a bridge without the support beams. It might stand up for awhile, but one bad blow and the thing topples down.

Trust is not something you should expect from a woman, but something you need to inspire. I notice how frustrated my men clients become when women don't trust them. In most cases, they make the women out to be difficult, or to have inherent trust issues. While this is undoubtedly the case with some women, most women who have inherent trust issues have them because their trust has been betrayed repeatedly by you or by previous men. There is no way for her to "fix" her trust issues on her own. You have to help her fix them by being trustable.

Every man wants a woman's trust, and it hurts not to get it. Her trust is an endorsement of your consistency and caring. It's an invitation to take her somewhere. Without it, it can feel like you're dragging her – and your relationship – through sand, and getting nowhere.

The opportunity the Sage archetype invites is to know that trust is the foundation of love. Instead of approaching trust as a "should" – or a dreaded task you must achieve with a woman – there is an opportunity to embrace it as your essential undercarriage for deep connection and intimacy.

You wouldn't try to build a house without a frame. You wouldn't shop for furnishings before you'd laid the floor of your house. Why try to push intimacy and love without trust? Let's look at how to build your framework of trust with your woman using three powerful opportunities that will open her body, mind, and heart.

The First Opportunity:
Keep Your Word

Every man knows that keeping his word is important. You know that keeping your word with your men friends is an absolute. Your word is your honor. It's a bond and a sacred trust. And yet, how often do you say you'll do something and simply "forget" to make it happen concerning your woman? How often do you slip up and get lazy and careless where it concerns keeping your word with your woman?

Perhaps it's because you don't understand the consequences. Of course, you won't notice those consequences initially because like a cracking foundation under a building, the breaks are invisible until the building becomes dangerous to inhabit.

When you don't keep your word with a woman, you leave little cracks in her heart that over time break her heart and her trust. Her very hope that you are the man who can care for and protect her comes into question. How can she trust you with her heart and her life if you can't do what you say you will do?

My clients, Jenn and Peter, seemed to be fighting over how to raise their children. They clearly had differing opinions on parenting, but when we got the bottom of the fight it had little to do that. It had to do with a lack of trust.

Jenn mentioned (seemingly out of the blue) in session how Peter was great at promises in a sarcastic tone. It took her a long time to get to this point, as she was really angry, but I stopped her and asked what she meant by that.

"He's just great at making promises is all," she said.

"You mean he doesn't keep them?"

"That's right. He doesn't keep them."

A silence followed.

"Jenn, please say more," I asked.

"He said we'd take the kids to Florida last winter and that he'd look into it and get it done. He didn't. He said he'd take me somewhere special for my birthday to have some time alone, and my birthday came and all he said was, 'sorry I'm very busy, how about if we just stay in tonight and cook dinner.' He said he'd consider a bigger house two years ago and that we'd start looking. When I asked about it, he said, 'Not now, I'm too busy.' So do I trust what he says? Well, would you?"

She quietly began to cry.

"I had no idea you felt that way," Peter said. "Why didn't you say anything?"

Jenn shook her head.

"How do you feel when Peter doesn't keep his word, Jenn?"

"I close down. I feel really hurt and I don't want to be near him. Usually I just act very busy."

"To what degree do you talk about what you're feeling?"

"I don't because he'll just promise to make it better, and he won't."

As we explored more deeply, it turned out that Jenn had lost faith in their relationship when Peter stopped keeping his word. She was hurt very deeply and profoundly disappointed in their relationship. She'd even considered divorce but didn't act on it because of their two children. For Jenn, it felt like they were just going through the motions of what a marriage should be. The excitement and the sense of adventure together had died for her.

Peter was shocked that he didn't know Jenn was feeling this way and that she'd not said anything. Time and again she had expressed her disappointment, but Peter didn't grasp the depth of it. He figured they were both a little disappointed but that she understood his need to put work first. She understood it practically, but that didn't make his not keeping his word feel right. It didn't erase her loss of trust.

The feminine looks to the masculine for a sense of security, safety, and protection. Your word is a bond. You may take it lightly when you say one thing and do another, but a woman does not. She also doesn't forget it, because your unfulfilled promises leave her feeling uncertain and upset. If you don't keep your word, how can she trust that anything between the two of you is solid or trustworthy?

When a woman gets really angry because you fail to keep your promises and you respond with anger, you're not taking responsibility. You may not like her anger and disappointment in you, but in truth, not keeping your word is a violation of her trust. You can't expect to keep her trust if you don't uphold it.

I notice that many men are afraid to give their word to a woman. They're afraid to commit themselves to follow through on what they say they want or what they promise to give. They're afraid to fail or to hold themselves accountable to a woman's expectations.

And then there are men who use their word to placate women with no intention of doing what they say. From a woman's perspective, not honoring your word means nothing you say can be trusted. You might be the kindest and most generous guy in the world, but if your word is like a feather in the wind, you can't be taken seriously or earn a woman's respect. The man whose word is solid and trustworthy gains a woman's fullest confidence and trust. And a woman who trusts loves more freely. She's less guarded and more self-protective. Trusting inspires her to surrender, to let go with a man. Trust is a foundation upon which she can anchor and free her heart.

Foremost, your word is a bond with yourself. When you do what you say you will do, you grow into a powerful creator. You develop confidence and trust. When you don't follow through on what you say, you feed a lack of self-trust.

Know that you can issue your word, follow through on what you say, and not lose your freedom. Your word is not a prison or a straitjacket. It's a rock-solid power base.

Your word can be renegotiated if need be, providing it's done in a timely, sensitive fashion – and not too often. Don't renegotiate the promise to take your woman to the opera on Friday – on Friday. Be sensitive that a woman holds on to what you say as a promise, and she counts on you to be consistent and follow through because this is the foundation of her trust.

You needn't fear this way that she counts on you, but rather let it inspire you to live in accordance with what you say. Every time you keep your word, you become more powerful to her. Her trust deepens.

Her "word" is a bit different.

It's best not to hold a woman to the same standards of keeping her word as you hold yourself. Yes, where it concerns her following through on important promises, you have every right to expect her to keep her word and to act accordingly.

But there's another kind of truth that women commonly express. It's critical for you to understand that women have an emotional truth – the truth of a feeling in a particular moment.

A woman's "truth" changes with her shifting feelings. If she says she wants to go out for sushi in the morning and changes her wish to pizza at night, did she break her word? No, she's simply expressing her ever-changing desires and communicating her truth of the moment.

If she says she hates you in the morning and then wants to make love that night, did she lie in the morning? No, she spoke the truth of the moment and that truth has changed. But if you say you'll be home at seven and are going to be late but don't renegotiate that, it has a different kind of effect and consequence.

It has a different effect because a man's word is a bond, a foundation of security for a woman. Her word for you is not like that. Yes, you'd like her to do what she says she will do, but if she doesn't, it probably doesn't feel threatening as it may to a woman.

The key thing here is: Don't hold your woman to the same standard you hold yourself as it concerns keeping your word. Is that fair? Well, maybe not, but fairness and attraction are seldom things we consider at the same time. Yes, count on her to keep her word when it concerns matters of true import, but don't make her wrong for changing her mind and truth shifting in accordance to her feelings.

Practice:
The Art of Keeping Your Word

Okay, this might sound really basic. Doesn't everyone know how to keep their word? Well, unfortunately, no. Most of the problems men have with keeping their word come down to some simple mistakes in communication rather than a glaring lack of integrity or honesty.

1. Do you know when you are giving your word? For a lot of men, giving your word needs to rise to a level of formality in which you look deeply into a woman's eyes and swear upon pain of death that you will do something, or that something is the truth. It's pretty obvious you are staking your integrity and trustworthiness on that declaration. But what about the comment you make in passing that you will pick up the dry cleaning, get the movie tickets, take her out for dinner, or make the plans for a family vacation? For you, this may be somewhat under the threshold of "giving your word," but, for her, it is definitely the same thing. She may cut you some slack if you occasionally forget things. She probably knows how distracted you are at any moment and won't be surprised if you don't always follow through completely. But if you let this become a pattern, it will infect your entire relationship. It's best to consider anything you say you will do as being no different than formally giving your word, which leads to the thing you need to know about keeping your word.

2. Don't make promises you can't keep or have no intention of really trying to keep. If everything you say you will do is going to be considered a promise by your woman, then don't casually say you will do things without being clear about what it means to you. Be aware that if you use "weasel" language rather than make a commitment ("I'll think about it," "We'll see," or "Maybe"), you

may be legally avoiding the trap of giving your word ("I never promised you; I said I'd think about it."), but you are going to create a different form of distrust in your partner.

3. Practice Conscious Communication. This means that when you are asked to do something, restate it back. Clearly say what you are being asked to do in a way that includes the task, the due date, and the way you will both know that you have done what was asked. Then, in that moment with real thought decide whether you can affirm and accept the task, whether you cannot accept the task, or whether you want to counter offer in that moment. Here is an example: Your partner says, "The dog needs her shots by the end of the month. Will you take care of it?"

    •   Restate: "You want me to make an appointment for the dog to get her shots and take her to the vet before April 30."

    •   Consciously Accept: "Yes, my schedule looks open enough to make that happen. I will take care of this. Will you get me the vet's number?"

    •   Consciously Reject: "I'm slammed with this project that also has to be completed by the end of the month and that's only five days away. I just don't think I'm going to be able to take the time away from work."

    •   Counter offer: "I'm really busy, but if you can make the appointment with the vet for Thursday afternoon, I will get the dog there."

4. Renegotiate your word. If you've committed to doing something and realize you are not going to be able to keep your promise, the time to renegotiate is as soon as possible but definitely before the deadline has come and gone.

These simple steps will help keep you in integrity in the busy day-to-day process of living in a relationship with another person.

The Second Opportunity:
Trust What You Know

Nothing you "know" is absolute, and yet you must often trust and act on what you know. If you don't, you'll find yourself standing at the edge of life paralyzed by having to choose.

I meet a lot of men who are frozen in a lack of self-trust. Getting them to act is monumental, like pulling a camel to a stream. What they know is useless because they don't trust it. They want guarantees like knowing it's all going to work out, and they'll succeed at whatever they do. Unfortunately, this kind of requirement means that you will never develop the self-trust you need to make a woman feel safe.

In order to develop self-trust, you have to trust – without guarantees. You have to trust what you know about electricity to plug in a toaster. You have trusted the pilot who flies the jumbo jet in order to board. You have to trust your powers of discernment to sign a contract for a business deal. And yes, sometimes what you trust won't be trustworthy or will fail to fulfill a promise. It's simply part of the process. We wouldn't call this opportunity "trust" if it came with a set of guarantees.

Wisdom is the culmination of knowing applied to life. When you trust what you know, act on it, and learn from it, you cultivate wisdom. Wise men don't get wise sitting in caves and refusing risk. They know there are lions and bears outside. But they trust they'll make their way back to the cave, uneaten, using the skills they have. You learn to trust what you know, even if it isn't always "right," and even if it doesn't always turn out well. This is the only way to cultivate wisdom and share that wisdom with your woman.

Trusting yourself is a power. My former partner, Brian, knew this and he aligned with this truth. He didn't have all of the answers, and he often didn't know how things would turn out, but he trusted himself to act. He would say, "Any decision is better than no decision at all," and was prepared to deal with the outcome of his choices.

Brian had his share of misfortunes. But he accepted the consequences. He'd often say: "You're either on the winning team or the learning team." I respected that when he was playing on the learning team, he continued to move forward. He didn't fall apart and feel sorry for himself. He recognized that every choice has a consequence and how you deal with that consequence is an opportunity to really learn and grow.

If you want to cultivate self-trust and your inner Sage, it begins with trusting that any choice you make (intelligently) is a good one – because this sets the ball of opportunity in motion. It sets a course for you to experience your knowing and to learn from whatever presents itself.

While I often asked for Brian's input, (and truly valued what he had to say), that didn't happen until I saw how masterfully he managed his own life and his own issues. I didn't necessarily want his opinions; I wanted his wisdom. The difference is that opinions tend to represent personal preferences and ego-driven points of view. His wisdom was his experience talking through his heart. It was this voice I heard most readily, as it wasn't tied to any personal goal to change or influence me. He would simply say what he saw as true – separate of any need to persuade me in any particular way. I felt he became a conduit for me to hear the voice of Spirit that I often couldn't hear, because he could offer insight without attachment.

When you can give a woman the seeds of your wisdom, it feels good to both of you, because those seeds are actually your self-respect and self-trust. When you trust, she trusts, too.

Invite Her Wisdom

A woman brings a distinctly different sensitivity to a relationship that can add terrific value to a man when he learns how to receive it and incorporate it. Naturally, if you're like most masculine men, you will resist asking for directions from anyone – especially the woman you love. Your nature is to seek truth and to do so with minimal interference from others. If you're like most masculine men, you'd rather walk a few more miles than admit to anyone that you don't know where you're going.

A wise man knows he cannot act alone in relationship to a woman, or in the world. He needs to embrace the wisdom of others who have been bestowed with different pieces of the puzzle of life. It's this willingness to ask and receive that increases his power and other people's support and respect. At the same time, inviting the input of others isn't easy for most men, but it is essential. The Sage doesn't randomly and promiscuously ask everyone for their advice and opinion. He is very strategic about when and whom he asks.

Think about the president of the United States. He asks for counsel on a daily basis. He cannot possibly know everything he needs to know about government, law, and foreign affairs to function without input from others. You also cannot act alone – and where it concerns women, it's best to embrace this wisdom wholeheartedly.

It may infuriate you that your woman's insight into relationships and people's emotional states is more highly attuned or intelligent than yours. It may not make a lot of sense to you when your woman says she doesn't feel good about somebody or when she explains that your mother-in-law's mood was triggered by your refusal to eat cake. But if you deny her input and her wisdom on these matters, it's like breathing through a mask with the air supply cut off.

Can you imagine having a wingman you didn't trust? A woman is your emotional and spiritual wingman. She sees your blind spots. She senses when you're in danger. She's like a thermometer in terms of giving you the temperature of how you're coming across to others. She lets you know when you're kidding yourself, when you're holding back, when you're not in alignment with your truth. You need her watching out for you, just as she needs you. Denying her insights, perspectives, and wisdom is as dangerous as ignoring your wingman when he says, "Bear right."

You'll recall in The Warrior chapter that we explored defending a woman's heart. I shared that a woman values her success at relationships above everything. It's her expert domain. Where it concerns what to say in sensitive situations, who to befriend, or how to deal with your children's hurt, she's likely more attuned than you to what the situation calls for. But it's not just the relational plane that women see clearly. Don't limit your woman's input by thinking her insight applies only to family or personal relationships.

Women have a third more area in the brain than men for processing emotion. This means women are more masterful at reading people, period.

We are all emotional beings, although men tend to forget this. When you need a read on how to negotiate with anyone – whether it's your mother, your boss, or your employees – it's a really good idea to take in what your woman senses and sees. Where it concerns the unseen realm of feeling and unconscious desires, it's like she's got the radar and you're just flying the plane.

Your woman helps remind you of what's most important. When you deny yourself this vital information, you misstep and step on toes, most especially hers.

Practice:
There's a Good Way to Ask

Asking for a woman's input is important, and how you ask is as important as the asking itself. Most men don't ask, and that's a problem. If you're not asking, it's probably because you're afraid of opening yourself to new information, you're afraid of being challenged, or you think you're an island. In any case, being guarded and closed off does not build trust. When you trust yourself to know what's best for your highest good – and for your woman's highest good – getting her input is not a threat. It's simply a wise practice, kind of like having a functioning rear view mirror on a truck. Before you get out on the open road, it's good to know you've got all your angles covered.

Good times to ask:

- When you need more information to make a critical decision;
- When you need insight into somebody's emotional state;
- When you feel conflicted about whether to trust someone or their motivations;
- When you need confirmation that your heart is in the right place or that you are acting with integrity.

Bad times to ask:

- If you've made up your mind and want only your woman's approval and agreement, this is a BAD time to ask for her input. It's a bad time because her opinions will have weight, and you are not open to them. She'll resent that you don't really want her input, and you'll resent that she has input to give.
- Another bad time to ask for a woman's input is when you're afraid to make a choice and you want her to choose for you, or when you hope to avoid personal responsibility for a choice and spread out the consequences. Her advice, counsel, and wisdom should be added to the "soup" of your process, not be the soup itself. No woman wants to feel that her man comes to her because he doesn't trust himself to choose. At the same time, she wants to know you're not afraid, threatened, or intimidated by the wisdom of her insights and perspectives.

The best time and the best way to ask is really any time you feel that inner urging for more information to put into the mix or to check yourself. It's good to tell her first, before you ask, that you welcome and value her feedback, and that you ultimately will make a decision that feels right for you. This way she's prepared should you choose to do something contrary to what she offers.

How to ask:

- The best way to ask is with open-ended questions, without yes or no answers. If you ask your woman whether you should say yes or no to a particular business offer, you are constraining her to one of two answers and negating her real strength, which is in giving you her emotional read. Better to lay out what you know and ask something like, "What am I not seeing here?" or, "What am I missing?" She may still want to give you a final yes or no answer, but the responsibility for "yes" or "no" is still yours.

A special exception:

- If you're talking about children you have together, you're on a different page. In this case, you may want to defer to her. Don't make wholesale decisions concerning family or children. Remember, this is her expert domain. Acknowledging her role and giving way to her wisdom – even if she herself isn't confident – tells her you recognize and respect what she loves.

The Third Opportunity:
Do the Right Thing

Most men will say they try to do the right thing. The operative word is "try." The question is: To what degree do you actually do what's right? Do you do what's right when it's easy and convenient, or do you reach for the right result even when you know it's going to require something of you?

There is no bigger turn off for a woman than a man who is lazy. I don't mean lazy in the sense of wanting to rest or enjoy a day reading. I mean lazy in the sense of not investing himself in what matters. I think of a client who told me he didn't help a dog who'd been hit by a car because it would have made him late to meet a friend for dinner. I was heartbroken to hear that he was so disconnected from what mattered.

Doing the right thing demonstrates that you can be trusted. It's scary to think of being with a man who wouldn't do the right thing because he's afraid of getting entangled, inconvenienced, or tested. I want to know that if you witness a rape or an assault you'll step in or do the intelligent thing – even though it's scary. I want to know that if you see a man kick a dog, you'll say something rather than empower him with your silence. It's not that what you do has to have a particular "right" outcome; it's that you mean to have a good effect and that you can't help but do the right thing.

I think of the time when my former partner, Brian, decided to take on the health department in his neighborhood because they didn't take care of a mosquito infestation as promised.

All the neighbors simply complained about the mosquito issue, but Brian decided to act. He knew it wouldn't be easy to deal with the bureaucracy and, in fact, just getting through to make a complaint took hours of his time. But he had to do the right thing. He couldn't sit on his hands and wait for someone else to address the problem. Brian didn't feel a right to complain if he hadn't exhausted his own resources. Nothing got done, at least not within a time frame I'm aware of. But I respected Brian anyway – because of thirty men involved and affected, he was the one man to act and invest himself in what mattered to him. Ultimately, to me and to our relationship it didn't matter whether he was successful as much as whether he gave it his best effort.

Sometimes doing the right thing is knowing when to do nothing at all. My client, Tim, knew that Jenny's boss was a womanizer. He'd heard all of the stories. He knew how this boss insisted on private dinners and dance outings when he and Jenny were traveling, because he wanted to spend time with her. But Tim also knew that Jenny was handling the situation. It would be just a few months until her sales manager was transferred out of town, and if Jenny played things right, the territory would be hers, and she'd inherit a team of ten.

At a Christmas party just a month before this, Tim was at the bar when Jeff, Jenny's boss, approached him.

"You should be proud of her," he said and nudged Tim on the arm, obviously drunk. "She's quite the catch, too," he nudged again and gave a smile. "Bet she's not easy to deal with, though, if you know what I mean," he said.

"No I don't know what you mean," Tim said flatly. "Tell me."

"Well, you know how moody she can be."

Tim looked around the room. His face was inscrutable. To say that Tim despised this guy would have been an understatement. He wanted to punch Jeff in the face. Moody? How dare he comment on his wife's personality? Here was a man who had caused his woman great distress over the years and now showed disrespect for her to his face. It took everything in his power not to hit him.

"Would you excuse me?" he said to Jeff. "There is an important call I need to make."

That night on the way home, Tim was quiet. He was angry that he and Jenny had tolerated this man's presence in their lives for so long. He was angry that he felt his hands were tied when what he wanted more than anything was to expose this man and his negative ways to the corporation. He was outright sexist, and Tim wanted justice.

He also held his tongue when Jenny asked what was wrong; he knew that to mention it would mean them having a fight, because Tim's energy around the whole thing was angry. Instead he chose to know that he did the right thing for his woman. He said wisely in session: "Sometimes being right isn't enough. Sometimes doing the right thing means not doing anything at all."

I agreed with Tim. Although from my perspective, what Tim did was something. He made a wise choice that had a good result. Jenny did get the territory. Jeff was transferred, and Jenny was able to have higher management look at Jeff's behavior when it wouldn't be attributed to her. It all worked out well. Of course, had Tim punched Jeff, we can assume Jenny would have lost her job and her opportunity to both manage the territory and have Jeff's behavior examined.

Sometimes doing the "right thing" is really difficult because it's not simply about whether you're right or wrong. Tim was clearly "right." It's about looking at the situation and deciding on an action based on the highest good of all involved. It means doing the thing that is beyond right and wrong – the thing that is bigger than circumstances of the personalities involved.

A woman doesn't need the outcome of your choice to necessarily have a positive result like Tim's. She just needs to know that you'll choose to act beyond your egoistic desires of the moment. This builds trust that you are a man who can and will love and protect her for reasons that are bigger than both of you.

Practice:
The Right Thing

For men who have even a basic level of integrity, there is a form of low-level stress that builds when they are forced to not act in situations in which something is clearly wrong. There are all sorts of reasons for this. Many men feel compelled to make compromises in the name of financial security for their families. This is a soul-deadening place to be, but it does happen. The challenge is that for many men and their women (and families) this low-level stress can have detrimental consequences in terms of physical and emotional health.

There is no easy answer to this challenge. Most men living in a practical and complex world can manage a small amount of moral ambiguity before it begins to have serious consequences. When I find a pervading sense of stress or habitual detachment in men I work with, I sometimes find it helpful to talk them through the process of identifying all the places in their day in which they feel compelled to act outside of integrity or feel disempowered to do the right thing. You might try this on your own.

For a week, keep a simple journal listing of all the times you are aware there is a "right thing" that feels like it should be done in this moment but which you feel you cannot do.

1. Your rights are being violated.
2. Your feelings are being disrespected.
3. Your integrity is being questioned or challenged unfairly.
4. You are accused of something you are not free to defend yourself against.
5. A loved one, family member, friend, or colleague is being treated unfairly or with blatant disrespect or discrimination.
6. A crime is being committed.

7. A policy with important safety or social implications is being violated.

8. A person or animal is being abused.

If you have a big list, it could be a sign that this is the source of a lot of unexpressed stress in your life. A friend of mine entered the police force with passion and high ideals as a young man but admitted after fifteen years on the job that a big part of the stress that ultimately destroyed his marriage and led to his alcohol abuse was caused by the moral compromises he had to make in choosing between loyalty to his fellow officers and the system and doing the right thing. Recognizing this was his first step in turning his life around.

The Dark Side of the Sage
Truth can be used as a weapon.

I think of a fiction writer I worked with years back who used "the truth" to avoid love and to avoid anything sticky with women. Right from the start he let me know how things were and how he saw them.

"Look, I'm here because I need to figure out how to better manage my relationships with women. I'm not here to dig up my childhood with you. And I have no plans of a long-term thing. I want to get the answers I need in a few sessions and move on. I'm not one of those guys who needs help with women. I need help with how to manage risk and liability."

"Risk and liability?" I asked.

"I'm a fiction writer. I spend a lot of time writing, and I do that alone. The problem comes when I've got a woman calling me all day, or dropping by my place to see me. The interruptions are a problem. I had a woman show up this week, crying and begging me to let her stay at my place while I wrote. What I need to know is: What am I doing wrong that is getting these results?"

"Results is an interesting choice of words."

"Let's be realistic. The truth is, I'm not looking for a relationship. I don't deceive anyone about this. I tell them right up front, 'I'm a writer. I spend a lot of time alone and I like it that way. And it's not very likely that will ever change.'"

"Is this before you sleep with them?"

"Absolutely."

"What results are you looking for?"

"I'm looking to have a good time and then have my space to work. I don't ask anything of them. I don't want them to ask anything of me. It's not like it's devoid of tenderness. We talk, we eat together, and we have good sex. I make it clear that this is what I'm available for. If they want the guy who dotes or brings flowers, or who gives up his life, that's not me."

Looking at Brett, I could see how women were falling hard. He was handsome, successful, thirty-eight, and an elegant communicator. It was easy to see the hook. About his situation, he'd said: "Not likely to change." That's really all a woman needs to hear to think there is hope. Brett looked, for all intents and purposes, like a great relationship catch. The operative word here is "looked." Women are often easily seduced by a picture that looks like what they've been searching for all of their lives.

"So you're looking to have a good time? That makes sense. And you're not looking for attachments? That makes sense. What is it that you imagine a woman is supposed to do with the feelings that arise for her in the course of your interaction?"

"I don't really care what she does with her feelings. I don't lead her on and tell her I love her. I'm honest. I tell the truth. The truth is that I don't want a woman in my life full-time, period. I've never lied about that."

"There is one woman in particular who is really creating problems for you. Tell me about her and what's going on," I said.

"She's been telling me that I'm leading her on. Her name is Libby. She's a writing coach. And it's bothering me. Why? I find myself thinking about it. I find myself feeling bad that's she's hurt and cries when we're together. I'm noticing that it's affecting my work. I wanted another opinion."

"What is it about this woman? It seems when these kinds of issues arose in the past, you simply let the women go. Why is she still around?"

"She's getting to me. It's the way she cries. It's so pure. I've never seen anything like it. Usually when a woman cries, it feels like she's this pesky little girl who needs attention. But with Libby, the tears are so deep and relevant and intimate. They make me want to see myself more clearly, and the effect I'm having on her. I had the thought to ask her to leave and break it off, but I couldn't. That's a sign that something is very different."

As we talked, I learned that Brett had never been in love. He'd "liked" a lot of women, but he had always avoided getting too close. When we looked at that, he realized that he'd never felt he was equipped to deal with a woman's feelings, to make her happy. The thought of a relationship felt to him like a death sentence of some kind. He remembered how his father wanted to write, and really could write, but was hogtied by his mother's constant need for attention. His mother spent much of her life in bed depressed, threatening suicide – to the point that Brett sometimes wished she would do it.

"So women have always seemed manipulative to you, Brett?"

"Yes. They use their emotions to control men."

"And it seems that you use your words, or what you call the truth, to control their emotions."

"Hadn't thought of it that way. But yes, it's damage control."

"Have you ever considered that it's a woman's capacity to feel that makes her so appealing to you as a man – that it's what makes her distinctly feminine?"

"I guess a woman's vulnerability is attractive."

"How would a woman have that were it not for the fact that she's emotionally sensitive?"

"Hadn't looked at it that way before," he said.

"When Libby cries, what do you feel?"

"I feel a desire to hold her and protect her. I never felt that with my mother or other women. Typically, when women get emotional, I feel a sort of contempt. It's like, 'Look, I told you I'm not available emotionally, so why are you acting all emotional?'"

"The problem with giving a woman boundaries is that her heart doesn't know any. If she's a feminine woman – open and receptive to love – she's going to feel love when you make love. She's going to feel love when you share yourselves. Asking her to express herself within a boundary is like sending a man into the world to succeed on a leash.

"Being truthful about your boundaries might release you from responsibility in one sense, but it doesn't excuse your lack of caring. It doesn't excuse the fact that you're acting as if a woman's love can be bound or contained and then making her wrong for being a woman."

"What can I do, then?" he asked, exasperated. "I do not want a full-time relationship."

"You can express this, but you also need to accept that if you want a woman's openness, her joy, and affection, it comes with feelings. You're going to have to deal with what arises in the course of your time together. The more you expect a woman to express her feelings within your boundaries, the more she is going to feel hemmed in. The more she feels hemmed in, the more she'll want to express and push your boundaries. Continue to be honest and speak your truth, but know it doesn't change how a woman is and how she will respond to intimacy."

"What about the fact that they agree to my terms? What about how changing their minds is like lying?"

"I think you'll get more mileage focusing on you and why you want to protect yourself from women. The more you're in a state of guardedness and self-protection, the more women feel a need to push your boundaries. You can create the no-strings relationship you want but not when it's coming from fear. Not when you're trying to avoid feelings. If you want this to work, your desire and your communications have to come from strength. In other words, don't push women away out of the sense that you can't handle women but from a place of honoring what is best for you. It doesn't mean that it will never get messy. Emotions are going to arise and you want to know how to navigate them, elegantly."

Brett's opportunity was two-fold: To learn how to sensitively deal with women's emotional needs and to come from strength in communicating his boundaries. Additionally, I helped Brett see how keeping his eye on his mission (his writing and his larger contribution to the world) was a healthy masculine impulse – unless it was used as an emotional defense or to avoid intimacy. It was good to take care of himself and not be derailed by women emotionally. To stay focused and on target with his mission in the world, he needed to learn to be masterful with women and embrace his power – how to be both flexible and permeable. A fortress ultimately restricts what you don't want but also what you do want.

Women are often attracted to men who speak their "truth," even if it's not the real truth, because it's disarming and can feel confident. In Brett's case, his "truth" was a way of guarding against emotional attachment and involvement. An unattainable man can be highly attractive to a woman who is unsure of herself because she's drawn to both his rejection and an unhealthy desire to prove her worth.

The true opportunity of The Sage is not to use "truth" as a weapon or defense but as a bond. No man has to give his heart if that isn't what he wants. But if he uses "truth" to create boundaries or to express desires, it's best if his truth is inspired from strength and self-love, rather than fear and guardedness.

With the archetype of The Artist, The Poet, The Director, The Warrior, and now The Sage, you have the foundation of what you need to know in order to truly live and give your masculine gifts to the world. These are all powerful archetypal energies that align directly with what the feminine seeks for a sense of completion in relationships.

The next archetype is less intuitive but answers one of the questions that most men eventually end up asking me: Why is it that women say they want a sensitive man, with whom they feel safe and protected, but over and over again pick a dangerous man who is just as likely to hurt them or treat them badly?

The answer to this question can be found in the archetype of The Dark Knight.

Chapter 6

The Dark Knight

The last thing on my mind was meeting a powerful man. My mission was to show up at my good friend Ana's house and oversee her purchase of a wedding ring from a broker.

I often had to play the bad cop in our relationship because when it came to saying "no" or noticing when someone wasn't exactly honest, Ana needed me to "pull out the guns." It's not that she was unintelligent; on the contrary, she just was generally unable to say "no."

I showed up at Ana and Derek's place at noon. We sat and sipped tea from little Japanese cups, wondering what kind of guy was going to deliver wedding rings to her door. He'd come highly recommended by a friend.

"Whatever you do, be nice to him," Ana warned playfully. I rolled my eyes. Be nice but don't let her be taken advantage of was my job.

When the doorbell rang, Ana rearranged her sweater and refilled our teacups, surely wanting to create a good bride-to-be image. I didn't have such high expectations of our guest. So the man I saw in the doorway was a shock. First thing that stood out was his confidence: legs spread ever so wide, one hand on his hip, a sharp black attaché in the other. He was dressed in dark jeans, a white collared shirt and blazer, and from a good ten feet away I could see a sparkle in his eyes.

Finally, after what seemed like a ridiculously long time, Ana jumped up and broke the spell.

"Tommy, come on in," she said with her usual disarming charm. She walked to him and kissed him on the cheek.

Tommy then came toward me. He took my hand and cupped it in his. I felt a bolt of energy shoot through my body and my face flush. I was like a schoolgirl meeting the captain of the football team for the first time.

Tommy quickly took charge and that was a relief. First he asked Ana to describe what she'd been looking at and what she had in mind. Then he listened, intently. It was remarkable to watch. I thought of a sales training I once had where we were told: you can't sell anything to a stranger. Tommy was collecting information on his subject. At one point he said: "Okay, I've got it. Now I'm going to show you four samples I think are in line with what you want. Don't react too quickly. Just take them in and sit with how they look. I have plenty more where these came from."

When he put his four pieces in front of Ana, she gasped. They were feminine, whimsical, and romantic. They were exactly what she had tried to describe but didn't really describe. She didn't wait to respond. "Those two are amazing," she said. As she took in the other two, she shook her head. "No, it's these two. I don't need to see any more." Ana was someone who couldn't say "no" easily, but when it came to knowing what she wanted, she was unparalleled. I had the feeling that Tommy knew exactly how this would go.

He suggested Ana spend time with the rings over the next week and that when he returned, they would close on the one she felt best about. It was all very elegant. As soon as the business of paperwork was complete, Ana insisted on opening a bottle of champagne. She wrapped her arms around Tommy and kissed his cheek. "You have no idea how far and wide I have searched for my ring."

"It's like choosing a man," Tommy said, not missing a beat. "You can take what comes along or you can wait for the one that sets your heart on fire." Tommy shot me a look that seemed to say he was speaking to me. Again that bolt of energy ran through me, and I flushed. Ana giggled.

As we held glasses in our hands waiting to be filled, I had a thought. It was five in the evening on a Friday night. If Tommy were married, he'd likely have declined champagne to get home for dinner. He wasn't wearing a wedding band and it would seem that a man in his business would. I began to ponder how to ask without giving too much away. But I didn't need to. Tommy asked me just after we made our toast. "So, Karen, are you married, engaged, in a relationship?"

That bolt of energy shot through me again.

"No, I'm not," I said, as neutrally as I could – perhaps with just a little too much control.

"That's great to know," he said, offering me a warm smile. I squeezed my thighs together so as not to explode with excitement.

I listened to Tommy and Ana talk about her wedding details for a good half hour, but I wasn't really present. As much I felt into Tommy, I also sensed danger. Not the kind of danger you encounter in a dark alley but the kind of danger you get when you don't play it safe in love. And yet I knew I couldn't save myself. Being with Tommy was a foregone conclusion.

An image comes to mind that prompts a similar sensation for me. There was a scene in one of the Dracula movies I saw as a girl where the vampire leaps through a young woman's window at night, white drapery blowing in the wind behind him. She awakens suddenly to the feel of his presence, to his command. There is but a flash of fear in her eyes and then a peace, a beautiful surrender to his absolute power. He has taken her with his will, and his pleasure is total.

She's aware that he's going to kill her, and yet the surrender is sweet ecstasy. She has drunk the drink of his power – his cocktail of desire, danger, and death – and she is drunk beyond hope. She turns her head and offers her pale neck to him. I felt a similar fear with Tommy, a similar desire to turn my head and invite his bite.

As I'd hoped, as Ana and Tommy concluded their talk about the wedding, Ana invited Tommy to the engagement party that evening. I was excited to know he'd be there. We had a few hours apart to rest and change and meet back at Ana's.

Right after Ana and Rick made their engagement announcement and served cake, Tommy came to me and took me by the hand. We hadn't really had any alone time.

"Follow me," he said. He led us out onto the terrace overlooking the city. Before I could turn around to comment on the view, I felt his hands lightly land on my hips – barely there and yet intensely erotic. I wondered how often he experienced this kind of intensity with other women. For me, it was extraordinary.

"I'm excited by you," he whispered in my ear. "You intrigue me, Karen."

I felt myself vibrating at the timbre of his voice, his breath tickling my ear. I turned toward him and looked into his eyes. I was both hot and cold, and defenseless. Slowly, I felt him move into me. I don't usually kiss someone I barely know, but this was different. We did know each other in a primal sense. We both loved the taste of danger.

Fast forward a month. Tommy and I are in bed on a sunny Sunday morning. I want him, really want him, but it's never that simple. He makes me tell him that I want him, and this can be torture for me. I'm not accustomed to having to be the one wanting anyone. I'm used to being wanted and chased after – and I'd gotten sort of comfortable with it.

Add that if I don't say I want Tommy in a way he feels as real or vulnerable, he withdraws and leaves me lying there in a pool of my own desire. I've never had a man own me the way he does. I've never given anyone this much power, and the thing is, I've never been this turned on.

I knew when I met Tommy that he was dangerous, but I didn't understand what that meant. I didn't know he would push me to open, and that it would be the most difficult thing I'd ever done. I didn't know he'd be the man to interfere with my games, point out my hiding places, and open me into real intimacy. Sometimes I had to pinch myself. This was not the man I thought I met at Ana's. I'd completely misinterpreted him. He wasn't a player or a seducer. It was deep engagement or nothing with Tommy.

One of my bad habits was to use seductive energy to get my way. Tommy forced me to clean it up. Did I want him or was I manipulating him? He caught it every time, and it was humiliating. Was I trying to hook him sexually or create intimacy? "Don't approach me unless you genuinely want me," he told me. "It doesn't feel good when you do."

In my former relationships with men, it was easy to manipulate. They didn't care if my sexual intentions had integrity. They just wanted sex. It was also easy to hide my true feelings. It seemed to me that men preferred "feelings" that were packaged in a tidy way – that could be readily fixed. Tommy didn't want this at all. He wanted me to crack open to him and spill out my darkest fears and feelings, so we could break the cycle of moving in and out of intimacy.

You get trained as a woman not to give much because men don't demand it. They don't demand desire, devotion, or emotional engagement. Often times they're so focused on getting what they need or getting it right or "making you happy" that they miss you're only half in, only partially committed. They don't notice that you're throwing them scraps instead of putting out the whole buffet. I was accustomed to that kind of loving. Suddenly, I was asked for the buffet and I was scrambling for what to do.

Things came to a head for Tommy and me at a dinner party I hosted so he and my friends could meet. I was nervous. Of course I knew that Tommy would impress. He was handsome, sharp, and elegant. Everywhere he went people were impressed with his presence, his charisma. But would my friends impress him? I didn't know. More importantly, would he find them as inauthentic as he had some aspects of my loving? He was a like a swordsman cutting away at what wasn't real, and I hoped it wouldn't be the people I called friends.

It all went quite beautifully. Tommy was even more charming than I imagined he'd be and expressed his delight at my friends. He made cocktails for the girls and engaged them playfully. He told stories that made the men laugh. He called me sweetheart and put his arms around me at the stove. He did all the things that would make a woman feel proud – and make her girlfriends give her their enthusiastic thumbs up. My friend, Tina, in the midst of many playful comments about love and relationships, said to Tommy, "So what is your intention for our girl?"

I felt an immediate tension in my gut and a tightening of my lip. This was not a topic Tommy would address lightly – even at a dinner party. I knew that much for sure. I was afraid of what kind of conversation would ensue. He paused a good long time, looked at Tina and said: "The only thing standing between Karen and me right now is her. She seems to think that she can have me and also play it safe. I'm not a needy or demanding man. What she doesn't understand is that devotion is the seed of love. Without it, we are just playing. I'm not a man who will wait around. So we'll see. It's really her choice."

I got a few looks of agreement from friends. He's right, they seemed to be suggesting. I quickly offered coffee and dessert.

The next day I called a few of my friends who had been there. Was I holding back? I got a resounding "Yes." Consensus was Tommy was a great guy. He wasn't asking for too much. Yes, you have a habit of holding onto yourself a little too tightly, I was told. But wasn't he pushing too hard? Didn't I need time to open, to trust?

"What you need is to jump in head first," my friend, Kim, said.

That night I asked Tommy to tell me how to surrender to him. Teach me. I want this, I told him.

"It's not something you're going to get in a lesson. It's a commitment. The first thing is you have to face your fear.

"I'm afraid you'll leave me," I blurted out. I couldn't believe the words had left my lips.

"That's a start," he said.

"That you'll ultimately find me undesirable, ugly, unlovable."

"Maybe I will. Would you be willing to love anyway? Would you be willing to love even if I would ultimately leave you?"

I knew my highest self chose "Yes," and yet I didn't know if it was a leap my ego could make. I laid there for a while contemplating the possibility and realized I'd always reached this point with every lover – and it was at this exact moment (although it looked different each time) I chose to leave, to find new horizons and easier, less complicated "love." Oh, I always had a good reason. He wasn't smart enough, rich enough, good enough in bed. Whatever it was – it was the fatal flaw. It was my exit and escape. Love couldn't work.

I recalled what a good friend had said many years ago to me, but that at the time didn't resonate. "You don't keep getting these kinds of chances. If you keep saying no to love, it won't come to you anymore. You asked for it; now let it in."

She was right. You don't pray for Mr. Right and then not answer the door when he shows up.

"Yes," I whispered to Tommy. "Yes, I want this regardless of what happens. I want it more than anything in the world."

Tommy held me, and I felt everything inside of me fall together. All the parts that had run from love and were in exile returned. For the first time in my life I knew that if I were willing to invite love it would be there. Without a focus on the outcome and my fear of that outcome, I could simply surrender into loving. It was a freeing possibility.

That night when we made love I found myself going into fear. I started thinking maybe it couldn't work. Maybe I was kidding myself. Tommy sensed it, and instead of pulling away, as he had before and insisting on my presence, he kissed me even more deeply and wrapped himself around me. Then at one point, without a word, he took my right arm, tied it to the bedpost and then tied my left. There was love in his eyes.

He left me like that for what seemed hours. I begged him to hold me, to touch me, but he refused. Initially I felt afraid. There was a deep, primal fear of being left to die, alone. I had emotional flashbacks, too, of wanting to be held as a child and being refused. I felt helpless and profoundly alone at moments. Then there was the fear of being seen in a way I didn't want to be seen – that fear was the worst of all.

Then anger rose up in me like an inferno. How dare he? Who did he think he was? But it didn't last. It quickly exploded into waves of tears. The walls were coming down, and behind those walls was an ocean of pain. There were tears of feeling unwanted, tears of aloneness, tears of separation. I wanted to cover my face and hide my tears, but they were out in the open. Tommy saw and heard those tears, and he heard my pain. When the tears finally subsided after a long time, there was just the sweetness of love. I could feel in the deepest recesses of my heart that I loved him and would love him. Finally, I said, exhausted, "Please come to me. Please hold me."

I had never asked for anything. Really. Not like that. Oh sure, I'd asked but never from a place of actual need. My asking had been more like a command. Asking out of need was vulnerable, and yet I felt my power so clearly. Tommy untied me, massaged my arms, and held me until we fell asleep.

I was his from that point forward – because I wanted to be his. Whatever I'd had to prove by holding back left that day tied to the bedpost. I'd have fleeting moments when I thought to pull away and mess with his heart. But I'd look at myself in those moments and decide better. The curtain was drawn, and hiding wasn't an option anymore. What I came to know in my relationship with Tommy is that anything less than surrender into love (at least for a woman) is a dress rehearsal. You can't experience the kind of trust and support and unflinching love you want, as a woman, until you let go of yourself. I am grateful that he helped open this wisdom in me and showed me the gift of the Dark Knight.

Who is *The Dark Knight*?
Why are women attracted to him?

The opportunity the Dark Knight represents is one of living at your edge. The edge is the great unknown. It's the mystery. The unexplored terrain. It's what beckons you and dares you to be all that you are.

The edge is the domain of the Dark Knight. He possesses the gift of knowing that a life not lived fully is not a life at all. Where other men can conveniently hide behind their women, financial security, or achievement, the Dark Knight is compelled to pull back the veil of fear and look it in the eye. He is beckoned to the edge – drawn to danger and even to death.

To some degree, every man lives at his edge. The edge is where you invite the unknown, where you cross the borders of what is determined to be safe. You push the envelope of your faith, your strength, or your love. It's that place where you know you're not operating on autopilot. You're flying the plane with everything you've got, and clearly you're on a maiden voyage.

When men climb the great mountains of the world or traverse the most treacherous deserts, these are obvious edges. Putting your life on the line is always an edge. And yet, your edge might be far less dangerous. It might be exploring that place inside yourself you've never dared to look – a debilitating addiction or a limiting belief. It can be committing in love to a woman (if that's a genuine, personal edge and not a hideout). To be fully alive, plugged into the creative force of your masculinity, you need to know your edge like you know the edge of your own face.

You might be a great achiever or even a mediocre one. This might be an edge for you, pushing to attain, to make something of yourself. Most men are familiar with riding a professional edge because it's related to money. But your true edge is not a place you go to win. It's not a place you go for recognition from other men or approval from women. You go there to embrace being alive, to express the creative force in you. You go there because anything less feels like you're cheating yourself or dying.

What you want to look at is whether the edge you're on is pushing you to be a better man, or does it simply satisfy your ego's desire to win and succeed?

If you say, "I'm at my edge," is it the edge of fatigue, stress, or being overwhelmed? That's not the edge we're talking about here. Your edge energizes. Sure, there's effort involved; but when you're living at your edge, whether it's relationally, professionally or creatively, you're a self-generating engine. You're not sliding the car into neutral and coasting downhill. There's a presence in how you drive and what you drive toward that takes nothing for granted. The Dark Knight is keenly aware of the finite nature of life, and he wants to be awake and engaged for the whole ride.

I find it's the rare few among men who reach for their edge – who dare to push the boundaries of what's possible. Most men get caught up in achieving and in the safe routine of responsibility and reward. While a woman might appreciate a man who provides well for her and who can achieve his goals, when you run from the edge (from your freedom, danger, and death) your woman and your relationship will suffer. Relationship becomes a hideout. This is not encouraging to a woman. It doesn't give her the feeling that you are either safe or powerful, regardless of how much money you earn. As scary as it might be, a man needs to find his edge and live on it. You don't want to trade in your pilot's license for a bond of security, regardless of how safe or comfortable it might seem.

Granted, if you're married and you have children, you have responsibilities and people who count on you. I'm not suggesting you abandon those responsibilities. I am challenging you to take a longer view. Life is bigger than your circumstances. If you become your circumstances and let them define you, you're missing the point. When you reach the end of your life, you won't be asking yourself if you reached your goals and earned enough money. You'll be asking yourself did I live? Did I love? That's what living at your edge is all about.

Awakening the Dark Knight

It's all about embracing life. When a man is living at his edge, I trust him. Like any woman, I experience the fear of losing my man to that edge where he is so alive and free. But frankly, that possibility makes him that much more desirable to me. To be with a man who isn't free in his mind and heart, who feels he's turned in his freedom, is to be with a man who is only partially alive. I've embraced men who felt they were not free, and it doesn't feel good. It also doesn't feel safe or secure, as I know in my heart of hearts that he's not happy. He might profess his love and his pleasure at being with me and being mine – and claim he is satisfied with our life – but if he's not living at his edge, he's lying. I know he's lying, even if he doesn't know it.

Sometimes, a man thinks he needs to tame his wild side to have love in his life. He believes his freedom is unacceptable to a woman, so he turns in his wings. But ultimately what he gives his woman in the way of his freedom he takes back in his withdrawal, his distance, his lies.

We women don't intend to rob you of that free spirit; we just want to be a part of it. We want to feel you pushing outward and testing your edges, and we also want to feel the warmth, protection, and caring beneath your wings. Sometimes out of fear, we insist you stop being free. And, of course, sometimes a man puts himself in a cage with no urging at all from a woman.

I've told you of my stepfather who supported my sisters, my mother, and me for a decade of his life. He did his job of bringing in a paycheck, but he was horribly bitter. I wanted to set him free – to tell him to go live his life – but I didn't have that right.

His heart and his soul were written into those paychecks, and I wanted nothing to do with them. "Keep your money. Run for the hills," I wanted to tell him. Set us free of your misery. Jack didn't know anything about living at his edge, but he knew he wasn't alive. Anyone could see he was a walking dead man.

I don't think my mother stole his freedom; I think he was simply afraid to live, so he used his circumstances and us as his reason.

If a woman is afraid of her man's freedom and his creative expression, she will hold him tight and try to keep him grounded. Her nature is to nest. Her nature is to capture your free spirit, to make you want to stay. And yet, often when you do, she wishes you would leave!

A healthy, feminine woman doesn't want you to become dependent on her nurturing or to be like a child she needs to encourage and push from the nest. She wants a man who has a healthy resistance to being captured, a man committed to the love of his freedom.

The Dark Knight is a powerful and yet frightening force for a woman because he presents the greatest risk of all in love – to love and potentially to lose love.

When you live at your edge, a woman feels her edge in love. She must expand the borders of her loving and untie her restraints on your heart. The smaller part of her might wish for you to be near and predictable at all times, but her heart (in truth) wants expansion. Yes, it's scary when a man is free. This doesn't mean he has other lovers or that he leaves a woman for other worlds; it just means he's not in a self-appointed cage. The Dark Knight is irresistible to women because loving a man who is free is, at a deeper level, true love. It's not love bound by fear. To love the Dark Knight in any man, a woman must put her heart on the line and risk losing what she has given herself to.

The First Opportunity:
Know Your Edge

You might be a doctor or an entrepreneur or an engineer asking yourself, "So how do I do this? Do I have to give up on twelve years of education or decades of my life to live at my edge? What is this adventure going to cost me?"

My clients often experience both fear and frustration with this opportunity – because on one hand they can feel how passionately they want to live at their edge, how compromise and self-deception is killing their spirit, and yet they have no idea logistically how that might work.

I think of a plastic surgeon I worked with who was really disturbed by the realization (through our work) that he wasn't happy being a surgeon. His profession was incredibly challenging, and the stakes were high; but he didn't feel he was living at the edge that was meaningful for him. He felt he had settled for doing what his father wanted him to do. He felt his edge wasn't doctoring, as challenging and rewarding as it was.

What David really wanted was to be a chef. He dreamed of owning a high-end bed and breakfast in Napa Valley where he and his wife could entertain people from around the globe. But almost immediately upon disclosing this, he said, "My wife would never go for it. She likes our lifestyle way too much."

Men often do this, of course, as I've shared. They look for reasons outside of themselves to shut themselves down, to stay safe. They say it's about their wives or their children. They say it's about their parents or the culture. The opportunity here is to look inside, to stop and ask yourself are you living as the man you want to be? Is that edge calling you to experience more of who you truly are?

David seemed the least likely person to drop what he was doing and chase a dream. He was highly successful with twenty-five years invested in being a plastic surgeon earning $750,000 a year. While his earnings might seem high to some, he was barely getting by – barely able to pay for his sessions. He and his wife were over-committed on a new house, a new car, and their children's educations. He confessed that if he were to quit his job, he could survive about six months; and that would be by selling some of his art and other prized possessions. He could do it, but it would be uncomfortable and a risk. He'd be putting his kids at risk, too.

We started looking at what he wanted, focusing less on how and more on what. Turns out he had a lot of experience cooking and working in the hospitality business, because it was a passion of his mother's. She had owned a little bed and breakfast when he was growing up. He spent many a summer helping his mother in the kitchen baking and prepping. What he didn't realize is, once he was clear he didn't want to be a doctor anymore and could say it out loud, a cascade of events would transpire to make it possible for him to realize his dream.

Turns out a client had met with his partners and threatened a lawsuit against David for malpractice. There had been complications with a patient's under-eye surgery that had left her disfigured with a droopy eye. After a careful assessment of the situation, the partners decided to settle with the woman for $500,000 and meet her stipulation that David be let go from the practice. It was the second time they'd had to make a settlement on his behalf, and they had lost confidence in his skill as a surgeon. David felt he was in the right – he had warned the woman of the possible complications of such surgery and had done nothing wrong technically – but the partners saw it differently. David had become a risk they could no longer afford.

David was devastated. He began drinking heavily and went on a binge that lasted four weeks. After spending a week at a friend's getting clean, he sat down with his former partners, ready to work out a settlement agreement. In order to break his remaining one-year contract, they offered $250,000 and all insurance benefits for his family for three years. David knew he could do a lot better. He left the meeting extremely agitated and concerned for his investments and his future.

He spoke with a lawyer, and with his advice negotiated a million dollar settlement: $250,000 at the closing of their contract and $250,000 every four months until complete. The settlement package didn't erase his feelings of shame at failing as a surgeon, but it was generous enough that if he worked hard could turn his life around. David bought a vineyard a year later and opened a gourmet store with a deli on that land.

You might think his being fired was a coincidence, having nothing to do with his declaration that he wanted out of doctoring, but I've seen these kinds of things happen to clients with such frequency I know it was no coincidence. The circumstances often look like they are unrelated to a man's decisions and thinking, but from my perspective, your thinking creates the circumstances.

Passion and clarity are powerful tools for manifestation. I experienced this, too, with my client, Jim, who had been a chiropractor for fifteen years. Nobody would have guessed listening to him that he was bored out of his mind with his work. He came across as competent and interested in what he was doing. But as I got to know Jim and worked with him on his relationships to women, I felt his insincerity and lack of passion bubble to the surface. So I asked him about it.

Initially, he denied any displeasure with his work. He had a lot to protect. He had a gorgeous home in the Bay area, a sailboat, and a chic car. To admit what he was doing wasn't satisfying could put his entire lifestyle at risk. Let's face it: it's not just admitting it. Like most men, if he admitted it, he'd feel compelled to do something about it. I didn't push him but waited for our relationship to develop.

About three months ahead Jim came to session kind of down. When I asked what was going on, he said, "I'm just busy, tired, that's all."

"How do you feel about being so busy," I asked.

"Tired," he said.

"Say more about that, Jim."

"Well, I see twelve to sixteen patients a day, and I just don't care. I'm not engaged and I'm not passionate."

"What is it you'd rather be doing with that time?"

"Sailing."

"And after sailing?"

"Writing. I want to write. It's what I do when I'm not seeing patients. But every time I think about doing that full time, I think of going back to being poor, to living without my toys and without the freedom to enjoy my life."

"What kind of freedom do you have now with sixteen patients a day, six days a week?"

"None. I haven't been on the sailboat in a month."

The thing most men don't get is that it's okay not to like what you're doing. That's the first step – just admitting you've painted yourself into a box. If you don't see the box you're in, you can't get out. It's hard for a man to admit he might have made a choice that wasn't the best choice for him. Admitting that means upheaval. It might mean having to shift his internal sense of self. This is what Jim went through over the next months. He vacillated between extreme excitement and extreme fear at the idea of picturing and ultimately taking action on a new way of life.

"Can you do this for another ten years?" I asked him.

He shook his head no. "It will kill me," he said.

"Okay then, are you willing to choose and then live with the consequences?"

"Let me think about it," he said. Jim did this for six months. He would come to that place where he'd almost say yes but then pull back. Finally, just before Christmas, he decided it was time.

When he said, "My answer is yes," I told him he didn't have to know the how just yet. His job was to simply know and accept that he was choosing it and to feel and celebrate his excitement. He wanted to write. So we began to structure his schedule so he could do that. He also decided to lighten his client load to ten patients a day.

Right away, he started to notice he liked his patients more. He also felt excited to speak with them about his writing on the topic of optimal nutrition. In the past, he'd said nothing about it and assumed their lack of interest. Much to his surprise, many of his patients said they wanted a consultation in order to have him examine what they ate and give them the score he had developed for their nutrition.

Soon, he was invited to be interviewed on radio (by one patient) which led to an article about him in the local newspaper, and that led to the creation of his own diet system designed to raise a person's health score. People were losing weight and claiming to have more energy using his system. He moved his clients who wanted adjustments to an assistant and found he enjoyed teaching and mentoring his assistant more than doing the adjustments himself.

By leveraging his time with the assistant and then raising his own rates to see select patients, Jim started making more money and feeling excitement about his practice. When last we spoke, he was working on his first book and had a publisher. When I asked what he had to give up to have such a great life, he laughed. "I didn't give anything up," he said. "The most important thing I've done is believe in the possibility of my dream – and of course, take the steps to make it happen. Every day I feed that belief and every day it feeds me back."

Anything is possible when there is clarity, passion, and commitment. Your edge isn't always a professional one – often it's personal, even deeply personal. I think of my client, Ken, who had been a father for thirteen years, almost without involvement. I worked with Ken over nine months to repair his marriage – to re-create intimacy and a sex life out of the ashes of a year of abstinence.

His incredible success with his wife created an opening and the clarity to see that the relationship he was having with his daughter was not in alignment with the man he was becoming. He didn't divulge all of the details of his situation initially; instead he simply mentioned that he and his wife were having issues with their daughter. I asked if he wanted to take a look at that.

He explained Leela was very angry and often threw temper tantrums that put him over the edge. As of late, she was refusing to attend school. She said she hated school and wanted to go somewhere else. She refused to discuss whether something had happened at school that upset her. When Ken and his wife suggested she speak with a professional about what was happening for her, Leela became wildly upset. "Get away from me!" she screamed. "I hate you!" Leela had had issues over the years socially and had been mostly homeschooled. The problem was that whenever she came up against not feeling okay socially, she quit. Ken didn't know how to handle her volatility, so he stayed in the background, often seething at his wife's lack of discipline and control. His fear was if he got involved, he'd be too heavy-handed. He'd act like his own mother who was a harsh, unforgiving disciplinarian. Not doing anything was a way of supporting his daughter. Not pushing her and letting her have her way was his way of honoring that she was fragile. He and his wife spent hours upon hours trying to figure out how to handle Leela in a way that wouldn't disturb her or force her to be even more emotionally volatile.

When I asked Ken whether he was living at his edge in this relationship with Leela, he said, "No. I've avoided her at all costs. And for this reason, I'm sad to say I barely know her."

He felt sad and ashamed. As I helped Ken to see, being run by his daughter's outbursts had many negative consequences. One, her ability to push him back by simply throwing a tantrum let her be in control. Not only could she control her parents, but she could also control the level of intimacy in her relationships with them. She could avoid what she was feeling, because everyone was afraid of her volatility. She also got reinforcement for the idea something was wrong with her, broken, or defective, and that she did in fact need to be treated differently. And because she wasn't encouraged to face and deal with what arose for her and learn from it, in a sense she was an emotional cripple.

Ken feared he didn't have the strength to weather her anger; there was a fear of being annihilated. He also feared his own anger and that unleashing it would make the situation worse. But at the deepest level was an old story that he didn't know much about women – that they were difficult and confusing – and to invite their emotions was akin to inviting a firing squad to shoot at his heart.

What I was able to help him see is that his edge was walking right into that storm. He needed to embrace the storm and find out what was at the heart of it. This was the only way to create intimacy and healing. His edge was overcoming his fear of women, the idea that he wasn't enough to deal with their feelings and needs.

The Dark Knight archetype is about walking right into what seems at times dangerous and even life-threatening territory. You know a girl isn't going to kill you, and yet it feels as if she might. It feels as if she might mince you into tiny pieces and leave you a mess of a man, but the truth is avoiding the relationship is more emasculating. Running from a woman in any form – whether she's your daughter, wife, mother, or friend – does not empower you.

Ken decided to stop simply tolerating and accepting his daughter's verbal outbursts and step right into the eye of the storm. He sat her down and told her he wanted her to listen and he wasn't going to be averted by her tantrums. He insisted on communication, and being supportive, and discovering together how to help her deal with what she was going through. By doing this he demonstrated that he accepted her emotions, could handle them, and that he didn't define his daughter by the way she was acting. He also became a protector instead of the enemy.

What he didn't expect was how much it would reward him with her affection and admiration. "The more I listen to her and insist on her being real with me, the more she wants to be with me. She walks up to me and hugs me for no reason. It's amazing."

Knowing your edge is knowing where in your life you're holding back out of fear. In Ken's case, it was easy to overlook: his daughter. Most people don't expect a man to have a particularly close relationship with a girl – so it was an easy weak spot to hide. Ken knew in his heart of hearts he was running, and the only reason he didn't have a close relationship with Leela was his fear. Reaching for this edge and coming face to face with what he most feared made him a more confident, loving man – a man his daughter could feel proud of and protected by.

Practice:
Living At Your Edge

There is a good chance you are in careful denial about the edges in your life. The first step in learning how to lean into your own edges is to identify them. An edge in your life is where you feel fear, trepidation, or anxiety around some task or confrontation. Habitually, we tend to avoid these things. We may avoid them because we feel inadequate in the face of them or because we simply hope that by avoiding them, they will somehow go away. As a way to get started with the practice of living at your edge, follow these steps:

1. Identify the edges you experience across different domains of your life. You probably have work edges, relationship edges, family edges, and perhaps even recreational edges. Many men address their recreational edges very successfully; they break their own records for performance by pushing themselves physically and mentally to live right at their edge in training and competition. Some men face their work edges fairly well, recognizing where they are weak and working to compensate for that weakness by taking on challenges that force them out of their comfort zone. Men are much less likely to push their edges in relationships, however. Try to identify your relationship edges. This might include a fear of certain feminine emotional storms or attitudes. Do you avoid certain emotional territory? Do you tiptoe around issues in relationships? That's an edge you are avoiding.

2. Lean into those edges. A good sailor doesn't seek out stormy weather. He does his best to avoid stormy conditions because of their unpredictability. But a good sailor knows that sailing eventually means dealing with storms, and when a storm comes up he is going to have to lean into it and face it with all the gifts and strength he has. In relationships, the corollary would be that no man goes out of his way to provoke a feminine storm, but every man who is willing to live at his edge realizes you cannot avoid the storm forever, and once the storm comes up, hiding below decks in your cabin is not an option. Can you stand in the face of the feminine storm of emotion? Can you honor the energy without being crushed, washed overboard, or drowning? If you can, you will both be better on the other side of the storm.

3. Expand your capacity to live at your edge. Every sailor who comes through a storm has huge respect for the power of the ocean but also a sense of satisfaction and self-confidence for having weathered that storm. This is the feeling you will discover in yourself when you are more consistently living at your edge. It will give you the strength and confidence to face more edges in your life. Remember that the Dark Knight lives by a simple code: If there is no way out of a situation, go more deeply into it. There you will find your true nature.

The Second Opportunity:
Live as a Free Man

The masculine in you values freedom in the way that the feminine values relationships and love. To some degree you likely feel a conflict if you're in a relationship with a woman – a desire to live unencumbered but to have that woman you care about at your side. Perhaps you believe it must be one way or the other, so you compromise one for the other.

It's not easy to navigate a relationship with a woman and your freedom – and not to lose something you care about in the process. It can seem cruel and unfair that you need to choose. Naturally, you want love and to have a woman in your life – and you want to embrace being free. I'm here to tell you that you can have both. It's a matter of how you're thinking and what you're choosing.

These two "tensions" will always exist if you're alive and well. The desire to be with a woman and the desire to be free are flip sides of a masculine coin. In the morning you might gaze upon her sleeping, and the love you feel for her is so deep and complete it hurts. That night you might go out to pick up ice cream and as you pass the freeway on-ramp, you feel a powerful urge to jump on and never come back. How you deal with the tension between these two impulses is important and will define you as a man.

Some men insist on a "freedom" characterized by having a variety of sexual partners or by refusing to be accountable for their own actions. Other men insist on a freedom defined by absence, whether it's silence, retreat, or emotional unavailability. The problem comes when your freedom is defined by resistance or rebellion, because then you're not truly free. You're simply fighting against whomever you think is your captor – namely your woman. If you act out against a woman or relationship by cheating and lying to gain your "freedom," that's not true freedom either. That's more like escaping to the yard of the prison but not scaling the wall.

Free is something you have to come to realize that you are. It's not something you do or something you find in remote lands outside of yourself. Your freedom is alive in you and needs to be fed by way of thoughts, feelings, and actions that satisfy that masculine impulse. Most men give this impulse "junk food": little runs in the prison yard that satisfy the recurring itch. For some it's a sensuous massage, a trip to a strip club, or a short-lived affair. Meanwhile, true freedom is never tasted, much less embraced.

To be free you have to know you always have a choice. If you're in an unsatisfying, emasculating relationship, this might be hard to imagine, and yet you need to see it to claim your freedom.

To think of life as a compromise closes the door of choice. To believe you compromise for love is a trap. Real love is not a compromise. Sure, you do things for love. You make choices that close out other choices – but that's simply the freedom of choice at play. Yes, if you marry and commit to one woman, you relinquish being with other women. That is a choice that comes of your freedom to love one woman. You don't have to have a woman in your life or a monogamous relationship. You don't have to have the responsibilities of children, or even a girlfriend. All of these are choices. You are free to make choices that align with what you care about, and you are free to modify what you choose over time.

To be free as a man you must find the space and freedom inherent in these choices (a freedom that is often overlooked).

Naturally, when you make certain choices, those choices come with a set of consequences. We call those consequences circumstances. You choose to love a woman, and that comes with a set of consequences. You choose to be single, and that comes with a set of consequences. You choose children, and that comes with consequences. Yet, within those consequences you still have choices. It's so important to remember this – because the moment you forget it, what you choose starts to feel like it has control over you, rather than you being the one making the choice.

You want to find freedom within you – because if you don't you can traverse the corners of the Earth and push the edges of human possibility and never feel free. Yes, being able to go places, to experience life and to enjoy it are all freedoms. And yet, there are men who have these freedoms who still feel trapped inside shells of loneliness. Being free must first begin with accepting a truth – that you are and always have been free. You may be making choices that hinder your ability to move about in life, to experience life, or to prosper in love, but the freedom to choose has always been yours.

My client, Sam, chose to work with me because he wanted to leave his wife of twenty years and couldn't make it happen. He claimed her abuses to both him and his kids were extreme and included spying on the children with hidden cameras and erasing information from their computers while they were at school. He was relegated to the couch and was often openly criticized in front of the children for being lazy, selfish, and overweight.

When he first described the situation, he was clear that he was the victim and she was the perpetrator, and he was caught in an inescapable trap. I could empathize that he felt powerless and the situation was emasculating, but I didn't agree with his victim position. I knew it was paramount that he realize his power of choice and see how choice got him where he was if he was ever to take his power back. So we looked there first. Then after a time we looked even more deeply.

"Have you considered that Susan lives with a man who chooses to be a prisoner of his circumstances? Have you considered that she lives with a man who is with her because he thinks he can't do better, believes he has no choice, and is afraid to leave? Can you imagine the response that might provoke in you?"

Sam didn't like looking at the situation from that angle, but he admitted he wouldn't like it if the tables were turned. "That might piss me off," he said. "I guess I've always believed I was doomed in the marriage, but if I just did what she wanted, someday she'd be happy and leave me alone. It hasn't worked."

"What kind of man wants a relationship where he's a servant to his wife's needs and expects nothing for himself?"

"I guess a pretty sad man," he said, true to form, playing the victim.

"If you're not playing the victim here, what kind of man stays in a situation like that?"

"One who doesn't have faith in himself, I guess."

In Sam's case, Sam refused to be free. He made his wife into a scapegoat for his lack of happiness and freedom. Like so many men I've worked with, he held the belief that if he just did the "right" things and enough of them, he'd finally get the approval he was seeking from his wife. He'd finally be in her good stead. Of course, this kind of "commerce" in a relationship never works. Look at it this way: When you're trying to do all the right things to gain your woman's approval or make her happy, you're creating a mother/child relationship with her. Yes, she wants you to do those sweet things for her, but when they become the product you trade for love or sex, it feels dishonest.

I didn't work with his wife, but from what I could glean, she did everything in her power to set him free. She pushed him out of their bedroom. She pushed him out of the guest room and out of her bank account. She treated him like a child and denied him his rights as a father. I think in her own not-so-kind way she was she was saying, "Don't fly on my wings." But time and again Sam got hooked by her criticisms and put his attention on pleasing her and righting his "wrongs" rather than finding the courage to live as a free man.

Sam continued to cling to his wife's abuses, even after realizing exactly what he was up to and why. He continued to feel afraid to let go, to claim his happiness as his own. Finally, after a year of coaching together, he filed for divorce and left his wife – but it came about because of an affair with another woman.

While I always hope my clients make the best choices for themselves and that they are inspired by our work to live in accordance with their highest knowing and values, there are those few who will continue to cling to fear. Sam needed another woman in his life to assure him he'd be loved – before he could leave his wife. I felt his leaving on these terms was weak and problematic. One, he didn't learn to trust that if he did the right thing he'd get the right result. Instead of leaving for all the right reasons and embracing that risk, he left to be with another woman (which was guaranteed). He could have left for the right reasons and done the right thing, and then taken up this relationship with the woman as a distinctly separate experience.

Freedom can be scary. It can be scary because it carries a lot of responsibility. There are risks and consequences when you live as a free man. You have no one to blame for your life, choices, or a lack of happiness. Sam was terrified of this.

Embracing freedom is about recognizing that you are already free. You're a creator. You have the power to think and feel in ways that bring about a positive experience. Those positive thoughts and feelings – and the actions that follow – can create a satisfying life.

When you think of freedom as a scarce commodity or something beyond your reach (outside of the deal you've made), you find yourself making little bargains with the woman in your life. Freedom becomes a transaction rather than a state of being. Think about the guy who mows the lawn and shops with his wife at Macy's in order to earn his day on the golf course, or the guy who runs himself into the ground serving his family in order to attend a conference once a year that is meaningful to him.

You don't have to buy freedom. You simply need to realize you are free and create a life that reflects that truth.

Ron, married with two children under five, couldn't believe he was free. Instead of hiding behind his wife's needs, like Sam, Ron acted as if freedom were something that could be taken from him, something he had to hoard and defend. When he wanted to take a business trip or go away camping with his friends, he simply issued an edict so as not to be interfered with. "I'm going away this weekend," he'd say. His communication was essentially: Deal with it.

You can imagine how well that went over with his young wife. His edicts meant she'd be stuck with the kids, alone, all weekend – after an entire week as a full-time mother. "He's like a sergeant in our home," she said. "I'm just one of his men."

Ron's fear of "no" and of losing his freedom made him act defensively. His wife would give in to his demands to keep the peace, but she would inevitably sabotage his trip with various dramas to draw his attention home. He got his "freedoms," but the cost was his wife's trust and his good time. Since he never fully relaxed or enjoyed these trips because of drama at home, he felt exhausted and always in need of rest.

I worked with Ron to learn how to be free inside of himself – to find freedom first in his choices. He saw he was choosing to feel and think of himself as a prisoner. His wife was a prison guard (in his mind), someone trying to rob him of his pleasure. His children he thought of as work and more responsibility.

He decided to see that he did have choices. He could walk out the door. That wasn't who he was, but it was possible. He didn't have to be a husband or a father. He didn't have to have a woman in his life. He could choose to leave and see his children part time.

But he decided he wanted exactly what he had already chosen. He simply had to act as if he had chosen it.

"Julie is different," he told me shortly thereafter. "I told her I was leaving town on a trip for business, and she said she'd miss me."

"So she changed?" I asked.

"Seems that way."

"What about you? What was different about how you were?"

"First of all, I didn't feel a need to attack her with the trip, to shove it down her throat. Truth is I felt bad that I had to go. I just said that I wish I didn't have to do this, but I need to take a trip this weekend."

"What you did was communicate that you didn't want to leave her – that leaving her mattered. All of your other notifications seemed hell-bent on getting away from her. It's no wonder she responded to you differently. You were different."

"Yeah, I was. The thing is she wants me to be happy. If I don't force my trips on her and consider her first, she's happy to support me and even encourage me to go away."

When you learn to be free and give that fullness to a woman, you then inspire her to be free as well. While a masculine man struggles with an impulse to be autonomous, a feminine woman struggles with the impulse to love freely. If she's with a man who holds back and refuses accountability and presence in the relationship, she will also hold back. She may fantasize about greener pastures or that "on-ramp" and other ways of protecting herself. If you're afraid of losing your freedom, she's going to be afraid of giving her love freely to you.

You being free and living as a free man in heart, body, and mind – full and unafraid –inspires a woman to love with abandon.

Practice:
Recognizing the Freedom You Really Want

For most men, "freedom" becomes a code word for certain dissatisfaction with being limited to one sexual partner. Men go to great lengths to defend this desire as being natural and to how it justifies either avoiding commitment or having affairs. The truth is that this desire is completely natural. The masculine desires feminine diversity in the same way the feminine desires masculine depth. Most men resort to pornography, strip clubs, or having affairs to get a flavor of feminine sexual energy they are not getting from their partners. Most women assume men want women who look different than they do (are younger, thinner, more attractive, or have features different from theirs). This is true only on the surface. Most men (while they are certainly drawn to different packages of feminine energy) are really more interested in the energy itself. So, to the extent that a woman can and is willing to give her man a range of feminine flavors and experiences, she is more likely to keep her man engaged and aroused. A lot of women, however, are extremely limited in the range of sexual energy they are capable of or willing to give to a man.

Most men tend to be very limited in the level of depth they are willing to take a woman sexually and so end up driving their women into the arms of more directional men willing to take a woman to a deeper place sexually.

One way of thinking about the freedom you actually want is to realize that if you can inspire and create a sense of exploration and trust in your woman, you are more likely to get her to give you the diversity of sexual energy you are craving. In this way you engage your partner rather than bypass her.

1. Own your sexual preferences. We all have sexual preferences. Are you honest about what yours are? Do you know what arouses you in sensual terms (smells, tastes, textures, sounds)? Do you know what arouses you in terms of situations and settings (fantasies and scenarios)? Most men do know these things and some obsess over them endlessly because they cannot honestly and openly communicate about them with their partners.

2. Share and discuss your sexual preferences. This often feels like risky territory for men, because you have been taught to be

ashamed of these preferences; and terms like "kinky" or "perverted" have been used to cause you to feel shame and embarrassment. What you do need to know about sharing your preferences is that there are things your partner could conceivably offer you and things that it is pointless to bring up. You might prefer a woman who is really thin and has big breasts; but if this is not your woman, sharing this is about as productive as her telling you she would prefer it if your penis were twice as big.

3. If acknowledging your sexual preferences and hers is new for both of you, consider starting small. Sometimes simple things like breaking old habits of sexual position, location, timing, etc., can feel like a breath of fresh air in a sex life that has become routine. This is not to say you can't introduce bigger variations into your sex life, but if you want to experiment with bondage, tying her wrists to the headboard with scarves is a step before complicated ropes and mechanical restraints.

The Third Opportunity:
Welcome Danger and Death

I could have called this opportunity by several different names. It could have been "Embrace What You Fear" or "Learn to Be Dangerous." If you look at your life, it's probably the most dangerous things you've done that have given you the most satisfaction. And by dangerous, I mean the moments in which you actually risked what had real value for you: your hard-earned money, your reputation, your status, your self-image, your physical safety, and perhaps even your life. It might have been the move you made to another city without guarantees. It might have been the backpacking trip you took solo into the deep unknown. Perhaps it was choosing a business or an investment opportunity that changed your life.

Danger comes when something of value is at risk. To be really alive, a man needs to accept danger and risk as part of the deal, even death. If you look at most of your self-inflicted diseases – overeating, procrastination, alcohol and drug addiction, philandering, excessive working, hoarding – you'll find they are all clever ways of avoiding danger and death, and avoiding or managing risk. You want to ensure an outcome, yet, no matter where you hide, danger and death come to visit. Risk is part of the game.

The willingness to die is not some kind of reckless pursuit. No woman is attracted for long to a man who takes unnecessary risks just to inflate his own ego. A woman can sense when a man is risking danger because he is trying to fill some empty place inside or is unwilling to face something even more frightening. But a man who is willing to risk what he values most in the name of something greater than himself is deeply attractive. A man who is willing to push himself to accomplish something great, even if that accomplishment carries with it great risk, is deeply attractive to the feminine. Are you willing to risk your life in order to live it? It's not that you leap in front of buses or trains, testing your luck, but do you love life so much that you are willing to die to live it full out?

The true, unfettered masculine impulse is to identify with emptiness. It is to give everything you have, to empty yourself in the name of something greater than you. The ultimate emptiness is of course death, so for a man to live deeply from his masculine essence, he needs to befriend death. Most men fear death, and in fearing death they fear to live fully. They seem to think that if they deny, hide, procrastinate and play it safe, they can postpone the inevitable. You know life will end. You see that demonstrated daily in the face of tragedy and unexpected death. Your own death is undeniable (simply look at the statistics). But are you rushing to live despite death or hiding in order to avoid what cannot be avoided?

You don't have to jump from a plane or run into a burning building to demonstrate a willingness to die or to embrace danger. It's true some men choose professions or hobbies that put them at continual risk in order to face their own deaths, but your expression of this masculine essence does not always need to involve physical danger. Just because you are willing to die does not mean you need or want to die. There may be no physical danger in putting your career or reputation on the line for something you really believe in, but there is certainly risk. Befriending death and embracing danger or risk does not mean the absence of fear. If there were no fear, it would indicate that nothing was actually at risk.

On the contrary, a truly dangerous man, in the sense of being able to live his life fully, feels the fear and acts anyway, not with recklessness but with clarity and purpose. You often find that men who put their lives at risk frequently or professionally spend a lot of time practicing and perfecting ways of minimizing risks over which they have some control; this is out of respect for their partners and for the nature of their endeavor and a real recognition that ultimately, there are aspects of the endeavor out of their control.

There is danger in all mystery. Isn't that why men exclaim that women are dangerous? There is danger in faith and in belief, too, because while these can be powerful energies, there are no guarantees. We often think of danger as something out of our control, something you accidentally walk into, like a blade in a dark alley. And yet, when you embrace danger and death as your allies and constant companions, you see that surprise is a very small part of living dangerously.

Why Women Love Dangerous Men

If you have fled from the danger that would give shape and excitement to your life, the woman in your life or the woman you hope to have in your life can feel it. Remember that feeling and energetic sensitivity are in the feminine domain. A woman is constantly feeling into you and where the lines of your potential begin and end. If you're avoiding danger and death, she'll feel the limits of your imagination, your courage, and your power. She'll feel the edges of the box that hems you in.

Women are attracted to men who embrace danger and death not because they are fearless (free of fear), but because they defy fear, they act in the face of fear. They exemplify manliness. Their bravery makes us feel safe and protected. A man who embraces danger and death is "dangerous" in the right way. He defies limiting ideas, slices through fear, and embraces what is possible.

We often think of dangerous men as bad or cruel. Yes, there are men who hurt others, and they are one kind of dangerous. But for the purpose of understanding a woman's attraction to dangerous men, the dangerous we're looking at here is the good kind of dangerous. It's true that women are often so starved for men who are willing to live fully and act in the face of fear that they are sometimes seduced by a man who is merely dangerous in a cruelly unpredictable or self-interested and self-serving way. But that is all the more reason for good and caring men to recognize and embrace their capacity for danger and risk.

Have you ever wondered why women are so attracted to men on motorcycles, men who drive fast cars, or men who excel at dangerous sports? It's because there's power in defying fear. There's a power we can feel. Women love power in men. There is actually an evolution- ary reason for this. Those of us alive today were selected because our Stone Age grandmothers made good choices in the men with whom they mated. They chose men who were risk takers and unafraid of danger because those men were the leaders and the hunters in the community. They could do a better job of providing food and safety and ensuring the survival of their offspring. So, in a very real way, this selection criterion is biologically programmed into women.

There is also an emotional component to these selection criteria. Every woman struggles with the two competing desires of having a man she can control and a man she cannot control. It is why a lot of women end up in safe relationships with the guy who is predictable and controllable but lust after the man who is dangerous and unpre- dictable. The former makes us feel safe; the latter makes us feel alive. If you want a deep relationship, figure out how to give your woman both things but don't ever sacrifice your power.

Most men find women difficult to understand, and that leads to a kind of fear of women. Recognizing that the woman you are with is part of the great mystery of life is one thing, but deferring to her out of fear is a relationship killer. Ultimately, the fear of women is simply the fear of failing. The fear of failing is so total in some men that they can't see a woman they're interested in or in relationship with as any- thing but possible failure. Facing danger – really taking it on – is also about working through this fear of women.

When a woman meets a dangerous man who is unafraid of her and of the world, he's like a bolt of electricity. She feels free and light in his presence. Fear is not his ruler. A man who masters fear makes no bargains with his heart and soul. He owns his life and he lives it – death be damned.

I'll never forget a hair-raising motorcycle ride I had with a young, sexy guy in Florence. His name was Niccolo, and he assured me he'd drive carefully, as I was highly resistant to the idea of mounting his machine. If you've seen how people drive their motorcycles in Italy, you will understand my fear. "I will be careful," he assured me, looking deeply into my eyes. "Believe me, I will drive slowly."

He was so convincing. But it wasn't a second or two after we slipped on helmets that he said, "Ready?" and then took off like a rocket ship out of hell. I clung to him for dear life. He wove in and out of traffic at speeds that were simply ridiculous. My choice was to become one with him and that bike or fall off.

I had moments when I seriously thought, "This is it," and moments when I was just furious at his lack of respect for my life and my wishes. The ride lasted about an hour, and when I got off the bike, I was shaking all over. Every attempt to yell at him and tell him how wrong he was just made me laugh. I laughed until I'd released all of the tension.

Truth be told, the way he maneuvered that bike was a turn-on and I was confused. Did I like being terrified? No. But I did like his skill – a lot.

"Wasn't I careful enough?" he asked sweetly.

The crazy thing is – he was serious. "You call that careful? I thought I'd never make it off that bike alive."

He laughed. "You like pasta?" he asked, a big smirk on his face as he pulled off his helmet.

"Of course," I said.

"Come by my family's house tonight and eat with us." It was a peace offering, I sensed.

I'd sworn while on the back of that bike I'd kill him before I'd ever go anywhere with him again. But suddenly, it was like I had amnesia.

"I'd love to," I said.

His family was a typical Italian family – demonstrative, engaging, passionate. The food was extravagant – meats, pastas, salads, cookies, cakes, sorbets. We ate for hours. They wanted to know me, and it felt sincere although pointed. Why was I in Italy? What was my passion? Did men in the U.S. lack masculinity as so many American women had reported?

Niccolo's mother, an elegant woman in her sixties, sat next to Niccolo and across from me and every now and again would turn to

Niccolo, grab his chin and say: "He has a killer face, no?" It was a line I suspected she picked up from an American film.

There were several toasts made to me, simply because I was a guest – and because everyone seemed fascinated to have an American to interview and prod for information.

At the end of the night, Niccolo said he'd drive me to my hotel on his bike, rather than me taking a taxi as we'd discussed earlier. He seemed surprised when I didn't hesitate to say "yes." Knowing his family, I felt secure in his desire to get back to them alive. He was no longer just some wild man on a bike. He was Niccolo, son of Francesca, brother of Antonio. I was also looking forward to that connection and the opportunity to wrap my body around his.

He drove fast and dangerously again, but it felt different altogether. I felt I could trust him. Feeling trust gave me a very different perspective on Niccolo. I could feel that he wasn't reckless. He wasn't showing off or taking adolescent risks. He drove that bike like it was made to be driven. To ride with any less focus or commitment would have been less safe in a sense. This time I clung to him, but it wasn't out of fear. It was out of desire.

When I kissed Niccolo goodnight that night, I was sad that I wouldn't be seeing him again. I was flying back to the states the next day. He didn't push for sex, which I appreciated – because as much as I would have liked to explore that with him, I would have wanted more time to know him.

It's interesting that of all the men I've known, and especially those I've met in my travels, Niccolo is so vivid in my mind. His combination of dangerous, sweet, and sexy is one that will always sit with me like the perfect day or the perfect kiss. He took me somewhere I'd never been, not just literally but in spirit, and those are moments you never forget.

Practice:
Making Friends with Death

There is no way to actually practice making friends, but I can give you two simple yet profound things to add to your daily living and loving regimen.

1. Meditate daily. Develop an emptiness practice. The true mascu-

line, the masculine that is so deeply attractive to the true feminine, is aligned with and drawn to emptiness and completion,
but too many men have become addicted to activity and self-dis-
traction. In order to be truly attractive to the feminine, you need
to cultivate that within you that is the polar opposite of the feminine. The feminine loves life and energy moving and fullness.
You can certainly relate to a woman by loving life and energy and
fullness, but she will see you more as a friend or a partner than a
lover. To really create strong attraction, cultivate your ability to
be comfortable with stillness and emptiness. A daily meditation
practice helps you slow down and befriend stillness. It gives you a
reserve of unshakable calm that women find irresistible.

2. Make love as if it was for the last time. When you take your woman in your arms, understand that in a relatively short period of
time you will both be dead. If you both live out your full allot-
ment of life, you may have years left together. But eventually she
will grow old, you will grow old, and life will leave your bodies. Make friends with this reality. Don't ignore it or suppress it.
Honor it. Make love as though this might be the last time. Honestly, it might be. Don't waste it. That doesn't mean you have to
talk about it to your partner or make a melodramatic scene out
of it, but let that subtle awareness carry your lovemaking to a new
depth. It is what she wants from you. Just as you want to feel her
life and her energy, her shine and her glow, she wants to feel your
depth and the steadiness you are at the core of your being.

The Dark Side of the Dark Knight

Brian was a client of mine for over a year. He'd been trained by some
of the best pick-up artists in the U.S., including the man called "Mystery," who wrote the book called The Game. He was confident, cocky,
and hard. I was able to imagine there were a lot of women in the
world who played and lost with Brian, whose hearts were trampled
by his lack of care and his skill at seduction.

He was handsome but not ridiculously so. What he had was this
uncanny ability to look at a woman and read her sexually. I know
because he read me over the phone, and we'd not even met. I can tell
you he was quite accurate – frighteningly so. Whatever face a wom-

an wore, whatever she used to disguise her flaws and her fears and hidden desires, Brian could unmask her. Women were naked in his presence, even if they didn't know it.

"I want to change," he said in the first session. "I chose you because when I read your profile and saw you on video, I knew I couldn't seduce you."

"How'd you know?" I asked.

"I just know these things. Look, you're a total pro. Your integrity is obviously impenetrable."

He was right. But admittedly, his power had an effect that wasn't always easy to manage. While we'd be talking about his story, I could feel his seductive energy like an invisible gas seeking to permeate, invade, and pervade my being. I could feel how less centered or present-minded women would be put under, unknowingly, by his spell.

What Brian wanted was to learn how to be in a relationship. He really had no idea about this. Of course, he knew how to get women into bed and even how to make them fall in love, but he had no idea how to create something called a "we" that would have ongoing interactions.

It was important to understand where he'd been with women, so I asked him to tell me how he took women. What was his process or his strategy? What had he learned about women from The Game? What had he learned about himself?

Brian decided to tell me about a woman he'd recently seduced, who for some reason affected him as none of the others had. It was the reason he decided to seek help. At our first session, this is what he told me.

Laura wasn't my usual conquest. She was a bit older, thirty-five to be exact, and she was what I would define as a good girl. The girl next door, tigress in bed. She surprised me and that never happens. I had her pegged for a girl who wanted to be bossed around, forced to submit, that sort of thing. But what happened wasn't that at all. Whenever I pushed to take her, she would stop and begin to cry. She'd ask me to just hold her. I was extremely uncomfortable with this, and it brought out something in me I didn't like. Her need and tears really turned me off. They made me want to hurt her. I had to stop everything and back up and ask myself what was going on.

I realized I was out of control. She had beaten me at my own game. I wanted to use her, to take her, and move on, and she was forcing me to do what she wanted. I hated her and I hated my discomfort with this. Part of me wanted to hold her, or I would not have stayed, but the bigger part despised her. That's what scares me most.

Look, I am accustomed to knowing what a woman wants before she knows she wants it. I see what a woman is hiding – her deepest sexual desires, and I expose them. It's like feeding milk to a baby. This woman tested me in a way I didn't like. She asked for something I didn't realize she needed. I left that first night on edge. I held her a little bit as she cried, and then I forced intercourse on her. She submitted to it, but it wasn't smooth. I needed to release tension and felt out of control. I planned to never see her again. Then the next day I found myself thinking about her – wanting her, wanting to take her, and even hurt her. I pictured tying her up and forcing her to cry again. I called her, almost unable to stop myself, and asked if I could come by and talk. She said yes. I hated that she was easy and I also felt turned on by it. She'd been crying, I could see it, and it provoked that same feeling in me. She was in this big furry robe that was like a little girl's, not at all the tigress I had pegged her as. I could see she wanted to be held, to be comforted, and I resisted. I also knew in my gut she liked it that I had forced myself on her, and she wanted more of that."

"What's with the tears?" I asked, though I didn't really care.

"I just had an abortion," she said. That thought made me ill.

I knew I could own her. I knew that with the right combination of soothing words and hard-core fucking, she'd be mine. That's the game. It's not just getting laid; it's getting in so deep with a girl she doesn't know what hit her. It's taking her mind, body, soul and leaving a giant void in your wake. I like to think that a woman is never the same after I have her, that it takes months or even years for her to put herself back together.

I know I sound like such an asshole, but it's all I know.

Anyway, so I say to her, "Honey, that's a nightmare. What can I do for you right now?"

"Hold me," she says, of course. What I could see is that she wanted me to play her daddy. She wanted to be held, yeah, but she wanted something else very dirty.

It's a crazy thing to know these things. And this one felt so freaky I was nervous I could be wrong. I'd been wrong that first night. Or had I?

I held her for a while and she cried a bit more on my lap, and then I said to her: "How's my little girl?"

There was silence and I had a moment where I lost confidence. Shit, did I get this wrong?

"Good," she said, in a baby voice with a little giggle.

Game on. I did all sorts of freaky things with her. She brought out this almost cruel side of me, and it's crazy but it made me fall in love with her. She was so bad. And yet so sweet. It ripped me open.

Every time I left her place I wanted to tear out her heart. I wanted to hurt her. I hated how she was hooking me with the daddy fantasy. Hated this feeling that she was trying to play me or get something from me. And yet, it was I pursuing her. She never said a word about getting together again. I'd just tell her what a sweetheart she was and that I'd be in touch.

The thing is, I have no idea how to deal with these feelings. I see what she wants. I see how she wants to be mine. With the others, I took delight in denying them, in walking away. With Laura, I feel limited. I want to take this feeling of wanting her and wanting to take her to a new place. I want to protect her from me and guys like me. It's new territory. I obviously need help.

So Laura and I got to talking last time I was there after we did the daddy thing and I beat her really good, and I felt manipulated. Here she was telling me that she's never been picked up before in a bar, that it wasn't her style. And yet, here she was letting me fuck her like I was her daddy. I had a lot of mixed feelings. She's a nurse, so I know she's got a good heart, but there's something about her sexually that confuses me. I've never been confused before. It's usually straightforward. They want to be dominated, or to dominate, or to pretend we're in love... but this way she seems to be leading me to do things feels out of control. I don't know who is playing whom.

I was trained to think of women like kids that grab onto your leg when you're leaving. If you don't kick them off, they drag you down. They rob you of your manhood; they take your friends, your freedom, and your access to the world from you. I've seen guys all around me wrecked by women who put their hooks in a little too deep – guys who were powerful brought to their knees. My dad was like that with my mom. If she was unhappy, if she didn't want him, he fell to pieces. He was a wreck half the time. I hated how mom's moods could affect him. Hated how much he was like a servant boy in his own house. I decided no woman would ever command me.

I give women what they most want, so it's not like I don't take care of women. I just don't let them hold onto my leg when I'm leaving. When it's time to go, it's time to go."

Finally, I interjected, "What is it women want, Brian?"

"Someone to take responsibility. When you get a woman to unleash herself in bed, she doesn't want to be burdened with the guilt of having done something really bad. If you're nastier than she is, the one in control, she can retain her innocence. I'm the guy who liberates those secret little places they share with no one."

"It seems that for you this is a kind of intimacy. It's like you get in where no other guy can. You see something other men can't get at. But perhaps it's not enough anymore. Seems you're starting to feel the hole it leaves inside of you."

"To be honest, for the first time I'm feeling like a predator. I keep eating, but I'm not getting full. So how does a guy like me with a huge chip on his shoulder learn how to love a woman the way you describe in those articles you write?"

"I think admitting that you're afraid of being controlled by women is a good beginning."

As I got to know Brian, it became clear that his father's lack of power in relationship to his mother was a primary, underlying issue. He was furious at how emasculated he felt as a boy in relationship to his mother and how his father continued to be "hogtied" by his mother's demands.

Brian had made a vow as a boy never to be a wimp like his father. He saw how his mother dangled the sex carrot to get him to do things for her, and he despised it. He felt that his mother had stolen his father from him by insisting on his twenty-four hour attention, by using her sexuality to control him. Essentially, he decided never to be in love. Love put a man in a weak position. It put his father in a weak position. So instead, he found a way to get close to girls and maintain his control – namely by seducing them and making them want him, but controlling his own interaction.

Every time we met, Brian talked about how Laura had overpowered him in some way – with her emotions or some hidden agenda. "I know what happens next, and I'm not interested," he said. "She gets me to care and then she laughs in my face. She leaves or hooks up with some other player – and I'm left holding the bag."

"So love is a trick? Is that it Brian?"

"You bet it is."

"What if Laura simply enjoys you and wants to spend more time with you? Is that a manipulation?"

"First it's my time, then what? My job, my friends, what else is she going to want?"

Brian's journey in our work together was first to recognize that his mother's manipulations were not ill intended, not intended to hurt Brian – but the only way she knew how to get her needs met. Like most people, she learned to manipulate as a child and carried that behavior into adulthood.

He was able to see his mother for the first time – as a woman. A woman who had needs and fears, doing the very best she could. This was a huge shift.

He saw his father was a man who knew intimacy only through

sex – a man who feared losing the lifeline and closeness that was so meaningful to him so much that he was willing to sacrifice his manhood to retain it. He felt compassion for the first time for his father.

Most importantly, Brian came to see how he was also a manipulator and a trickster – not because he was a bad guy, but because he didn't know how to be powerful in love.

So we began filling Brian's toolbox with tools and practices for how to both let go in love and stay in his power.

Brian had a talk about sex for the first time in his life with Laura. He asked Laura about her daddy fantasy (as I had advised) and what it meant to her, and he was totally surprised by what he learned.

"It's not my fantasy at all," she said. "I thought it was yours. I just want to be with you. I don't need any of that, but I do it because you seem to need it."

"And what about being dominated?" he said. "You must like it."

"I love that you can control my body and how you play with my mind, and admittedly that was the attraction initially, but what I want most from you is your heart. I want to know that you love me. That would turn me on more than anything."

"Can you believe this shit?" he said, in session.

"I see now why I was so attracted to her, why I fell in love, and why none of it made sense. She's a sexual healer. She saw me. She's been waiting for me to get off my game. Amazing. It's why I felt so much confusion with her."

"For all those years I thought I knew women inside and out. The thing I didn't get is that they're not like men. They aren't looking for the ultimate fuck; they're looking for love. Now, I'm ready to give her the fuck of her life, but it's not at all about controlling her mind or her body. It's about loving her enough that she can let go and give me what she's never given any other man. That's 'The Game.'"

The Dark Knight nearly completes our menu of archetypal energies. With a healthy expression of living at your edge, you now have most of what you need to truly open a woman and engage her heart and her passion. What remains is to finally own your sexuality, with integrity, and that is the topic of the next chapter.

Chapter 7

The Lover

It was an early Sunday morning, and my partner, Phil, and I were snuggling in bed. I was sad because a friend of mine had died a month before, and I was riding a fresh wave of grief. Add to that my mother was ill with cancer, and my cat was going blind. I was also dealing with some issues with my own health. It was one of those moments where I wanted to be held but also wanted to be alone. So I was irritable and uncomfortable.

Phil and I had been together about nine months. I pretty much knew how he would respond to me and in this case expected he'd just hold me. But something about that annoyed me. I didn't want to be just embraced; I wanted something more. I wanted something I couldn't put my finger on.

I felt Phil's arms around me but they were suffocating. His breath was hot and for the first time did not feel good on my neck. What was going on with me? Was I moving into my old pattern of withdrawing and isolating myself?

I didn't grow up with affection. Nobody held me or comforted me as a child. So I learned how to be alone and how to self-soothe in moments that were crushing or devastating – which seemed like most of my childhood. I'd also learned how to be held, as a woman, and had broken down many of my walls to love. In that moment it felt like the walls had gone up once again, and I was pulling inside of myself.

Phil suddenly turned me toward him – which I didn't want or like. I felt exposed. I didn't want him to know how sad I was. If he were like most men, he'd hold that against me. "What's going on?" he asked gently.

There was a welcome kindness in his voice. He wasn't angry that there was something wrong, and he wasn't challenged (as I had experienced in prior relationships); he was open to knowing and also seemed to invite it. But could I trust it? Would he make me feel wrong for what I was feeling?

I breathed deeply for a moment, wanting to tap into the essence of what was going on for me and then began by sharing the things that felt the heaviest. There was my mother's illness – we'd never been really close but I loved her deeply, nonetheless. How long did she have? There was my cat's loss of seventy percent of her sight. Would she go blind? Could I have been a better pet owner? All of this, of course, brought up my own fear that I would never be happy and never fulfill my life's dreams – that I would die never having truly lived.

What I loved about Phil is that nothing I said, no matter how dark, heavy, or even negative, overwhelmed him. He was steady and focused. He had an incredible emotional bandwidth.

"What else?" he said. He wanted me to empty myself of all of it.

"Just hold me," I said.

Being heard in the way Phil could hear made things fall away. Where it may have taken an hour to process the very same information with another man, I felt emptied, open, and available.

Phil wrapped himself around me. Our lips found each other. We kissed deeply, like swimming in a warm sea, dissolving into each other. Soon, we were entwining our bodies, and it felt like the right thing to be doing.

Phil never wanted just sex. He wanted me. So we'd never had those awkward moments where I felt I wanted to say "no" and didn't. He only wanted me when I wanted him. He'd look into my eyes and read me. When there wasn't a mutual desire to engage physically, he'd just kiss me and say goodnight, or he'd ask, "Is there something you'd like to talk about?"

There was one night I'll never forget when I was feeling pretty needy and insecure and reached for him. He was lying with his hands behind his neck, looking at the ceiling, and I was pleading for his attention – flirting, giggling, rubbing his belly – letting those caresses slip down over his underwear. I didn't really want sex; I wanted affirmation and reassurance, but I was slipping into an old habit of acting sexual when I needed nurturing.

Phil took my advances and began kissing me deeply. I was not into it. I didn't know what to do because I'd never said "no" before. He'd always been so attuned. Of course he thought I wanted to make love – I was all over him. At one point he touched my nipple, and I flinched. It shocked both of us. He looked at me and I at him, and he stopped. "Sorry," I said right away. "I'm a little sensitive for some reason."

I lied. I couldn't believe that I'd lied. But Phil didn't miss it.

"What do you mean, sensitive?" he asked. He knew what I'd said, but I could see in his eyes he wanted a better answer.

"Let's just do it," I said, not wanting to process or tell him how needy I felt, and it sounded a little impatient. It was definitely a pivotal moment. Up until that point I'd been able to hide my insecure feelings and deal with them on my own.

"Just do it?" He made a face as if the idea made him ill. "Since when do we just do it? Is that what you do with me? Because if that's what you're up to, I don't want any part of it."

"No, that's not it. I'm just saying that we don't have to stop just because I'm not feeling that great."

"Really. Is that how you think I am? That I'd just go through with it, regardless of how you feel?"

"No."

"Don't ever, ever make love to me out of obligation, Karen. I will not tolerate it. Don't ever go through with it. Do you hear me? I really need you to hear me."

I took Phil's words in deeply. I'd never heard him angry before, but this had made him angry. I had to admit I loved him more than ever in that moment. It was the first time a man stopped me from hurting myself sexually.

We had a long talk. Phil explained how he'd had a lot of disconnected sex in his twenties and early thirties and was over it. I hadn't known that. The thought of it was hard to imagine and made me feel a little ill. Of course, I should have known better. You don't get to be the kind of lover he was without walking around the block a few times, or a lot of times. Phil said that he wanted to connect with me more deeply. He wanted to take me somewhere he hadn't gone with any other woman. But he couldn't do that if I didn't want that, too. And if I was clinging to "safety."

"I want you to trust me, Karen."

"I do trust you. What do you mean?"

"I mean, know that I want only the best for you in every way. I want to have your trust and your heart."

It was one of the most beautiful things I'd ever heard.

We were quiet for a minute as I took that in, as I let myself feel into what it might be like to surrender myself to this man, to actually trust him. I felt a sudden and powerful urge to marry him.

"What do you need from me?" he asked finally. "What do you need to feel safe here?"

"I don't know," I said. But, of course, that wasn't true. I was afraid to say what I needed. I needed so much. I needed him to tell me I was beautiful, often. I wanted to hear that he was inspired by me. I needed to know I was really seen – that the real me wouldn't take him by surprise someday soon and make him want to leave. It was one of those moments where my needs felt monumental.

"I need so much right now," I shook my head and fought off tears.

Phil held me. I felt I was home. He wanted me to trust him, and I noticed that when I did, he was there for me. He was inviting me into something real, not some romantic fantasy. I knew that if we had challenges down the road, we could negotiate those challenges intelligently and sensitively. That was clear.

I went inward to my deepest knowing. I sensed the opportunity to learn more about love and to open in a greater way to my pleasure. So I told Phil I wanted to give myself over to our relationship. I told him I wanted to open my heart to him.

"That makes me very happy," he said.

Like all the men I have highlighted in this book, Phil taught me something of significance. It's impossible to tell our whole story, and really unimportant. What is important is how I grew in knowing him and what he embodied that can be offered as a gift to other men, and their women.

Phil showed me – through who and how he was – that a man can own his sexuality. He can learn to recognize his sexuality as a powerful energy and use it for good. He can be a sexual healer for women if he chooses – as Phil was for me. By insisting on sex that was loving, Phil helped me break my pattern of self-abuse with men. He didn't want me to "do" him, or to pay him with sex. He wanted me to share my body and my heart with him. This changed who I was. And it changed my expectations of loving men, and of loving relationships.

Who is The Lover?
Why are women drawn to him?

The Lover is a man in full ownership of his sexuality. As his sexuality is so deeply a part of him, it's not a wedge that gets between him and a woman. It's not a manipulation or a deal. It's an invitation.

The Lover archetype has discovered the sacred nature of his sexuality. He doesn't need to bargain or deal to get his sexual needs met. He doesn't need to prove his manliness through sex. He finds being a man and his sexuality are gifts he can give a woman.

Owning your sexuality is a powerful choice. Most men will never give this a thought. Most men will chase sex and women all of their lives, as if they don't already have sexual resources right at their feet.

Owning your sexuality is not about putting your sexuality under lock and key or about diminishing sexual returns, on the contrary. My desire is to show you how freeing and empowering ownership is, and how men who own their sex enjoy a life of great sexual abundance.

A client of mine once said, "It's like the difference between owning and renting your home. When you rent, you're always thinking, Hey, this is temporary, so you don't really care about the place. When you buy, suddenly there's a respect and an appreciation. You want to make something of it."

Yes, ownership is a whole different level of engagement, and it's exactly the direction you want to take to get a woman's complete and undivided attention.

Awakening the Lover

Ownership shows up in strange places. It is a crisp, sunny morning in Marin County, and as usual the dog park is teeming with people and their "best friends." I don't have a dog, but I love dogs and people watching, so I drop into this park now and again. On this particular day I notice a man being dragged around by his thirty-pound, red-haired dog. The man is in his forties – fit, and well-dressed, intelligent looking – someone I imagine most women would find physically attractive.

All fifty of the other dogs at the park are running around off leash, playing up a storm. His dog is the only one on a leash. He seems perturbed as he chases his dog's every whim. This doesn't go unnoticed by the crowd, a group who takes dog parenting pretty seriously.

"Yeah, problem with that dog is his owner gets too uptight."

"He should play with that dog more."

When the red-haired dog neared other dogs, it was clear why he was on a leash. "Johnnie" mounted every female, frantically. "Stop Johnnie! Johnnie NO!" his owner yelled. But the dog continued humping like there was no tomorrow. To make matters worse, when the dog was finished mounting dogs, he ran over to the women in our group and pounced on them, leaving dirt marks on their clothes. The man apologized but then spewed out a litany of excuses.

"So sorry, I took him to training, but nothing seems to work. He's just nervous around other dogs, I think. He's not usually like this. Really he's not. I've been out of town this week so I think he's just running off some energy." He let out a deep breath as if he'd been holding it for a long while.

We were all pretty much silent, smiling gently. Silently thinking that the dog was neurotic like his "dad." He bid us farewell, and we watched in horror as the dog literally pulled him out of the park.

My attention then went to a confident man just across the way, in blue jeans, white T-shirt, and red baseball cap. He was a vision of calm, hands resting deep in his pockets. His dog was off leash (a pretty, medium-sized blonde dog) and was playing cheerfully among the other dogs. He was talking with a group of attractive, sexy-mom types, glancing only occasionally toward his dog to check her whereabouts. It was clear he had no worries about what his dog might do as she cruised the park.

At one point he called his dog ("Honey") and gave a little slap to his thigh. Honey perked up, looked at her man, and came running directly to his side. She sat by his leg, wagging her tail; he gave her a treat and a pat on the head. The ladies gasped with delight at Honey's obedience. He then directed Honey to return to playing by throwing his arm out and pointed in the direction of the other dogs. She took off running like a little ball of joy.

Every guy wants to be this guy, the guy who can control his dog in the right way. It demonstrates a healthy connection and relationship with his dog. It demonstrates confidence and discipline. In the same way, owning your sex is like having that well-behaved dog. Not owning it is like being pulled around on a leash by your impulses.

Ever let your dog off leash and he misbehaved? Did you take responsibility or serve up a litany of excuses? Or worse, did you pretend he wasn't your dog? Likewise, how often have you disowned your sexuality and acted as if you weren't the one choosing the experience you were having – as if you weren't in charge?

Owning your sexuality is about taking responsibility for your sex life, every ounce of it. If you're not happy with how much sex you're getting, the quality of the sex you're experiencing, or whom you're having sex with, you need to own that. These are all factors within your choice and control. Without acknowledging and embracing this, you won't have your total power at your disposal.

Think about this: How do you want to be viewed by women? As that guy pulled along by his impulses? Or like a man who commands the best from his relationship with his sexuality and women?

We're going to take a look at three key opportunities to help guide you to take ownership of your sexuality and literally transform how women view you. The first is to recognize that you have a choice around sexuality. You are not a victim of your sexual desires and drives. The second is to recognize that you can have a higher purpose for your sexuality than the mere scratching of a genital itch. And the third opportunity comes when you realize that you can give the best of your erotic and sexual energy as a gift.

The Lover archetype is a rare, highly desirable breed of man. Women are magnetized by his sexual integrity. You can know that when your woman feels the qualities of The Lover playing through you, she's going to take positive notice and make herself more sexually and romantically available to you.

The First Opportunity:
Recognize Your Sexual Choice

I meet a lot of men who are sexually frustrated. Many of them exist in a state of sexual exile with no idea how to get home. One day their partner says "no," and she never stops saying no. They don't know what went wrong, and they have no idea how to turn it around. They're angry and feel tricked. How does a man get here? How does he become so sexually powerless in relationship with his woman that he doesn't know what to say to her, much less how to turn around her "no?" How does a man find himself groveling for sexual intimacy, having lost all confidence and dignity?

One of the biggest issues most men have with women is: how to respond to a woman's "no." As simple as this might seem, it's actually quite complex. Your sexual relationship with a woman is a dance. How you move, and how you choose to lead when she resists, has everything to do with how flexible and giving she's going to be with you sexually.

Women who once seemed to really enjoy sex and actually have a hunger for sexual intimacy may have many reasons for suddenly saying no to sex. Some of those reasons may honestly have nothing to do with you. Men find release from stress in sex where most women can't enjoy sex when they are stressed. The hormonal changes of pregnancy, menstrual cycles, and menopause affect a woman's sexual desire. And, some women, in order to get a relationship commitment, become the kind of sexual creature they think men want, even though they know they cannot sustain it. Men, of course, do the same thing when they become the kind of romantic and sensitive partner they think a woman wants when they know they cannot maintain it. As a man you will probably want sex more than she does, and this creates a kind of tension. So first, it is important to understand that, in part, why a woman begins saying no to sex has nothing to do with you. Your time and energy is much better spent on the factors that are within your control.

When you're feeling sorry for yourself, betrayed, or tricked by your woman's lack of interest, or her waning interest, these feelings contribute heavily to furthering her lack of desire for you. You may not realize it, but you're feeling this way because you don't feel you have a choice. She gets her way, and you feel forced to accept that.

When you decide that a woman is the sexual boss and you follow her mandates, she acts like your boss. You don't get to decide when you have sex, if you have sex, or how you have sex. You go along with her program and get whatever sex you can. When a woman knows that this what you'll settle for, you lose power in her eyes! You might think you're doing what a loving man should do by being compliant and non-demanding, but these passive actions have a negative effect on how she views you and feels about you.

You know, for example, if a woman is confident or not. If she doesn't respect herself, and she's not a challenge for you, what happens? You lose interest. You might keep her on a string and pull that string when you want her, but she's not going to excite you. Women are like this, too, in how they respond to men. When you don't demonstrate confidence and sexual leadership, and you let a woman lead, a woman's sexual attraction for you dies. So while you're trying to be Mr. Nice Guy and pretend you're not chasing her tail, she's fantasizing about a guy who won't take her crap and crumble at "no."

What do you do if you're caught in this trap? You need to start exercising personal choice. Recognizing your choice does not mean indulging in a variety of women. That might be an option, but the opportunity here is to learn how to exercise choice within the parameters of satisfying your woman's needs and your own.

But She Doesn't Want Me!

You can't force a woman to have sex with you – obviously – at least not morally or legally. Your having a choice has nothing to do with disregarding hers. Your choice is characterized by how you choose to think and feel – and also how you choose to respond to her choices. This is precisely what distinguishes a sexually powerful man from a not-so-sexually powerful man. When was the last time you saw a hero cry over a woman's "no," or beg a woman for sex? Your response to her choices has everything to do with how she perceives you sexually and how she decides to treat you.

You have control only over you – how you think, feel, and act. But make no mistake: this power is monumental. If you believe, even a little, that you're at the mercy of a woman's sexual choice, you can't help but appear less manly to her. A woman wants to know that you're not at the mercy of her needs and choices but a master of your own. Your opportunity is to watch her responses and respond in a way that makes you look and feel powerful and desirable in her eyes.

I often get a lot of eye rolling and "yeah, buts" from men at this point in our work together. They simply can't imagine how making choices will get them more sex or awaken their woman's desire. And frankly, it's because they know so little about women. Remember: a woman feels best in the company of a confident, powerful man. It makes her feel feminine, open, and relaxed. When you fall apart at "no" and choose to feel rejected, it tells her that you're easy to break and not very powerful. It also tells her that you have way too much invested in sex.

Once she knows you're fragile in this regard, you seem less in command. She now feels she has to take care of you – to make you feel okay about yourself. It's a dynamic of diminishing returns, and ultimately it kills the sexual attraction. No man likes "no," but how you deal with it is critical to your sexual relationship with a woman.

You always have choices, and you should know what they are. If your woman doesn't want you when you want her, you can choose to be upset. You can also choose to be a relaxed, loving partner. Most importantly, you can choose not to take it personally. This gives you perspective. It also tells her that you're strong and not easily broken.

You have many choices. You can take care of your own pleasure and become more sensitive to avoid pushing your sexual needs in the wrong moments. You can choose to channel your sexual energy into other pursuits, into achieving goals. Sulking, withdrawing, acting out, and getting angry are choices, too. They're just not going to get you more of what you want. What's important is that you know you're not a victim of your woman's choices. By choosing how you feel and respond, you are in your power.

Now, let's make a distinction here: There are two types of sexual interruptions in your sex life. One is a temporary interruption when someone in the family dies, financial disaster hits, or one of you is ill or under significant stress. It could be depression, weight gain, or waning hormones. It could simply be the end of the romantic honeymoon phase of the relationship, during which you both channeled a lot of energy into being what you each thought the other wanted.

As beautiful and as bonding as this period is, it is also almost always unsustainable. These pauses in your sex life will happen throughout your time together. There will always be peaks and valleys, and if you want to inspire the best from your woman, you'll work with accepting the low periods as part of the deal. A woman will be more emotionally affected by these dramas, and being sensitive to this is a powerful choice. You can fight these fluctuations and protest them as wrong, but that won't change the fact that they'll keep surfacing – as they do for all women and for all couples.

There is also a more permanent interruption in your sexual relationship that bears attention. And that's when you're not having sex and you're not talking about it, and you've stopped connecting. If you haven't had sex in more than a month (without an expressed reason), or worse, more than three months, you definitely have intimacy roadblocks. If neither of you knows how to get unstuck, I suggest you get counseling to uncover what's between you. There is no shame in having someone help you reconnect in a meaningful way. We all get stuck. Of course, if after counseling your partner decides she doesn't want you sexually or she plain doesn't want sex, you have choices. It's important to keep seeing and acting on your choices. Avoiding the situation and being passive with a woman – about sex or anything else – is always a relationship killer. The more you act on choices, the more you preserve your masculinity and your power in her eyes.

I had a partner, Jeff, who would mope around the house and silently punish me when I didn't give him sex. All the niceties he would typically demonstrate – like telling me how beautiful I was, making me tea, running errands for me – would all go out the window. He'd just sit, ignore me, and even watch me struggle with things until he ultimately got his way. Once he got his way and his tension was released, he'd become Mr. Chivalry. While I loved how attentive he was after sex and knew exactly how to get my way with him, the set-up made me lose my attraction for him. I couldn't respect a man whose sexual needs were so shallow and whose love was so conditional.

Practice:
Choosing to be okay with what is
actually happening.

As a practice, this may feel like a bit of a stretch. When it comes to sex, most men have a "bursting dam" mentality. They feel the urge for sexual release as a kind of pressure that builds and builds. If they can't find sexual release, that dam gets higher and the water backs up and the pressure builds as anger, irritation, annoyance, or frustration. With the build-up of that pressure, almost any action becomes justifiable and even reasonable. That includes obsessive masturbation to Internet porn, engaging prostitutes, or having affairs. Granted, most men probably don't take it to those extremes, but many men build up a lot of frustration and resentment and develop manipulative behaviors around sex.

Who do you want to be? Are you the guy in the dog park with the out-of-control dog or the guy whose dog seems to be under his gentle but firm control? To be the second guy, you have to understand that having sex with a particular woman at a particular time is never going to be solely your call. What is always your call is how you deal with that fact. That is where you have a choice. You can continue to see yourself as a victim or you can reclaim your power.

1. Don't confuse the need you have to release tension with the desire to make love to your partner. It's the difference between eating whatever you find cold in the refrigerator because you are "starving" and cooking a gourmet meal for someone you love.

2. If you truly believe you need the release of an orgasm, then masturbate and be done with it. But do it without anger or resentment. It is your itch you are scratching. You might wish that she would scratch your itch, and sometime she might be willing to give you that gift or favor. But it is not the basis for an intimate relationship.

3. If you are truly called to spend intimate time with your partner, then do that without expectation of anything else happening.

4. At a higher level, men can learn – through meditation and breath work and the internal direction of energy – to circulate the energy of an orgasm through their body without an orgasm. It's beyond the scope of this book to get into those specific techniques,

but the point is that you do have choices with what you do with your sexual energy.

The Second Opportunity
Have a Sexual Purpose

There are many ways to have sex. You can have sex that is just about pleasure. You can have sex that is about pain. You can have sex that is about expressing love. The more you know about why you're doing it and toward what end, the more you are the director and creator of your experience.

Very few men have a known sexual purpose. Meaning that very few men give the kind of soulful attention to sex they give to their career choices or their finances. You might think about sex itself, a lot. But if a woman asked you for your highest reason for making love or having sex, what would you say?

Maybe you'd think, "I don't know. It feels good."

Of course it does. And while there's definitely value in pleasure, if you want to keep a woman happy sexually, you've got to have a bigger scope. When you're looking down a narrow lens, you tend to see just the target. You don't have your eye on the abundant field that is all around you. Men look to become proficient in bed and then keep driving their experiences to the same point. A feminine being craves more than this. Her nature is to reach for the edges of where there is no edge. So what you see in your mind's eye is what you ultimately give her in bed. If what you see is expansive and soulful, it changes how you feel, how you touch, and where you take her.

Usually men look to enhance lovemaking externally. You make love on the kitchen counter or buy toys and pretty lingerie. This can definitely heat things up. But if you don't expand on the inside, too, you find yourself coming up against her sluggishness over and over again. You can change the whole feel of your lovemaking and make it a lot deeper by expanding the picture you hold about it in your mind's eye and following that trajectory in bed. What really undermines pleasure for a woman is the feeling that your sexual experiences are a dead end.

Where does a woman expect sex to go? She hopes it will go to the stars. In other words, that the love you make continues to expand and surprise her. Ideally, the possibility with you feels infinite. Will there be mundane moments? Yes, of course. And without a sexual purpose, there will be plenty. Pleasure alone is just not enough to sustain a woman's interest. It needs to be fed by a purpose that gives you something to reach for and to take her toward.

Marcello was in big trouble in his marriage when he came to see me. He identified himself as a sex addict right off. "I don't know if there's anything we can do about this, but I'm here," he said.

His definition of "sex addict" was being out of control. I agreed that being out of control wasn't powerful sexually but asked that for the sake of our sessions he let go of the label "sex addict."

Marcello didn't like that. He'd been given that label by a psychiatrist, a man he deeply respected but with whom he got no positive results. They had worked together for two years, and Marcello was no better off.

"You think I can just forget I'm an addict? I don't know if this is going to work."

"How is identifying with being an addict working for you?"

He was quiet.

Marcello stuck around. And he noticed that when he didn't use the label to block progress, thwart responsibility, or excuse his lack of consciousness, he felt different. He didn't feel like a pervert or a fiend; he felt like a man who needed to make some deep inner changes.

When I asked Marcello what his purpose was for having sex, he was confused. "What do you mean?"

"What is your most important reason?"

"Well, I don't know. It seems to do me instead of me doing it. When I think of the porn issue and the obsession with escorts, the most important reason seems to be avoidance."

He paused for a while.

"I'm avoiding intimacy, it seems."

"Powerful revelation," I told him and asked, "What do you want your most important reason to be?"

"I want to learn how to be close to a woman," he said. "I want to feel what it's like to relax completely and enjoy myself in bed. I've never felt that."

At the time, Marcello was dating a woman he was afraid to let in.

Instead of initiating any kind of deeper engagement, he found ways to keep her at a safe distance. He decided he'd talk to her and ask her to be exclusive with him. It was what he wanted, but he was also afraid of it. Chasing sex and feeling frenzied were distracting him from his fears of intimacy. Feeling out of control also felt familiar and somewhat safe.

A month later, Marcello told me: "The fear is definitely still there, but when I just dive into it and commit to being there, the payoff is incredible. I keep remembering my purpose, and it seems to ground me. She told me I'm the best lover she's ever had. When I asked her why, she said sex didn't seem that important to me in the way it is to other men. Amazing, right? She said, 'I know you love it, but you love it differently.' And the funny thing is that it's true; since I dropped the label and started being aware and focusing on what I most want, I'm a different man altogether."

Where Do I Get a Purpose?

Even men who are not spiritual or religious, when guided, realize they do have a higher reason for sex. Once they get past the obvious – that they like sex and need it to feel good – they realize they want something more from sex that exists at a deeper level. Just like women, men want a spiritual experience in bed. It's not that they expect to see God at the point of orgasm or to transcend the body, but they want what they describe as deep connection or union, to become one with a woman. While women often dissolve into men with little effort, men need to focus and practice to transcend the mundane.

I think it's safe to say that most men don't have spiritual experiences because they don't focus on having them. If you look at Tantric practitioners who regularly have mind-blowing sexual experiences, it's not because they're physically extraordinary, but because that's where they put their attention. They want spiritual experiences. They want to get beyond orgasm, so they cultivate practices that elevate their experience.

Your purpose doesn't have to be spiritual (for you) in the least. I've known men who said their higher purpose was to merge with a woman. While for one man this might not be spiritual, for another it is. The most important thing is that you have this place you can look toward that gives you a sense of leaning into something bigger than yourself and beyond one moment of pleasure. This will give you power and confidence in the bedroom and give your woman the sense that you are taking her somewhere of meaning.

Men having relationship problems are often embroiled in a bad habit I call "Bargaining for Sex." Bargaining is essentially making deals for sex. It's so deeply ingrained that most men do it without even knowing it. Some men do it by buying women things. Others by doing favors, little things they hate. Others by lying (or going along with what a woman wants) in order to get what they want. In any case, there's this ongoing, never-ending boogie, where you're try to earn your way into her pants.

When you have a higher purpose, you don't operate this way. You don't need to. You become a more confident sexual being – that is, if you're acting on that purpose and living as if it's true. But when you're working for sex, you're not very sexually appealing to any woman.

If you'll remember in Chapter 4, we looked at the qualities of The Warrior. He fights for what he cares about, and women line up to be in his company. The Lover is a warrior of sorts, too. He cuts away what doesn't empower him (bargaining, begging, not choosing) and what isn't in alignment with his higher meaning. This is why women trust him and feel Goddess-like in his presence. His more elevated sexual energy presents a promise – that a woman will feel deeply seen, deeply known, and taken somewhere in body, heart, and mind she's never been.

The Power of No

When you decide to step it up sexually, you'll find your challenge is learning to say "no" to what doesn't align. If you're like most men, you've been conditioned to believe that any sex is good sex. Saying "no" to sex can feel like turning down food when you're starving. But for those men who want to up-level their sexual offering, "no" is essential, – especially if you've been in the habit of taking half-hearted handouts, bargaining, and groveling.

It's not that you need to reject women. You need to honor yourself. Sometimes, in that process of self-honoring, a woman gets hurt – it can't be helped. The "no" means you're aligning with your truth and you're no longer in a scarcity mindset. When you're choosing from an abundance viewpoint, there will be moments, and women, that simply don't fit. Trust that when you honor yourself as a sexual man, what a woman will offer you will be very different. Instead of the scraps of her energy at the end of the day, you'll elicit the nectar of her desire. You can also know that as long as you continue to choose to settle, she'll treat you as a man who will settle.

There was one man in my life who turned me down for sex. The fact that I'm telling you this makes it clear that I never forgot Rick and what I learned from him. I'm not telling you about Rick because I felt rejected. In fact, I didn't feel any ego around his "no." The way he handled it, and the reasons he expressed, gave me no reason to feel bad.

We'd been seeing each other for just a week or so, and I was feeling a strong desire to be sexual with him. We talked a lot about our work and realized we were both on the same path – the path of our own sexual healing and helping others. It was meaningful to meet a man of a similar heart. It also became clear, based on Rick's training, that he was a master of his body. Unlike my current partner at the time, giving me what I needed in bed wasn't going to be a problem. The prospect of that drove me to distraction, and I found myself trying to seduce Rick a little too soon.

Looking back, it was clearly not the right moment. We hadn't even been affectionate or kissed, and suddenly I was pushing a sexual agenda. We were on my couch and I leaned in, looked in his eyes and kissed him. He went with it for a bit, but as I began caressing him on the chest, I felt his energy stop. He wasn't participating. I pulled back and looked at Rick's face. He looked concerned.

"What's wrong?" I asked.

"Well," he said, "you're in a relationship for one. And, I don't just do this. I have to have some kind of emotional involvement."

I'd never had a man say no, and it had an unexpected effect on me.

"My relationship is over for all intents and purposes," I started to explain. "He's moving away. I do feel something for you. I feel a deep connection to you." But even as I said it, I felt insincere.

For a moment, he seemed to buy it. I saw a glimmer of hope in his face. But then on second thought, he said, "If we're right for each other, if this was meant to be, we can slow it down."

I felt very masculine – charged by his "no." I wanted to push. It was true that I felt a certain kind of closeness to Rick, but it wasn't the kind he was looking for. His "no" made me want to win.

I started rubbing his thigh. He allowed it, but there was no weakness. No giving in, like other men might. He held himself steady and watched. I poured on the seductive energy – pressing myself against him, biting his neck, putting his fingers in my mouth – but he remained unmoved.

I pulled back and took a deep breath.

"Wow, this is a first," I told him, exhilarated by what had come out of me.

"Doesn't surprise me," he said.

It took me a while to calm down and let go. Ultimately, I was grateful that he turned me down. But for a moment there, I was hellbent on having my way.

Yes, my relationship was ending, but it hadn't fully ended. Being with Rick would have convoluted things. Even more importantly, I learned something from Rick that day I'd never forget. I learned that a "no," given out of self-love, isn't a rejection. And that a "no" doesn't close the door; it simply turns up the fire. As a woman, I saw how I never needed to compromise myself for a man by going along with his agenda. I could always exercise my truth to a good end, to a positive effect.

I also saw a man honor his heart and his body for the first time in my life, and it changed what I saw as possible for men.

I realized that a kingly man, a man who loves and honors himself, inspires the love and respect of a woman. She not only wants to present him with her best, but giving to him is a pleasure unto itself.

A man who begs or takes what he can get without thought for his honor, whose hunger is insatiable, will never inspire a woman's most queenly seduction.

Practice:
A Shared Sexual Purpose

Sexual energy is a powerful force. You can direct it toward your own spiritual or material purpose. It is, again, beyond the scope of this book to instruct you on specific sexual techniques, but this might give you a taste of what I mean by having a sexual purpose.

1. Decide on something you both are waiting for, something you both deeply desire. This can be something material, emotional, or spiritual.

2. Put this into words and talk about how you would feel or act if that desire were suddenly fulfilled. How would other people recognize that you had realized this dream or desire?

3. Once you feel the thrill of your desire made manifest, begin to make love.

4. Try to hold that desire and that feeling as you make love. Stretch out, as long as possible, the time that you make love. The longer you build and circulate that energy without releasing it, the more powerful it is.

5. When you are both ready, agree to release that energy as an orgasm while remembering and feeling the force of that gratified desire.

6. After orgasm, reconnect with the feeling of the gratified desire and how it changed you in the moment.

7. Now, and this is the really important part, continue to act, living your life each day, as if that desire had been gratified. Act in the way you would if you had realized that desire, whether it has manifested or not.

The Third Opportunity:
Give Sex as a Gift

Until this point in your life, maybe you thought sex was a gift a woman bestowed upon you. Getting sex was a thing to celebrate like your birthday or winning the lottery. Why and how, you didn't know and maybe you didn't care. You felt lucky when it happened not so lucky when it didn't.

While feeling celebratory about sex is a good thing, if you're tired of intimacy being a crap shoot, you need to recognize and honor the fact that you also have a sexual gift to give.

Sex given in the spirit of love is a gift for a woman. More than just sex, it can be a deep healing, a profound opening. Yet, if you don't realize this potential within you, how can you give it?

The secret here is that in order to give your sexual energy as a gift, you must understand the complementary feminine and masculine roles. The first thing to understand is that the energy of a sexual encounter is the domain of the feminine. That is her responsibility. When men find themselves trying to "spice up" their sexual relationships with role-playing, new toys, new positions, etc., they are taking on the feminine responsibility. This is usually a good sign that their feminine partners have abrogated responsibility for this. The masculine wants to sample all the flavors of the feminine; and if he doesn't get them from his partner, he'll seek them out in other partners (affairs), in surrogates (strip clubs), and in fantasy (pornography).

He'll also fantasize about his partner while making love to her and end up disconnecting from her in the process. The feminine challenge in a sexual relationship is to learn to express the full spectrum of erotic energy through her body and give those flavors as her gift to her partner. If she chooses not to do that, she should not be surprised if her partner seeks feminine energy elsewhere (even if he does not actually break the covenant of the relationship).

So what is the masculine challenge? The masculine is responsible for the depth of the sexual encounter. That means a man is responsible for creating the kind of container into which a woman can freely dissolve all her boundaries in sexual intimacy and melt into delirious union.

Every woman you have ever known can give herself an orgasm or bring herself physical pleasure. Ultimately, she does not need you to do that. What she needs, what she most deeply desires, is for you to take her someplace she cannot take herself. Does that feel like a tall order? You bet it is. But that is why I've built up to this point with every archetype I've shared so far.

Embodying All The Archetypes

To really take a woman to a depth in your sexual intimacy, you need to see her as clearly as she sees herself (the Artist). You need to be able to celebrate her unique beauty and make her feel profoundly chosen (the Poet). You need to be willing to offer clear and loving direction (the Director), because she will not always want to be taken to that depth. She will want to wallow in her constriction or waste her energy in a flood with no direction. You need to convince her that you have the strength and the desire to fight for her and for what you believe in (the Warrior) and that you have the kind of solid and grounded integrity that will ensure that the *container you create – for her complete and delirious surrender to love – will be safe (the Sage). When you add to these qualities the ability to risk and to live at your own edge, you give her the confidence to allow you to take her to her edge (the Dark Knight).

When I suggest that you begin to see your sexuality as a gift, I'm referring to your ability to take a woman to a deep and transcendent place. Does that mean every sexual encounter is going to last four hours and leave you both drained and exhausted and deeply, intimately connected, with all your barriers and shells dissolved in the glow of love? Well, no, but if you never have that kind of sex – that kind of depth – don't be surprised if your woman seeks that kind of depth elsewhere or anesthetizes her sense of lack with shopping or chocolate or dancing or tennis lessons with the club pro who at least takes her someplace she cannot get to on her own.

How Do You Achieve Depth?

You don't take a woman deep simply because you fall into the water. Like a diver, you learn how to navigate depth. Being able to navigate depth combines a variety of skills, as discussed in chapters 1 through 6. Depth happens when you bring the well-honed skills of seeing (The Artist) and communication (The Poet) and direction (The Director). It also requires passion (The Warrior), integrity (The Sage), and risk-taking (the Dark Knight). If you bring direction but can't embody the Artist, the Poet or the Sage, a woman will feel only the demand of your desires rather than the love.

A film director is a great example of a man who inspires and cultivates depth. As a visionary, he holds the whole picture in his mind. Because he's the director, he can't simply push what he wants to happen. He has to pull the scenes out of his actors. To open to him, his actors have to feel heard and know they are seen and celebrated. He doesn't inspire their best by being insensitive and single-minded.

The actors, on the other hand, immerse themselves deeply in the acting process itself and forget the big picture. Their job is to experience total immersion in the feelings and nuances of their roles. It's the director's job to guide and give shape to their passions – and also maintain the integrity of the vision, the finished film. The director, if he's good, creates depth by listening, seeing, and responding creatively.

Lovemaking is much the same way in the masculine role. A woman is an emotional, sensual being – and like an actress acting, her pleasure is found deep in the immersion. She doesn't want to have to direct herself or tell the director how to direct her. She wants to dive into her experience and let go of where it's all headed. That's why if her masculine partner takes responsibility for the depth, she can relax and access her passion. Yes, she can help pull you under and match your depth, but you need to direct the scene and the movie.

Think of how challenging it is to stop thinking. Think of how challenging it can be to get still. A woman can't both lead the scene and also let go. Therefore, depth is your work. Like that film director, it's about noticing what's going on in the scene, taking a reading, and acting boldly on what is perceived.

My client, Margo, was exhausted and bored with her relationship and her husband, Steve. When they came to see me, she could barely muster the energy to describe their sex life and shook her head as if it was useless. "I don't know. I just can't imagine how we're going to work this out."

Margo was talked out. She and Steve had tried everything on their own to negotiate their sexual issues, and nothing ever worked or changed. It was Steve's idea to come and see me, so she was also feeling some resistance.

As I usually do, I saw each of them on their own early on. My first solo session was with Steve who clearly was not an aware man. He was dull in his senses – not sensually alive, nor conscious of his thoughts and feelings. He seemed heavy in all respects, slow to respond and to move.

Without being prompted, Steve began talking about Margo's "issues," as if the session were going to be about her.

"She even needed to know how long our session would last. She's got to control everything," he said, as if he were talking about a child.

When a man says a woman is controlling, it's because he feels controlled. He doesn't feel masculine or powerful in her presence. Her need to control may also have a lot to do with his unwillingness to play the masculine role and be directional. I could see that Steve was not a man who was comfortable taking the reins.

"Let's jump right in and talk about what's going on in the bedroom. That's really the bigger issue at hand," I said.

"It's simple. She hates everything I do. And I'm not thirty years old anymore."

"What does that mean, not thirty years old anymore?"

"I can't last like she wants me to."

"How do you feel about that?"

"I'm fine with it. I can't help it that sometimes I'm more sensitive than others."

"Well, you can. But let's address that a bit later."

"You say she hates everything you do? Tell me about that."

"About a month ago, I was doing the same thing I've done for twenty years that works for her, and she pushed my hand away. I said, 'What?' She said it didn't feel good. She didn't say what she did want, so I just stopped altogether. I walked away.

Then we tried it again. I was rubbing her nipples, and she pushed my hand away. I looked at her and she said, 'It hurts.'"

He said, "Come on, this is what we've been doing forever and she loved it before. So what's going on? Suddenly I'm not good enough for her? Some weeks ago I tried to get her into a new position. We've been in the missionary position for years. She wasn't having it. She got irritated and pulled the sheet over her head. Is there something wrong with wanting a little variety sometimes?"

"What kind of verbal feedback are you getting from Margo about your sex life?" I asked.

"Verbal feedback? I don't know. We don't talk about sex, but she makes it known how she feels about it."

Shortly thereafter I spoke with Margo, who held nothing back. "He's the most boring lover I've ever had. He does the exact same thing every time we have sex. It makes me cringe. A few weeks ago he tried to get me to do it doggie style. Are you kidding me? After all these years of one, two, three and it's over, he wants me to give him something new? In the early days I tried to tell him what I needed, but nothing ever happened."

"Did you try to tell him, or you told him?"

No, I told him. I told him I needed it to last longer; I told him I wanted him to go slower and to be gentler. I even bought a book on Tantra for us to explore, but he ignored it. After it sat on the nightstand for months, I gave it away."

"What is Steve saying to you about your sex life?"

"Saying? Nothing. He's more of a grunter. He seems to want it, but he shows no passion. It's like he goes for it and expects to be turned down. He's disappointed before we even begin and, frankly, it makes me feel ill."

Steve and Margo had a lot to work out. But we began by helping to repair the loss of excitement with newness and creativity. I guided Steve to stop trying to get it right. He was taken aback that I was giving him permission to stop performing.

"Steve, it's not contributing to closeness, and it's locking you out of your creative intelligence as a lover. The more you try to 'perform' to please or to get it right, the less you feel good about yourself, and the less Margo can feel you as present with her."

"Okay, but what do you suggest I do? She complains if I can't make her have an orgasm or if I come too soon."

"She complains," I explained, "because there's a void of intimacy. And your ability to last will be enhanced by relaxing and dropping performing. It's like when you're on stage: you're tense, you're afraid of messing up the performance. When you let that go and show up simply to be intimate with Margo, you'll be surprised at how responsive she will be."

"But how do I do that?"

"I want you to lie down with her and look at her to start. See what you see. Study her face. Follow her breath. Notice how she smells. It's best not to talk if you can avoid it. You want to learn to reactivate your senses. Look deeply into her eyes and find her underneath all of the noise of thinking. Find her in the silence."

"Are you kidding me? She'll never go for that."

"Let me ask you this: How well are things going now?"

"Okay, I'll try it. But I think she's going to hate it."

"If you're comfortable with it, or at least sincere, she will come around."

That night, Steve invited Margo to "rest," a code word they use for getting intimate. Much to his surprise, she said, "Yes." He lay down on the bed and invited her to join him. At first there was some awkwardness with moving the cat and the fact that it was not routine, but they eased into it.

"Typically," Steve explained during our next session, "we would have each taken a shower and been in our bathrobes," so telling her to just lie down with me made her a little uneasy. I let go of thinking I needed to do something, and it was very different. I looked into her eyes and she started giggling. And she giggled on and off for a long time. What's interesting is that I saw the Margo I used to date twenty years ago, right there. I just stayed steady and observed.

"Then I got this impulse to tell her she was gorgeous. Normally, I would have ignored it. This time I said it: 'You're a gorgeous woman, honey.' She was startled. She looked behind her to be funny. 'Moi?' 'Yes, you,'" I said.

"Much to my surprise, she kissed me and she gave me her tongue. It has been ages since she did that. I was a bit shocked. Next I felt the urge to put my hands on her face, one on each cheek, so I did. She seemed scared at first, but then she melted like a girl and her eyes got soft.

"Then I was thinking, 'What now?' I started to panic but then remembered what you said: follow what was there and what I felt. So I chose to hold her tight in my arms. It's what I wanted. And she cried. We broke through something. She hasn't cried like that in years. I'm just thrilled. She's been hugging me and kissing me ever since."

Steve interrupted a pattern of disconnecting by opening himself to his creative impulses and trusting those impulses. They were simple: tell her she was gorgeous. Cradle her face. Wrap his arms around her. Was it what Margo wanted? Maybe it's not what she thought she wanted. It was certainly unexpected. What's important is that Steve listened, and he trusted his read.

What if he had put his arms around her and she had repelled him? Well, that's information. Then he could have asked: What would feel good? Trusting creative impulses doesn't mean you have to shut yourself off from verbal feedback. On the contrary: use feedback and ask for it, just don't use it as a crutch for not sensing and acting.

Margo and Steve had a lot of other issues to clear up, but their

positive start gave each of them great hope that led to our being able
to make many more powerful inroads over the next four months.

Practice:

The Art of Being Attuned

I'm often astonished at how little my male clients notice in the realm
of lovemaking. I'll ask, "What was she doing with her body?" And
I get blank looks. They have no pictures or physical memories. If a
woman has her bottom in the air when you're stimulating her with
your finger, there's a reason. If she reaches her hands over her head
and grips the headboard when you're inside her, you can bet there's a
reason. She wants something from you. Your opportunity is to learn
how to read these signals and respond intelligently.

If you're simply diving into your own sensations and not directing the scene, you won't notice when she's doing something to indicate a lead she wants from you. To take her deep (as a director might
take an actress) you need to see what's emerging. Where is she? What
next move would elicit even more? And where can you take her that
she's not even thinking about?

You're not always going to know exactly what to do, so forget
about that. But you will get a sense, an impulse. Your job is to trust
what you sense and to act. The more you do, the more you discover.
It's similar to how you've learned to trust and act on the signals from
your own body like when the hairs go up on the back of your neck.

If instead of looking at a woman's face as you make love, you
think: What should I do now? Or if instead of checking out what
her body does in response to yours, you think: What does she like?
You're running blind. Thinking about what she likes will only make
you anxious about what you're doing.

In a bit of a deviation from previous chapters, I'm going to embed
the practices of being attuned in this section. There are three skills
you want to develop in order to take a woman to depth: Listening,
Seeing, and Responding (creatively).

Listening:
It's More than Your Ears

Most men are good at listening for a woman's sounds. You listen for
moans of pleasure, signals that what you're doing is working. The

problem with this is that some women make noises because they think they should, or because they know you need to hear them to feel good. Women are pleasers. Some women don't make noise because they think it makes them seem easy or bad in some way. You can't rely on moans to know if what you're doing works. You need to engage a much deeper kind of listening.

When your own engine is revving, it's hard to "hear." Hearing is about attuning, like a tuning fork to a woman's body. You don't just listen with your ears. Your whole body becomes a listening device.

- Don't just listen for sounds of affirmation and approval anymore; listen to subtle body temperature changes, changes in texture, changes in posture, changes in breath. And under all that, listen for your woman's "core rhythm." She has one, and if you don't tap into it, you'll always be either moving a little too slow or a little too fast for her body. It's like dancing with someone who isn't dancing to the music. Think about your own body. You also have a core rhythm. When that rhythm is matched, it engages your pleasure like a lock and key¬ whether it's you touching yourself or a woman touching you. If you're stroked too quickly or too slowly, or if your lover is dancing to her own music, it's distracting. It doesn't let you relax. You're looking to attune to the rhythm that makes her whole body sing, not simply the stroke that brings her to orgasm.

- When your own engine is too loud and revving, you go deaf. You drive your rhythm on her body, and it drowns out her subtle and profound pleasure. You might have totally different rhythms. This is Okay. They can be blended. They can become synergy if you know how to attune.

- Imagine driving a car. At 30 mph you feel a certain way in that car. At 50 and 70, a bit different. The way your body responds varies. If you were to attune to your most pleasurable rhythm in that car, where you were most in sync with yourself and the road, it might be 55 mph. Now and then, you might get the impulse to kick that speed up or slow it down. This is how a woman's body acts. Her "core rhythm" might be simmer, though sometimes she wants you to run up the fire to boiling.

- The key here is to turn off your engine and listen to her. What do you hear in the way of feedback? If you're quiet, what can you sense in the way of subtle responses? What is the rhythm pulsing through her, and what external rhythm does her body most respond to?

Attuning at any level gives you a sense of power – because you can do something and because you're getting into the practice of trusting what you sense. When you don't attune, you feel locked out of you own intelligence. Then, naturally, you feel anxious about what to do. Think of the director here again. He feels into what's needed. Maybe he gets it right, maybe not. The key is he trusts his instincts and then adjusts accordingly. He listens and responds. This is the nature of a creative process, and it's one you want to develop as a lover.

Seeing:
Open Your Eyes

I love to watch a confident man work with tools. If he's fixing a leak in a sink and one wrench doesn't fit, he goes for another. If that doesn't fit, he goes for the next. It's simple. He looks for the tool that will get the job done. But when it comes to sex, men lose confidence all too often and all too soon. They're unwilling to experiment and test. They want to know it all instead of trying out what will fit in the moment and learning from that experience.

- Keep Your Eyes Open. If your eyes are always closed when you make love, it's hard to see the changing landscape of a woman's face. You also won't see her hands gripping or her toes curl. Your eyes can tell you a lot about what a woman is experiencing in her body – if you choose to look.

- Trust and Try. It's important to know that lovemaking is not an exact science. One woman's arched neck might mean she wants a deeper thrust, while for another woman it means she's pulling away, not present. How do you know? You can only know by trusting your instinct and trying something. If you trust and try and get it wrong, you will know in a microsecond (as long as your eyes are open). You can easily course-correct without ruining the mood.

- Study Her. If your woman looks like she wants you to use more force because she's gripping the headboard and thrusting her hips upward, try that. Go with your gut. If she is lying completely still with her hands flat and open, maybe she's hoping for a feather-light touch, to be tickled. Try that. Watch what emerges in her breath, on her face, and in her eyes.

- Take A Chance. You can't develop into a great lover and take a woman deep if you're not willing to take risks. If you wait for some kind of assurance every time you act or hope for blow-by-blow instructions so you cannot fail, your lovemaking will lack fire and excitement. Some women don't mind teaching, but most secretly want you to figure it out. Most women want you to find their hidden sweet spots and unleash them. Is this fair to you as a man? Well, not exactly. But it's the nature of the feminine in women, and if you want to be a lover who enjoys women abundantly, it's worth learning to attune!

Responding:
The Creative Impulse

By definition, to be creative is to make something that did not exist before.

Where it concerns sex and lovemaking, this doesn't mean adding a position to the Kama Sutra or getting a woman's body part named after you.

It simply means showing up in a state of sexual openness and being willing to follow the impulses and opportunities that arise. It's like the difference between having a travel itinerary mapped out and driving without a specific destination. A woman wants to be taken and swept into lovemaking. If she can track your every move, her mind and her body cannot surrender. If you're like a lot of men, you try to figure out how to get to the goal and then do those one or two things repetitively. This is not only annoying, but a woman's body becomes resistant to what she recognizes as routine. Your efforts to "succeed" can actually force her to put up walls of physical protection and refuse sex.

- It's the feminine desire and hope to be distracted from her relentless mind. It's the only way for her to truly let go. You don't have to come up with fifty new positions or hang her from a chandelier to achieve this. You need only to learn to respond presently and creatively (and then notice what arises when you aren't trying out canned routines). What happens when you're daring? When you get an impulse and you act on it?

- To be creative, you need to let go of that safe outcome. You have to drop the need for her orgasm, and even for yours. While women love orgasms, your insistence on them and predictable ways of achieving them rob sex of its mystery. I can't tell you how many orgasmic women I've coached who were bored out of their minds with their lovers. Don't assume orgasm is the end-all and be-all. For too many men, it's a creative crutch.

- In order to open to your creative intelligence, you need to engage your senses. Look and listen as you never have before. Let thoughts fall away and do not rely on them. They will only lead you astray.

The Dark Side of the Lover

Paul had a reputation in the North Bay Tantra Community as the "Enlightened Samurai Cocksman." It was not a name given in admiration or out of respect. The fact that a spiritual teacher was being mocked as some kind of porn star did not bode well for Paul. More importantly, it was blight on the community already struggling with a troubled identity.

Paul had slept with several of his students, I would learn, but one woman in particular, feeling disregarded by Paul, brought her story to a powerful group of women in the community and demanded that something be done. Paul's mentor was immediately contacted (the man who he taught with), and a meeting was scheduled. It was determined that several key things needed to happen to cleanse the community of Paul's wrongdoing and deal with Paul's issues; among those was getting Paul some help.

I had the good fortune of Paul being referred to me because of my reputation for working with professionals and getting results, and because I was not directly associated with the community.

If you don't know anything about Tantra training, one of the key embodiments is to become aware of oneself as connected to everything. It was clear as soon as I encountered Paul that he was a master of his craft, a man who embodied the Tantra teaching. It's not a joke that he was enlightened – in the sense that he was full of light – and deeply self-aware. I could feel he was definitely a powerful teacher. But like any human being – teacher or not – Paul had his shadow side. There was a part of him in the dark, and that part acted out in ways not in alignment with his oaths and higher intentions as a teacher.

We looked at Paul's history. He grew up with his mother and sister. His mother was a waitress who worked most nights, and Paul learned how to take care of himself early on. Knowing he'd likely not go to college as they didn't have money, he developed his skills as a musician and as an artist making portraits. He always had work and friends eager to create with him. He took care of his mom however he could – whether making her soups or rubbing her feet at the end of a shift. Girls came easy for Paul. They were plentiful, like grapes on a vine. He lost his virginity at fourteen and by nineteen had lost track of his number of lovers.

In our first session, we started to look at how he became the sexual man he was.

"What is it, from your perspective, that attracts women to you?" I asked.

"My friend, Michael, would ask me when we were nineteen, 'Why do these babes go for you? I don't get it. You're not great looking, and you don't have money. What's the deal?'

"I had no idea. I thought it might be because I was a good flirt, but then so was Michael, and he rarely got sex. He was also better looking, a really great-looking guy. I didn't get it until I was thirty that other guys were trying really hard, and that effort made women run away. I never really tried."

"You understood something it takes some men a lifetime to understand. Were there any older women in your experience?" I asked, looking for sexual abuse.

"Why do you ask?"

"I'm wondering if anyone, specifically, contributed to your precociousness."

Paul paused. It seemed to me that he was trying to decide if he could trust me, if talking about what he was about to reveal would be safe.

"There was a teacher in high school, Ms. Green."

"Oh."

"She was my art teacher."

"She seduced you?"

"You could say that. One day she saw me on campus wandering through the parking lot and offered me a ride in her blue Mustang convertible. I'd always found her attractive but never thought she'd be into me. I was just a kid. On the way to my house, she asked if I'd like to go for a little drive with her. My heart leapt for joy.

"When we got to the lake, she pulled a blanket from the car and spread it on the grass and patted it. 'Sit,' she said. We sat together looking at the water, and our fingers touched. The sexual energy between was off the charts. Before I knew it, we were kissing, and then we were making love. I still remember it as some of the best sex I've ever had."

"What made it memorable for you?"

"I think that it was so taboo. But also that she was this angel to me, older and experienced. She had been the inspiration for me as an artist. She seemed to truly appreciate my talent. She was also very beautiful, maybe twenty-four years old. But it was the way she just let me have her with no tension or guilt or shame, unlike girls my age. She just let me have all of her. It changed my life."

"What do you mean, changed your life?"

"I grew up instantly. I understood that sex wasn't supposed to be so tense and a woman could actually receive and enjoy and let me enjoy her without shame. It made me a better lover, because I knew after that what to go for."

"So what about the fact that she was a teacher and she seduced you? How do you feel about that piece of it?"

"I don't see it as wrong. She didn't force me."

Paul got quiet. For the first time, he made a connection. What he was up to with his students was linked to this experience.

"That's embarrassing," he said.

"What?"

"That I never made the connection. In my mind, she was this angel who gave me a gift. But the fact is she eroticized what should not have been an erotic experience."

We paused.

"Paul, it was a powerful moment for you sexually. I can under-stand why you would unconsciously re-create it."

After Paul had integrated that revelation and was more at ease, I asked him to tell me about what happened with the woman who blew the whistle – his Tantra student.

Paul became very tense. He exhaled and looked down at his thighs.

"I don't know. I didn't do anything to her that she didn't want. It's not like I forced her."

"Nobody said you forced her, Paul." It was interesting to watch him forget everything he had just discovered.

"Well, they're making it seem as if I damaged her in some way."

"Let's forget what they think. You're a powerful teacher. What do you think of your behavior in this situation?"

"I think we were two adults."

I found it interesting that Paul was receding from his role as a spiritual teacher and becoming very defensive.

"Okay, so using your own measure of integrity, you're saying you're fine with this."

He sat still, but his face was tense.

"No. I'm not saying that."

"What are you saying?"

"I'm saying I didn't hurt her."

"Well, apparently she is hurt. What do you think that's about?"

"I think she's not taking responsibility for her part. She could have said no."

"I agree. She could have said no. But this isn't about her. It's about you. What stopped you from saying no'?"

"I don't know."

I was quiet, letting Paul sit with his feelings, and then some things became clear for him.

"The power trip is an incredible high. Here it is, a girl or a woman who thinks of me as an ideal man, a god, and a sexual paragon. If you could see the look in her eyes ... it's like a drug. She's hooked. So she starts hanging on my every word. Touching her own body, she does not even notice how turned on she is. And then I just become on fire. It's like if you touched me, I'd orgasm. The fire is so hot, I'm unstoppable – completely out of control.

"But I don't drop the role. That's the part that makes me angry. I keep playing her and teaching even as I'm seducing her, acting as if I'm not virtually taking her clothes off and penetrating her with my energy. I'm so good at it that it's almost sickening. And I've never been able to tell anyone this.

"If I say 'lie on your back and breathe' or 'thrust your hips in the air and release energy,' these women do it. They trust me. The power in that should be respected, but I get so turned on by it that it overtakes me.

"This woman, Sienna, is wickedly smart. She wasn't easy to seduce, and that made it all the more irresistible. I really had to teach and pull out everything I had to get her. Finally, there was a moment where she became mine. I could see it in her eyes; she surrendered to me. I should have walked away. In fact, I thought to do it. I knew in my heart this one was wrong, really wrong. I'd made her fall in love with me – not just lust for me. And taking her was going to be a problem. But I didn't stop. And then, feeling so much shame the day after, I avoided her for a week. I didn't even give her a chance to connect with me."

We were quiet for a minute.

Then I asked Paul: "How does a man control this kind of energy?"

"With his heart," he said without hesitation. "He always has to remember who he is and let his love for women lead."

"Beautiful. You said you didn't hurt her. Did you love her by doing what you did?"

"No. I loved being with her. But if I loved her in the Tantric way, I would have protected her heart. I would not have taken her. She was open in a way that was vulnerable and susceptible. It wasn't fair."

"What's the right thing to do here?" I asked him.

"I need to invite her and the women she went to about this to a ceremony where she can speak her mind to me. I have denied her a voice. I need to hear her and look her in the eyes and ask for her forgiveness."

"What if she says no?"

"I keep asking until she says yes."

Sienna did say yes to the ceremony. Paul was surprised by her tenderness. She didn't want to punish him; she wanted compassion. She wanted him to hear how he had betrayed her trust.

Paul came to understand that he needed to lead with his desire to love women, putting it ahead of his desire to make love to women. This understanding gave him power over his impulses. Suddenly that energy which had felt so all encompassing –like he was back with his teacher – was only a feeling, and one he could manage. He broke the pattern that had begun back in high school.

When a man lets his desire lead, he often finds it robs him of power. When he leads with love and the desire to love and honor women, he retains energy and is able to channel it in ways that preserve his integrity and create even greater sexual abundance.

Sienna did forgive Paul, and she later became his teaching assistant. I witnessed Paul grow from a man who claimed to love women into a man who truly loved women in practice. It was a beautiful process to help facilitate.

Now, with The Lover archetype, you know the seven archetypal masculine energies that will open a woman and arouse her desire and inspire her love. And more importantly, you now know how the feminine responds to those energies. You know that the feminine has a deep desire to be seen and celebrated, which is met by the masculine gifts of The Artist and The Poet. The feminine wants to be guided and taken someplace she cannot reach on her own, which is met by the masculine gift of direction (The Director). She wants the man she chooses to have a passion for life and a mission in the world, which shows up as The Warrior energy in the masculine. She wants a man who is trustworthy and has integrity, but at the same time is not always predictable and who is not driven by fear and averse to risk. These are the qualities of The Sage and The Dark Knight. When these aspects of masculine potential are awakened, the feminine can fully open to the lover archetype, and she can surrender in love to a man who is deeply desirous of her without being needy or obsessed by her.

Conclusion

This book is meant to empower you. If you've taken the material and the practices to heart, you're in a more powerful place even if you haven't mastered them yet. You should be clearer about where you stand within yourself, and you should see the path to feeling more confident in your relationships to women.

You are now aware of the fundamental points of how this all works, but knowing about these things is just the beginning. I know from my experience working one-on-one with men that a lot can arise as you embrace new ways of being. If you're in a relationship, some of this material may have brought forward upset or feelings of regret. You may have been inspired and yet felt paralyzed to act. Perhaps most of what you read here really went against everything you have learned before, and you haven't felt the confidence to engage it.

Take heart. Sometimes when you open doorways to new consciousness, it can create discomfort. Suddenly, you start connecting the dots, making sense of past misunderstandings, and it can be a bit overwhelming. This doesn't mean you're headed in the wrong direction; it simply means you've exposed yourself. It's like you've crawled out of a cave into the light and the buffeting winds.

You can't grow and remain comfortable. The degree to which you're willing to be uncomfortable will be a direct measure of how big you live your life. You can be sure the men who conquered cities or traversed oceans were extremely uncomfortable much of the time.

Your bigger problem isn't being uncomfortable; that's actually a good sign. It means you're on a positive trajectory. The bigger problem is feeling nothing – when you're just "trying." My clients often tell me, "I'm trying," which I interpret as code for "I'm doing nothing" or "I'm acting right up until the moment there is a challenge or a conflict, then I'm backing off and relying on my habitual ways of being."

"Trying" to be more intimate or "trying" to speak your truth is about as effective as thinking about exercise. You have to have skin in the game to make a difference. Anything worthwhile comes with risk.

Let me address another key point concerning obstacles. If you apply yourself heart and soul to these practices, you might discover something completely unexpected: that your partner and your relationship can't support the changes in you – not because you shouldn't be who you are, but because the old agreements created a container just too small to contain the new reality. Sometimes we're able to hold a relationship together by being less of who we are, or by supporting our partner to be less. By being true to yourself and asking your woman to be true to herself, you force a break in the contract. Your partner may not want to step into what's next with you because it's not part of the deal.

I'm reminded of a client I worked with who was a functioning alcoholic for twenty years. When Aaron got sober, he thought sure his wife would be thrilled. He thought sure he'd finally be capable of giving her the fulfilling relationship she'd always wanted. He thought they could heal their lack of intimacy. Well, none of that was true. She wasn't thrilled. She was accustomed to his being half alive. She was accustomed to babysitting him, to having to monitor his behavior like a parent would a child. She'd grown used to no physical intimacy. The blackouts, the vomiting on the furniture, and his bursts of rage had killed any romantic sexual attraction she had for him. His newfound desires for closeness and physical intimacy felt dead wrong and impudent. The only reason she was still with Aaron was their sixteen-year-old daughter, but his new state was making that impossible for her. Instead of opening to Aaron, she asked him to leave.

Aaron was tempted to start drinking again, to avoid the inevitable, and to keep Melanie in his life. But ultimately, he knew the time had come to move on and he agreed to a divorce.

Now, this isn't permission to leave your relationship just because change is difficult and you don't want to change. And this is an extreme case. But if you've done everything in your power to live in alignment with your higher truth and your heart and everything possible to be a more loving man for your woman, and she has no interest in meeting you in that higher place, it might be time to consider moving on.

This should be a last resort. Before you opt for leaving a relationship, you need to be certain you are actually living to your highest potential (as opposed to just fooling yourself about it) and that you have given your partner the time to acclimate to and trust the new you. This way you know without a doubt that you aren't leaving as a victim. You aren't leaving having just "tried." You aren't leaving because you lack courage. You're leaving because you have become who you are, and the relationship is not a fit. That is a powerful place to leave from and to lead your next relationship from.

I'd also like to address time. This work may take longer than you would like. It's understandable that you'd like quick results; it's your nature. You'd like to put the practices into play, have your woman sense it immediately, and get immediate results. But relationships, and certainly women, don't operate that way. If your woman has an expectation of limiting behaviors from you, such as not seeing her or not reflecting who she is, telling her she's beautiful four times over a weekend will not be viewed as change. She'll know you've extended a gesture; you can count on that. Women don't miss little kindnesses, or a man who is suddenly more confident, but she's not going to jump for joy the first time you try a new way of being. What your initial gestures will do is put her on alert. Now, what she wants to know is, can I trust this? She'll know only by testing it over time. This is how trust is built. It's not built on what's new, but what's old, what's patterned. Most guys give up way too soon – before they've had a chance to wear in a way of being that a woman can sink her trust into. Your woman wants to be certain your "good deeds" aren't just a set-up for a personal payoff.

Let me be absolutely clear that you don't have to buy or earn your way into a woman's heart. You can make choices that honor who you are, and the right women will line up to love and support you. The idea that love is a compromise of who you are or that you need to dilute your masculinity to appeal to women are errors in thinking. Living these errors give us relationships that are safe and pragmatic, but which end up feeling empty and unfulfilling. Your masculinity needs to be fully intact and fully engaged for you to succeed in a relationship with a woman. Anything less is, frankly, an unsustainable compromise. The better you understand the nature of your power and how to leverage that power with women, the better you will feel about yourself and your relationships with women.

Questions

One of the things I've discovered from working with men around these archetypes is that certain questions come up again and again. Here are some of those questions.

• *Are you expecting me to be some kind of superhero by taking on all of these masculine qualities?*

No. If anything, my hope is to inspire your vulnerability as well as your strength. I want you to be the man you are, only more empowered. There is no expectation of perfection or invulnerability. If you only see yourself more clearly and appreciate what you bring to the masculine/feminine, that would be a significant enough gain.

• *What if my woman resists or resents my doing the practices?*

As I said above, you can do all the right things and be who you are, and it doesn't mean that you'll get the love you want. You have to choose to do the right things – not to gain approval or win love – but because anything less is a compromise of who you are. A woman's love and her desire are often benefits of being true to yourself, but if they are your main reason, you'll likely be disappointed. Don't expect a payoff. Do what is good for you, give of yourself genuinely, and see what comes. The gift has to be in the giving, or it won't feed you in the long run.

Your woman may resent the new you or the new gestures you're putting forth, because she thinks they're tied to some sort of payoff. Check in with yourself and be clear on your intentions. Then be consistent and don't let her doubts throw you into a tailspin. It's key to stay focused and committed to an empowered state of mind. Also, keep in mind that she may test you to see just how trustable this new you is. She can't really relax or surrender into your love if she doesn't trust it.

- *I've done some of the practices and they didn't work. Now what?*

Some guys are resigned to "trying" a few things and seeing what happens. If this is you, you're not going to benefit much. If you had an employee who did just what he had to do to get by and win your approval, you'd see right through his game and ultimately fire him. You don't want obedience in an employee; you want dedication. A woman wants dedication, too. So look at how you've engaged the practices and your expectations. What did you think would happen? How much of your attention is going toward the outcome? If it's more than ten percent, back up and remember that this journey is for your empowerment first. Find the personal benefit in doing the practices. What are you getting out of being more loving, or expressing more authentically?

- *My partner hates men who are violent and hates war movies and heroes. If being a warrior means fighting for what I believe in, she isn't going to like that. She places a high value on sensitivity in men.*

First of all, it isn't the warrior or the hero that she is uncomfortable with; it is the oppressor, the one who uses his strength to manipulate and control others for his own gain. Women often feel that wars can be avoided if diplomatic measures are taken. We have greater respect for a man who would exercise a peaceful possibility – first. That said, you can trust that if something went down on the street putting the two of you in harm's way, every woman would want you to protect her and get her out of there safely. We don't like men who resort to violence for egotistic reasons, but we do like men who fight the good fight. The good fight, fighting for what you love, may never come to violence, but unfortunately, sometimes it does. If you look at Nelson Mandela or Desmond Tutu, both men fought to end apartheid. Their fight was for peace, but they were commonly met with violence of one sort or another. It's simply the nature of doing the right thing. Yes, we want a man who can be sensitive in that he can hear us in a meaningful way, but we also want him to know what's right and what's wrong and to be willing to stand on the side of good – even if that means joining a fight.

- *When I tell my wife she's beautiful, she gets angry. She tells me to stop. When I ask her why, she says, "I don't believe you."*

First, I want to suggest that you look at your motivations. Are you seeking her approval or looking for a payoff? Are you thinking something other than what you're saying? When you say that a woman is beautiful, don't tie it to images of other women. Don't compare her with some ideal beauty. Say it from the place of recognizing that beauty is energy. It might be the light in her eyes or the turn of her lips. It might be her compassion or the tone of her voice.

Second, remember that as the Artist, your challenge is to see her unique beauty, and as the Poet the challenge is to give voice to that in specific language and detail. Telling a woman she's beautiful is a generic compliment. Telling her that you love the color of her hair in the later afternoon sunlight or that the curve of her calf is as close to perfection as you can imagine is a specific and detailed compliment. Instead of repeating that she is beautiful, you should be always trying to surprise her with your observations.

Sometimes a woman is uncomfortable receiving a compliment. You can tell her it hurts you that she doesn't receive what you offer. Ask her to simply get into the practice of saying: "Thank you for noticing." It always generates laughs, and it will get her into the practice of receiving. Whatever you do, don't be deterred. Stay centered and let her deal with her inability to receive in the ways she needs to. It's not easy to stay the course in the face of a woman's refusal, but it will make you a stronger, more loving man.

- *Sometimes when I do these practices, I feel like I'm faking it. Is that Okay?*

Yes, absolutely. First off, these may not be ways of engaging that have ever occurred to you. It's like speaking a foreign language. You're saying the right words, but they don't sound real to you in the beginning. As you use them with greater and greater frequency, they will start to feel connected to what you're feeling instead of just being words spilling out of your mouth. It's the same thing with these practices. You will connect to them eventually and ultimately feel the power of what you're giving.

- *I want to animate the Dark Knight in my relationship and bring more of an edge to our sexual relationship, but when I asked my wife if I could tie her hands to the bedpost, she got upset with me. What can I do to express this part of myself and not offend her?*

The Dark Knight is much more than a bondage expert! He brings the gift of living at the edge. What edge are you gracing in your life? If you're not living at your own edge, your lead in this way is not going to feel right. So first look at where you're hiding from your own edge and ask yourself: If I weren't afraid to be fully alive, what would I be doing? A woman needs to feel your power in your own life before she'll submit to you sexually.

Perhaps you are living at your edge. Perhaps you are living at your edge everywhere but sexually. So how can you engage this energy in a sexual way that is safe and appealing to your partner? Imagine receiving a deep tissue massage. If the therapist goes too deep too fast, your body tightens in protection. However, if she starts with light pressure and slowly deepens that, letting her touch sink in, you remain open. To push the sexual edge with a woman, you have to do it incrementally. You don't jump from Mr. Sensuous Caresses of many years to a man with a whip. Hold one of her hands down in yours. Use a bit more pressure as you kiss. Tell her you want to take her. Lightly pull her hair or bite her neck. Then notice what happens and see if there is a positive response. Build trust that you can do what you're doing confidently. Then she'll feel greater and greater trust to allow more of the Dark Knight to be present in your bed.

- *What's the best way to take on this material?*

The best way to take in any new information successfully is to read it, and then read it again. I'm including a quick overview of the seven Masculine Archetypes below, and I suggest you read through them. What wasn't clear on a first read might be clearer on another pass. Some of the chapters will have felt very comfortable to you. That means you are probably already comfortable animating that energy in your life. You'll obviously see yourself in one or two of the archetypes and know, "Yes, that's me," and feel empowered and good about that archetype.

What I suggest, then, is for you choose a chapter that felt most challenging to you –the one that angered you or felt ridiculously not you. The challenge I give you is to take on the archetypes that are unfamiliar – those that might confront your limiting beliefs about yourself and your masculinity. If you always hated the Dark Knight archetype because he was the guy who stole your girlfriend in college, that would be a good place to start. Read that chapter again. Read it as many times as you need to take it in fully. And then dive in.

Again, don't "try" to engage this material. Do the practices in a sincere way or don't do them. Do them for you. Don't go into the challenge looking for a reward or a specific result. Step up with the idea of investing in yourself and your relationship. When you invest in an IRA, stocks or bonds, you don't get an immediate payoff. Be in it for the long haul. First notice yourself and what you feel: How are you changing as you take on these new ways of being and acting in the world? Then, gently notice how women are affected. Whatever you do, don't look for approval from women. This will only make you seem insincere and desperate. If you want approval, find it within yourself. Be self-congratulatory for taking on a more powerful way of being. Celebrate your progress privately. And trust you'll have much to celebrate!

The Seven Archetypes: A Quick Reference

The Artist

His gift is the ability to deeply see a woman. There are men who truly see women and men who see only what they want in women. The latter don't get a lot in return. If you see only a body or a shell when you look at a woman, what would inspire her to share the gift of her innermost self? Remember, a woman thrives on being seen and known; a void of this reflection and caring leaves her feeling empty, unfulfilled, and resistant to you.

The Poet

His gift is his capacity to give voice to what he sees. You might see a woman's feminine essence, her unique beauty, and her inner beauty; but if you aren't able to convey that to her, she won't know or feel the depth of your love and desire. When you do choose to see and express who a woman is (at her essence) in words, you offer her a gift she cannot give to herself. Sure, she can know and cherish herself, but her feminine desire to be celebrated is different. "To be celebrated, honored, and valued with language and gesture" is a gift she cannot give herself.

> **Note:** *The Artist and the Poet are clearly intertwined. Seeing and celebrating a woman are practically one in the same. And yet, one without the other leaves a void. Animate the Artist and the Poet together and feel inside you how deeply seeing a woman and being emotionally expressive with her unlocks your love and your power, and opens her.*

The Director

His gift is the gift of direction – taking a woman somewhere she cannot take herself. The Artist and The Poet give shape to your loving, but without the forward motion and focus of the director, your relationship will lack directionality. The director takes a woman somewhere, sometimes literally, and sometimes within herself. Yes, a woman can direct herself; she has a masculine aspect. But your gift of directionality opens doorways, experiences, and feelings a feminine, flowing woman may never access on her own.

> **Note:** *The Director and The Poet are natural partners. Giving voice to what you see and know about a woman builds trust. She relaxes. The Poet opens a woman's desire to let go and turn herself over to a man's directionality. Without this, The Director will meet with resistance. Remember, following is a choice. Letting go with you is a choice. A woman follows a confident dancer; she resists a weak one. Let her know you see and understand her, and she will open to your lead.*

The Warrior

His gift is the gift of passion and a commitment to something larger than himself in the world. The Warrior fights for what he loves. He has a mission that is bigger than his woman, his relationship, or himself. He's not a fighter for the sake of fighting, but he aligns with what he cares about. By loving something bigger than himself, he inspires respect, honor, and a woman's devotion. The Warrior is about living life on your own terms.

The Sage
His gift is the gift of integrity and an unbreakable trust. A man can see a woman's beauty, communicate his love, and direct and offer his passion, but all that is nothing without trust. A woman never fully surrenders herself until she feels trust. Trust is not simply upholding vows of monogamy. It's trusting that you truly see and know her. It's trusting you can take her somewhere she can't get to on her own. It's trusting she can relax into your leadership and directionality. The opportunity of The Sage is integrity. Trust what you know. Use your word as a bond and do the right thing.

> *Note: The Sage and the Warrior are partners in spirit. The Warrior, without integrity of mind, body, and spirit – and without the power of his truth – can do only harm. If you've struck out to fight the good fight and found yourself beaten by anger or misdirected energy, or you have lost the support of your woman, you likely lacked the integrity of The Sage. With greater alignment of values and actions, you can act on what you care about in a good way and have an impact you cannot have without it. If you're not getting the support and the speed you want in your mission, check on where you might be lacking integrity.*

The Dark Knight
His gift is that he pushes a woman's emotional and sexual edges. The Dark Knight lives at his own edge. The Dark Knight is named the dark knight because he's ready and willing to face danger, and even death, to be fully alive. You don't have to risk your life to traverse this edge. You need only to be willing to pull back the curtain of fear and look at where you're hiding or what you're hiding from. A man who lives at his edge is exciting to a woman because he demonstrates courage and bold resolve. He knows how to push a woman's sexual and emotional edge and open her to hidden aspects of herself – because he doesn't avoid his own.

The Lover

His gift is the gift of sexual integrity. The Lover owns his sexuality. He takes responsibility for what arises in him sexually and how he acts on that – never pretending that his sexual excitement controls him. By being in sexual possession he can give a woman something most men cannot: sexual freedom. The Lover is a powerful amalgamation of all the types, but most especially The Sage and The Dark Knight. His integrity builds trust, like The Sage. His fearlessness inspires passion, like The Dark Knight. His willingness to take responsibility sets a woman free. Your opportunity in embodying this archetype is parlaying ownership and responsibility into a very deep sexual connection with a woman.

How We Can Continue this Journey Together

Although I have been as thorough as I can be in a book in my quest to empower you and give you the tools you need to be successful with women, this is, frankly, still only a book. Add to that the fact you are an individual with many unique complexities to navigate, and it will be obvious that many questions will arise within the course of your journey with this work.

My standing offer to you is that I am here to offer further support. I offer updates on my blog to answer your questions. I offer workshops, both live and virtual, and when my schedule permits, private or group coaching. It's key we stay in touch. I really mean that.

I'd like to continue to communicate with you! I'd like to know how this book has affected you and find out how I can assist you further. I offer this teaching as both a live and a virtual course because some men find that live interaction with others is a powerful catalyst. I also do the live courses because I love meeting you and witnessing your growth.

For those of you who desire one-on-one time, I offer private coaching when possible. If you go to *www.Loveandintimacycoach.com* and sign up for my updates, I'll keep you informed of classes and other opportunities; and you can request private session time. You'll also receive a special gift that will help further this process for you. Don't miss this step, as I'd really like to be in touch with you, and share other powerful ways to enhance your love life!

Additionally, if you loved the book and what it's done for you, you can gift me by reviewing it on Amazon.com. I will enter you into a monthly draw to win a free class with me. Your reviews really make the difference in getting this book into the hands of the men who need it.

Lastly, I want to wish you well. I hope, at the very least, I have impressed upon you that your masculinity is a gift. It is a gift to the women in your life, your children, your friends, and the world. I hope you choose to share it in this vein. I know if you do and if you continue to honor yourself, you will undoubtedly be lavished in the attention, respect, and desire you so greatly deserve.

About the Author

Karen Brody is a leading voice for the empowerment of men, and awakened masculinity. Karen believes most of the issues men experience concerning love and women are because men don't understand the nature of their own masculine power, or how to use that power to magnify attraction, desire, and love.

In her 14 years coaching men in relationships, Karen has helped thousands of men stop living diminished lives in relationship to their women, work, and life, and learn to embrace masculinity and the power of a fully embodied, fully realized masculine self. Karen inspires men to stop apologizing for being men, and to wake up to the masculine gifts within them to share with their women and the world.

As Karen has written, "When a man embraces the idea that true masculine power is not about domination or force, or measured by financial success, but is about living and loving with an awakened heart, his relationships with women deepen and blossom, as does his success at everything he does."

Karen's professional background includes a MA in Counseling Psychology and BA in Journalism, alongside a lifetime of personal growth work. Like most people, Karen's gift was inspired by her own wounding, and her loss of trust in men. Her commitment to heal her body and her heart, to forgive men and love the masculine is her life's journey and a gift to men.

"I am the ideal advocate for men because I am no longer under any illusion about men being somehow inherently good or inherently bad, and that makes it possible for me to adore, respect and love men exactly as they are. When men are whole and powerful, women benefit. And that of course, is my ultimate mission – that women get the love they crave and men get the love they deserve!

To get a powerful free gift, now, receive Karen's live course and webinar updates, or her speaking schedule, please sign up at *www. Loveandintimacycoach.com.*

To book Karen to speak at your event or on your radio or television show, please also head over to *www.Loveandintimacycoach.com,* and leave your request under "Contact."

Made in the USA
San Bernardino, CA
18 May 2019